WOM
FOR A NEW LIFE

WOMEN STRUGGLING FOR A NEW LIFE

AI RA KIM

State University
of New York
Press

Published by
State University of New York Press, Albany

Production by Susan Geraghty
Marketing by Dana Yanulavich

Printed in the United States of America

For information, address State University of New York Press,
State University Plaza, Albany, N.Y. 12246

Kim, Ai Ra, 1938–
    Women struggling for a new life: the role of religion in the
cultural passage from Korea to America / Ai Ra Kim
        p. cm.
    Includes bibliographical references.
    ISBN 0-7914-2737-4 (alk. paper). —   ISBN 0-7914-2738-2 (pbk. :
alk. paper).
        1. Korean American women—New Jersey—Religious life.
2. Methodist women—New Jersey—Religious life.   3. United Methodist
Church (U.S.)—Membership.   4. Methodist Church—United States—
Membership.   I. Title.
BX8247.K67K55   1955   95-3470
305.48'8957073—dc20   CIP

10   9   8   7   6   5   4   3   2   1

I dedicate this book

to Father (Kim, Hyung Yoon: 1910–1979),
  who empowered me to be "who I am"

and

to Mother (Kim, Yei Yang: 1914-1992),
  who sacrificed her entire life for her
  "created gods"—her husband and her five
  children.

CONTENTS

PREFACE

My father often told me this when I was young:

You should never marry. In this society, marriage, to women, means the end of her life. You should go to Law School and become a first woman-lawyer in Korea and work for the transformation of Korean society.

Under my father's liberal life-principle, I grew up in an egalitarian family, in terms of sex; this implanted in me a strong sense of self, pride, and dignity as a woman. Also, from junior high school to college in Korea, I attended girls schools. I grew up in the world of women. Therefore, as far as I remember, I never experienced sexual discrimination until I became an "actual social member" whose fate—especially for women—is often determined by marriage.

Disappointing my father, after college graduation I came to the United States in order to marry a man recommended and arranged by my mother. With a filmy dream of cottonlike clouds, I arrived in America in January 1962. At the San Francisco airport, looking around for my fiance, whom I had never met, I saw a group of Asians, young and old, who came out to welcome me in this foreign land. What a disappointment! Compared to the gigantic airport building and huge white Americans, those orientals looked so small and shabby. They didn't seem to belong to America. Seeing them, I saw myself as one of them. At that moment, I experienced the sudden awareness of who and what I really would be in America.

From that moment, surrounded by gigantic people—mainly whites—I became "nobody." On streets, in shopping malls or restaurants, wherever I went, no one cared for me. Nobody knew who I was. Ai Ra Kim, the three paramount letters upholding the pride and dignity of my being, disappeared in America. I was so sad and angry.

Furthermore, I had a new name, a new identity, Mrs. "So-and-so",* which was so foreign to me. At first, I was shocked by this new name because in Korean culture marriage never alters a woman's maiden name. Therefore, I was upset and furious. I felt that my

* Throughout the text, letters are occasionally used in place of proper names, particularly when this helps to protect the privacy of individuals consulted for study.

personhood was totally robbed by an invisible force. I fought back by insisting on keeping my name, Kim. Then, I faced a severe problem with my newly married husband, still a "stranger." Above all, people in the Korean community and the Church, as well as in American society, simply ignored my good will and treated me as so-and-so's wife. In return, they expected me to act as Mrs. "So-and-So."

Soon, I became "wise." The only way that I could survive in that reality was to accept and to adjust to the new cultural-social game. Furthermore, I tried to be what Anne Wilson Schaef has called an "ideal woman" who represents her socio-cultural norms and rules.[1] Consequently, throughout my twenty-five-year marriage, I have consumed all my energy and intellect in the effort to belittle and demolish my "self" for not being the real person, Ai Ra Kim.

Ironically, however, the more I put myself down or tried to erase my self-image, the higher and stronger the desire to be myself sprang up from the abyss of my consciousness and annoyed me: Who are you? What are you doing? Are you satisfied with your self? Be yourself! Constantly, these voices bothered me. I couldn't stand them; I had no peace with myself at all. I desperately needed pretexts justifying my living-suicide.

Here, the Korean immigrant churches became my saviors, supplying the fixed and rigorous apologetic principles legitimating my self-denunciation, principles such as woman's submission to man (Eph. 5:22–24) and women's silence in public (1 Cor. 14:34–35), derived from the Bible. Also, the church's hierarchical system and structure enhances and justifies women's subjugation to men. The more I was involved in the church and adopted the church's patriarchal teachings and doctrines, the more easily could I placate my quest and yearning to claim my own personhood. In this case, as Karl Marx proclaimed once, I became addicted to "religious opium" prescribed by the church.

There are still numerous Korean immigrant women who are taking religion, Christianity, as their opium in order to escape from the unbearable sexual oppression at home, in the church (the major Korean community center)[2] and in society in general. The church, implicitly and explicitly, supplies the justifying principles of women's self-demolition. By legimating women's inferior status, it perpetuates institutional sexism at home, in the church, in Korean immigrant community, and in society.

I wrote this book, therefore, for the purpose of encouraging Korean immigrant women's self-reflection and for elevating women's self-awareness. At the same time, I hope, this book can help the Korean immigrant church reevaluate its mission and take its prophetic role seriously so that the church may contribute to helping women recreate their self-image and to transforming the immigrant families and their community in the new land, America.

Second, it has been almost a century since the first Korean immigration to the United States in 1903. However, resource material about Korean immigrant women is very scarce. Further, the general image of these women has been distorted. They are commonly thought to be docile, subservient, and passive. I hope that this book not only adds a literary source to feminist studies but also alters the stereotypical description of Korean-American women.

Above all, I wrote this book for social transformation. By disclosing the predicament of Korean *ilse* women, a socially powerless minority group, the church and society may together work for understanding and change in existing problems such as the sexism, racism, and white cultural imperialism permeating American society.

Finally, I express my deep and sincere thanks to, and share the fruitful joy for the publication of this book with, my teachers at the Theological School and the Graduate School of Drew University, Dr. Joanna Bowen Gillespie, Dr. Karen McCarthy Brown, Dr. Hesung Chun Koh, Dr. Michael Ryan, Jerome Baggett, the women-interviewees, Alice Yun Chai, Linda E. Thomas, and Janet Clark, and Linda Buskus, David W. Goodrich, Susan Geraghty, Christine Worden, and the United Methodist Church. Above all, with my utmost gratitude, I would like to share the most fulfilling moment of my life with my daughters, Katharine and Caroline Moon (my life-long colleagues and friends), and SUNY Press.

CHAPTER 1

Introduction

Sociologists understand that human beings are social products. Particularly, George Herbert Mead asserts that human beings become "who they are," that is to say, develop "self," through the social process of adjustment and adaptation to one's social context. Mead, therefore, explains self as follows:

> The self is something which has a development; it is not initially there at birth but arises in the process of social experience and activity, that is, develops in the given individual as a result of his relations to that process as a whole and to other individuals within that process.[1]

Nevertheless, Mead's theory of self shows a double-edged process of self-formation: objective and subjective.[2] Objective process is a mechanical adjustment. People simply adjust to the social environment by adapting to the norms and patterns such as gender roles prescribed and sanctioned by the society.[3] Playing those roles, an object self, that is, a social self, emerges. Social self, therefore, is passive and receptive. After making the mechanical adjustment, for betterment, people reshape themselves by changing or renovating the social situation. Mead names the self developed through the latter process, internalization, as "subjective." Through the subjective adjustment, an autonomous self, "I," evolves. "I" is a rationalizing and active self. Therefore, self is constructed through the objective and subjective cycle of social adjustment and renovation. Mead's theory highlights that human "self" is constantly renewed and reshaped according to the change of social environment.

Mead's theory of self has some problems for me. His view of the objective process may be convincing in understanding the self-formation of the powerless. Because the powerless do not have power or autonomy to alter their social situation, they merely adjust themselves to the given social situation. Then, they develop their selves passively. However, as the Communist revolution in Eastern Europe and the former Russian republic in the spirit of *perestroica* and, especially, the 1992 riots in Los Angeles powerfully demonstrate, people are not simply mechanical beings. Though they may still not change the social situation for their own betterment, they do not simply accept it.

Then, what kinds of self are developed by the powerless who neither accept their lot nor change their social circumstances? Furthermore, how do the modern people who live with multiple values and in multiple cultures react to their social circumstance and develop their selves? Mead does not say anything about the above problems and, particularly, self-development in complicated social situations.

Nonetheless, Mead's view of the inseparable correlation of social force and its impact on the social members's lives astounds me. Korean immigrant *ilse* (일세: 一世) women, who grew up in the collective Confucian culture, today live in individualistic American society.[4] Yet the Korean immigrant church which upholds the old cultural values and traditions is a powerful social context to most women. Women live in these two indispensable social realities. How do these social realities affect Korean immigrant women's lives? How do these women adjust to their new social environments? How do they react? Do they change their social environment for their satisfaction, or, if not, do they revolt? What kinds of self do they develop? These are the focal issues explored in this book, a revision of my doctoral Dissertation, *"The Religious Factor in the Adaptation of Korean Immigrant Ilse Women to Life In America"* (1991).

To most of the women I studied, living in the United States means adapting to new social contexts. In order to disclose Korean *ilse* women's adaptation for survival in their new immigrant situation, I employed a semi-open qualitative interview method. I selected twenty four women, aged forty to sixty, whom I have known for years from three United Methodist churches in northern New Jersey. Because most Korean women not only are unfamiliar with the concept of the interview but also do not reveal their private thoughts and lives unless they trust the interviewer or conversant, I chose my acquaintances as the objects of this study. Except for two college drop-outs, all have completed college or graduate school. All have lived in the United States more than ten years. Except for one, all had or have marriage experience at the time of interview.

Since social context is the primary variable for this study, it is appropriate to note that these women can be grouped into three categories:

1. six housewives whose major social context is home and the church, that is, Korean old culture
2. six entrepreneurial women among whom three have businesses mainly in the context of Korean customers and employees and three women engage in business which is not Korean-oriented
3. six professional women, such as medical doctors, nurses, and people in educational occupations, whose major context is non-Korean, that is, in mainstream American society
4. additionally, four women were interviewed as pre-tests. They were not necessarily United Methodists.

Interviews were held, mostly, at the interviewees' houses. They were conducted in the Korean language, tape-recorded, and translated into English for the purpose of citation in this book. Since the Korean community in America is relatively small and its members are closely related to one another, interviewees are identified by pseudonyms only.

Also, I have given the churches pseudonyms that indicate their uniqueness. For example, "Fellowship Church" signifies the church's strength in serving as a social gathering place. "Word Church" refers to the popularity of the pastor's sermons, which act as that church's main drawing point. "Holiness Church" stands out as one of the most fundamentalistic pentecostal Methodist churches in the northern New Jersey area; it stresses the centrality of the Holy Spirit, rather than fellowship or sermon, in church life.

As secondary sources, I used the existing literature, which is both scarce and fragmentary. For the theoretical work, the western theories such as those of Durkheim or Peter Berger contribute to understanding and analyzing the issues.

Following the first chapter (Preface and Introduction), the second chapter provides a historical description of the self-identity of Korean women through their social experiences in the Yi dynasty. The role of Confucianism and Korean Shamanism in forming women's identities will be examined. The third chapter discusses the social experiences of the contemporary *ilse* women prior to their immigration and in their churches in America. It deals with the contrasting and conflicting situations inside and outside the church. The fourth chapter explores the impact of the Korean immigrant churches on women's lives, particularly in marriage and family in the United States, and women's reaction to the religious influence. The fifth chapter discloses the dynamic of immigrant women's adaptation to both of their immigrant churches and the host American society. The focus there is on the woman's process of self-development through their experiences, particularly in education and work, in two major social contexts. The last chapter is the conclusion, accompanied by the questionnaire and a brief description of the interviewees.

Before going into the main text, I want to make clear certain problems. First, *Women Struggling For A New Life* is an initial-- not a complete--work to disclose issues and problems of Korean immigrant *ilse* women and the influences of the church and society on their lives. Since the interviews and observations were limited to twenty four women and three United Methodist churches in the area of northern New Jersey, the facts in the book can not be used as the basis of a concrete generalization of the Korean church and its women.

Moreover, it is neither a comparative study of gender and ethnic acculturation nor a theoretical study in feminism. It is, of course, not a history book. Therefore, certain issues such as abortion or problems of Korean men or historical details, though related to those of women and mentioned in the book, are not developed further because they are not my present focus. My work is a sociological study whose value and significance lie in "uncovering" the hidden lives of Korean Protestant immigrant *ilse* women in the United States for the first time in Korean immigrant history since 1903. This book, I hope, serves as a conduit for further studies of Korean immigrant women and the church.

CHAPTER 2

Women of Yesterday: Women of the Yi Dynasty

It has been well demonstrated by the theory and work of George Herbert Mead that the study of human self-development requires the study of an individual's social contexts and social experiences. In this chapter, the past social experiences of Korean women will be reviewed in order to understand contemporary Korean women's adaptation to immigrant life in America. What are the experiences of Korean women of the past, and how do they differ from those of contemporary Korean women? While taking into account the various social experiences of women of premodern Korea, this chapter will focus upon their view of gender roles and their social status in family, education, work, and religion.

THE SOCIAL PRINCIPLE

The Chosŏn Dynasty (1392–1910), the last Korean kingdom, was established through a military coup d'etat led by General Yi Sŏng-Ge.[1] In order to expunge the kingdom of the all-pervasive influences of the previous Koryŏ dynasty's state religion, Buddhism, Yi employed Confucian scholars in his new Yi dynasty. Confucianism, therefore, became the ruling principle in Korean society. Since then, Confucian ideas have critically affected the development of Korean people's consciousness (mind) and lifestyles, akin to the way in which Max Weber asserts that Protestant Christianity influenced the thinking and behavior of northern Europeans, and the people in capitalistic society, particularly in the United States of America.[2]

Confucianism views the family as the basic social unit. The establishment and maintenance of good order in the family was regarded as the Yi kingdom's primary means of safeguarding social security and stability. Accordingly, the value of marriage and family was elevated, and gender roles and status were clearly defined for the purpose of maintaining order in these two social institutions. The social principle, *namjon yŏbi* (남존 여비 : 男尊女卑), "Men should be respected; women should be lowered," which was derived from the Confucian belief in hierarchy, functioned as the leading ethical principle, while *hyŏnmo yangch'ŏ* (현모 양처 : 賢母良妻 : wise mother-good wife) became the motto for women's role performance. The Yi dynasty enforced these principles and rules by law, and punishment for violating them was severe.[3] As a consequence, the establishment of a family based on the above principles became indispensable to an individual's survival in that society.

MARRIAGE

Marriage was customarily arranged by fathers. Children had absolutely no voice in choosing their spouse. Marriages prearranged by prospective fathers even before the birth of a child were not uncommon. The legal age for marriage was fourteen for girls and fifteen for boys.[4] However, exceptions to marry even younger children could be made in accordance with particular agreements between two families. As a father, a man had power over his children's fate, especially that of his daughters, for marriage determined a woman's destiny.

The Yi society was patrilocal. For a girl, marriage meant not only moving out of her parents' household, but also completely separating herself from it. Marriage was equivalent to total deracination from her own family and transplantation into the home of her husband; therefore, married girls and women were called "*ch'ulga woein*" (출가외인: 出家外人), meaning "stranger after leaving natal home." Returning to her natal home, for any reason, only brought shame and disgrace to her family, so women were not permitted to go back. This meant that women had to endure any situation in marriage and perform their roles faithfully, while men, whether or not they were satisfied with their marriage, could have other women as concubines. In that society, maintaining the marriage was a matter of survival for a woman. A well-known proverb advised women about how to adjust to married life: "Blind for three years, deaf for three years, mute for three years." This instruction clearly commands the self-renunciation of women. They were not to think, speak, feel, and respond contrarily to what their men deemed fit. Men, both father and husband, fully determined the conditions of women's existence.

Also, the traditional Korean marriage mandated that the husband must be older than the wife. In other words, a man was to be higher than a woman in status and experience. This accords with the cardinal principle of women's conduct, *samjong chidŏk* (삼종지덕: 三從之德), "obedience to father; obedience to husband; obedience to son," derived from the principle of *namjon yŏbi*. It was not uncommon for men in their fifties to marry fifteen-year-old girls. With women securely beneath men in age, education, experience, and social resources, the Yi dynasty enforced the hierarchical structure of family order and, in turn, sought to preserve the social order.

However, during times of economic need, especially for those in the lower classes, families would marry young boys to older girls, for the wives would add to the household's labor power by undertaking domestic chores and by giving birth to children. Moreover, the wife was to play the role of "nanny," taking care of her child-husband the way babysitters or childcare centers today look after children. Hence, it was not uncommon to see ten-year-old boys married to sixteen-year-old girls, nor was it unusual to see a boy-husband being carried papoose-like on his girl-wife's back. That practice remained popular even until the 1930s. Age reversal in marriage signified the role of woman as baby-maker in the service of the ancestral lineage and as nurturer of men.

The most important biological role for women was reproduction, especially giving birth to sons. Since the Yi society was also patrilineal, primogeniture determined the status and future wealth of sons as well as the fate of the lineage. For example, in case a man, the first son of the family in particular, had no sons, that is, no heirs, it was customary to adopt one of his younger brothers' sons, who would then carry out the family name and tradition. It was very important to have several potential male heirs. Since the infant mortality rate was very high in premodern Korea, a girl, upon reaching her menstrual age, was eligible to start producing male heirs. With a young boy as father, the chances of producing sons increased. In other words, the more sons a woman produced, the more security the family had in transmitting its name through several generations.

In addition, women were viewed as caretakers and nurturers.

From childhood, girls learned to take care of their families. They cooked for them and washed their clothes and cleaned houses. They had been taught to care for their fathers and siblings, especially brothers. Girls were trained to become "mini-mothers." After marriage, teen-age girls cared for their child-husbands, the in-laws, and other family members of the extended family. These young girls not only fed, bathed, and clothed their even younger husbands, but also played with, taught, and scolded them. In other words, these young females greatly influenced the physical and emotional development of boys and learned to control them while still young and needy.

In short, women's roles consisted mainly of reproduction, caretaking, nurturing, and homemaking. That is, women devoted themselves entirely to others. The fact that women served men guaranteed their inferior status, for people in service occupations or positions usually came from the lower classes and depended on their masters for survival or death. In order to survive, women had to deny themselves, and even death could be required of them.[5] If we accept Mead's theory that the self is a natural emergent of social experiences, it is not surprising that the women of the Yi dynasty should have developed selfless self-images. Jean Baker Miller's explication of women's psychology as a process of self-negation and self-devaluation through participation in the development of others also sheds light on the reality of Yi women's self-abnegation and martyrdom for the family.[6] Given the legal and moral demands of the Yi dynasty upon women, one might well draw the conclusion that self-abnegation and self-sacrifice served as the only viable means of survival—and, perhaps, even fulfillment—for the women of that time.[7] For a woman in Yi society, separating herself first from her natal family, then, later, sacrificing herself for marital family and husband was tantamount to suicide.

In summary then, marriage, with its attendant roles and duties, was the primary means of survival for women in the Yi society. The result was that women developed collective identities with their men and families. Women lived for the family, especially for their men; yet through them, women also survived, and some even found fulfillment. It would seem, therefore, that Mead's theory of the role of society as "self-producer" applies most aptly to the "self-in-the-family" consciousness of Yi women.

PUBLIC LIFE AND WORK

The sexual division of roles and status was established not only vertically, with men placed above women in the social hierarchy, but also horizontally, in terms of spatial realms reserved for men and women. The outside world belonged to men, and women belonged in the home. It was common to call a man (husband) *"paggat yangban/ŏrun"* (바깥양반 / 어른 : outside aristocrat/mature adult) and a woman (wife) *"an/chip saram"* (안 / 집사람: inside/house person). These appellations indicated the social distance in terms of space between men and women. At home, women dwelt in *an ch'ae* (안채: inside quarter) and men in *sarang ch'ae* (사랑채: outside quarter). In theory, there was neither spatial nor social connection between those two quarters, and no mutual visitation occurred between husband and wife unless necessary. For couples who abided strictly by these social rules, that is, those in the upper classes, a husband could not enter his wife's quarter without her consent. That is to say, women's space was strictly women's space and off-limits to the public eye. Even a police guard would not be able to enter a woman's room to apprehend a criminal who was hiding in it. Women were confined deep inside the house, and *an ch'ae* was considered as a woman's sanctuary. Women's appearance in public, therefore, was not even imaginable, and, in fact, women were prohibited by law from exiting their own homes in the daytime. They were permitted to go outside their homes only when there was no public, that is, at night (from 9 P.M. to 2 A.M.), when men stayed at home.[8] When women did go out, they were obliged to cover their bodies from head to toe—especially their faces—with a *chang-ot* (장옷: shawl-coat).[9] When women in the *yangban* class[10] (양반: 良班) ventured outside, they travelled in *kama* (가마: palanquin) and were accompanied by their servants. Women in the upper class, therefore, were neither free to move about nor visible on the streets. Given these physical restrictions, women's work or activities outside the home were strictly prohibited (to those who were not servants or peasants). Violations of these rules could result in punishment of eighty lashes in public.[11]

Women of the lower classes, however, were somewhat exempt from, or marginalized by, those strict rules. The paintings of Kim Hong-Do, the most famous artist of eighteenth century Korea, portray women drawing water from village wells and washing clothes in streams. Women of the lower classes also worked on farms and in the family trade, either as the main rice-winners or as helpers of their families, in addition to meeting their homemaking responsibilities.[12] Thus, lower-class women had some freedom in outside activities, yet their dual roles as homemakers and rice-winners imposed on them great physical and psychological burdens.

In addition to farming and assisting in the family trade, four other categories of women's work were sanctioned by the state: *kungnyŏ* (궁녀: 宮女: royal court servants); *munyŏ* (무녀: 巫女: shamans/priestesses of Shamanism); *ŭinyŏ* (의녀: 醫女: medicine women, mid-wives); *kisaeng* (기생: 妓生: entertainers/prostitutes).[13] As is apparent from the nature of these jobs, women's work outside the home was closely tied to their role as caretakers, nurturers, and service persons.

In the Confucian Yi society, only *ch'ŏnmin* (천민: 賤民: lowest-class people) engaged in service-related jobs, and so people in service positions were not respected. The service-oriented nature of women's jobs reflects the inferior status of women in that society.

In short, home was the only proper place for women, and their primary responsibility was to serve others. Women's leadership in the public arena, a career, and autonomy were unthinkable, for such activities would require women to separate themselves from their families. They had no individual selfhood in the western sense.

EDUCATION

As Mead has indicated, after making the primary adjustment to the social context, people, if not satisfied, try to amend their attitudes or to renovate the social circumstance to better suit themselves. In this process, rationalization such as analyzing/intellectualizing/legitimating is essential. Rationalization, therefore, is closely linked to education, since education provides individuals with rationales and rationalizing capacity.

Further, Max Weber and Peter Berger explicate how powerfully religion, particularly Christianity, has been tied to education.[14] The point made by Weber and Berger is that religious ideas provide the basis for educating believers and rationalizing their self-identity. Just as in the West Christianity educated believers and supplied them with rationalizing principles, the Yi dynasty used Confucian ideas to educate and legitimate its women's roles and status. The separation of gender role and status was clearly established in education. Although it is difficult to state that there was an official system of education in the Yi dynasty, it is certain that several different forms of education for men existed. The *Sŏnggyun-kwan* (성균관: National Academy), which prepared men for the *kwagŏ* (과거: government service examination), was the primary and most advanced form of formal Confucian education. The *yang-ban* men also studied Chinese classics, literature, philosophy, and fine arts at home under private tutors. They often went to China to pursue not only Chinese studies, especially Confucian thoughts and rituals, but also advanced Western scholarship (in the late Yi). After completing their formal and informal education, the scholar-mandarins were employed by kings to serve the court in positions of power and high status.

The government also established *hyanggyo* (향교: village schools) in every administrative district. Boys between twelve and twenty years of age, from all social classes except the *ch'ŏnmin*, were allowed to attend the *hyanggyo*; but *yangban* boys were predominant, for lower-class people rarely went to school. Village elders generally taught the village boys Chinese classics and Confucianism. In addition, there were private *sŏdangs* (서당: study halls) supported by individual families or the entire village. Just as in *hyanggyo*, boys in *sŏdang* studied Chinese letters and Confucian morals and rituals and prepared to go to the *Sŏnggyunkwan*, where they would prepare for the *kwagŏ*. For men, especially *yangban*, education was a tool of self-cultivation and moral refinement as well as a means to enter government service.

However, the *ch'ŏnmin* and all women were excluded from participation in formal education. The only education that the state required for women was moral cultivation for the fulfillment of their socially sanctioned roles and status. This could be performed in the home. One of the books written by Yi Ik, the most famous Confucian scholar of the eighteenth-century Korea, clearly illustrates the moral purpose of women's education:

> Reading and learning are the domain of men. For a woman it is enough if she knows the Confucian virtues of diligence, frugality, and chastity. If a woman disobeys these virtues, she will bring disgrace to the family.[15]

In order to cultivate their morality, *yangban* women were taught *ŏnmun* (언문),[16] differentiating them from upper- and middle-class men who learned Chinese. Women in the lower classes were not even allowed to learn the Korean *ŏnmun*. Through such exclusive and hierarchical education systems, the Yi state prohibited the development of women's intellectual capacity and maintained women's status as inferior to that of men.

The Yi state also translated and published Confucian ethical codes such as the *Sam Gang Haeng Sil To* (삼강행실도 : 三綱行實道 : The Three Principles of Virtuous Conduct) and *Nae Hun* (내훈 : 內訓 : The Instruction for Women [1475]) intended to educate women on virtuous conduct.[17] The former was published in the reign of the fourth King Se-jong in 1432. However, because it was published in Chinese, it had little effect on women's education, for women could not read Chinese. In 1481, it was republished in a combination of Chinese and *ŏnmun* and distributed to women, especially *yangban* women. The *Sam Gang Haeng Sil To* placed emphasis on women's loyalty, filial piety, and chastity. For example, to commend women who committed suicide in order to follow their deceased husbands to the afterworld, it bestowed special titles on them by royal decree; in such a way, the Yi society commemorated and worshipped women's martyrdom and matrimonial piety. The offspring of such self-sacrificial women benefitted by having their taxes reduced and service in the *puyŏk* (부역 : mandatory labor service to the state, e.g. building bridges and constructing roads, and waging war) exempted. The image of the chaste woman was greatly elevated, and remarriage was considered an irrevocable disgrace to herself and her family. The offspring of remarried women were prohibited from taking part in the Government Service Examination.[18] That is, such offspring (and the family name) were condemned to the lower ranks of society; respect, dignity, and glory to the family name through government service would remain out of reach on the account of a woman's remarriage.

The following portion of The *Pu Haeng P'yŏn* (부행편 : 婦行編 : The Rules of Women's Conduct) in *Myŏng Sim Bo Gam* (명심보감 : 明心寶鑑 : The Right Mind and Precious Behavior), further informs our understanding of women's roles and status through Confucian education:

> "Women must keep their chastity and be obedient," "Women must not expect anything other than the assigned identity,"

"Women must not go outside of their own houses for social activities after reaching adulthood," "Women must have pleasure only in cooking food and making wine and clothing for men," "Women must not become interested in political or social affairs, but only in family activities inside the house" . . .[19]

These rules illustrate the content of women's education.

Furthermore, *Kyŏng Guk Tae Jŏn* (경국대전 : *The Encyclopedia of the National Conduct*) was published in 1485 during the reign of King Sŏng-jong. It was a codified text book of morals with legal implications. In this book, detailed descriptions about women's education were carefully prescribed. For example, the head of the family should teach the women and girls in the family. If the head was not eligible, the respected village elder was to go from village to village to educate girls. Women who went out to mountains or to the riverside for a feast or other social gatherings were to be punished with one hundred lashes.[20] Through education, the dynasty enforced rules and laws to educate women to become obedient and selfless service persons to men and the family.

Novels and biographies such as *Yŏll Yŏ Jŏn* (열여전: 烈女傳: Five Biographies of Faithful Women) and *So Hak* (소학: 小學: Book of Lesser Learning), which portray women's obedient and sacrificial roles and highlight the rewards for their faithful role-performances were also published and distributed to women in order to emphasize proper conduct.[21] Official and unofficial forms of women's education, royal laws, decrees, and local mores all produced one monolithic ideal of women and women's education: self-sacrifice and selflessness.

With the introduction of Christianity into Korea in the late 1800s, women's education underwent great improvements, for the missionaries promoted formal and modern education for women. In 1886, Mary Fitch Scranton, an American Methodist missionary, established the first school for women in the history of Korea, the *Ewha Haktang* (이화학당: 梨花學堂).[22] There, women were taught the *ŏnmun* (Korean alphabet), English, and elementary western knowledge (e.g., biblical teachings and ethics, and philosophical thinking), along with native and foreign sewing and embroidery. Yet, Mary Scranton stated clearly that her aim in educating Korean women was to Christianize them in order to make them into "better Korean women who could be proud of things Korean."[23]

What Mary Scranton meant by "better Korean women who

could be proud of things Korean" is not clear. Perhaps, she meant modern-traditional housewives. As a missionary, she was influenced by the fervor of nineteenth-century evangelism. At the same time, as a nineteenth-century woman, she must have been influenced by Victorian notions of womanhood and family.[24] Therefore, the goal of women's education for her may have been to produce traditional homemakers with some understanding of Western and Christian knowledge. Significantly, the above source points out that the *Ewha* curriculum focused on sewing and embroidery skills. Furthermore, the clothes of all the students and faculty were made and cared for by the older girls at the school. Although *Ewha* women were introduced to modern knowledge, it is quite clear that those "modern" women were equipped to become better housewives. In other words, early Christianity contributed to the creation of "modern homemakers" supported by Christian ideals and some modern knowledge.

With the forced entry of foreign powers into Korea, particularly Japanese and western, the official Korean education "system" experienced numerous changes. With the increasing corruption, decline of authority, and instability of rule in late Yi society, the royal house lost its autonomous power. The 1876 *Kanghwa* Treaty (강화 조약) with Japan required Korea to open its doors to Japan and western powers; thus, modern Western ideas and practices infiltrated Korea. As a consequence, in 1894 Korea witnessed a radical administrative reorganization, known as the "*Kabo* Reform" (갑오경쟁). Government organizations were restructured from six ministries to eight, and the administrative districts of provinces were altered. Currency and tax systems were also transformed.

After the *Kabo* Reform, education was handled by the Ministry of Education. *Kwagŏ*, the civil service examination, was abandoned, and, in 1895, elementary schools were first established, based on the concept of equal opportunities for all classes. However, the *Kabo* Reform affected only men's education, so no attention was paid to the formal education of women: there were still no official schools for women. *The Tongnip Sinmun* (독립신문: The Independence Newspaper) pointed out the government's conspicuous gender discrimination policy in education:

> Though the government just started to teach the children, girls are still neglected. How could they discriminate against girls in the future programs for the education of the coming generation?

It is proper to match a school for girls whenever they found a school for boys. . . .[25]

Despite attempts to modernize Korea through administrative and educational reforms, the late Yi government continued to neglect the formal education of women.

However, during the period of Japanese annexation of Korea (1910–45), elementary schools were open equally to boys and girls, and women also had access to advanced education. Nonetheless, as late as the 1930s, 90 percent of the women remained illiterate.[26] For the most part, women continued to be educated informally at home. Prevailing patriarchal beliefs and practices weighed heavily against the actual formal education of women even in the early modern education system, and traditional Confucian values and norms continued to shape women's consciousness and behavior. In retrospect, early Christianity and modern education in Korea failed to challenge, but rather confirmed the traditional self-images of Korean women, even as they introduced modern knowledge to those women.

For the majority of women, accepting the traditional rules, roles, and status prescribed for women served as the initial step to adjusting to that society. To become an obedient wife and sacrificial mother was a matter of existential survival. From the Meadean point of view, one may easily assume that women in the Yi dynasty had developed strong social selves because the Confucian society controlled and shaped women's self-identities. In one sense, those women can be viewed as dependent, passive, and mechanical social animals who had not yet developed the western individualistic and autonomous "I" that is engaged in the process of thinking, choosing, and innovating.

However, in reality, those women were not mere mechanical/social animals. They may have been dependent on men for their livelihood and status and passive in outlook, but in their own way and within the spheres assigned to them, they were autonomous and active. Some women even became poets and artists in addition to fulfilling their roles as sacrificial mothers and obedient wives (although the number of female poets and artists of that period is small).[27] Such women of talent and family devotion were highly regarded and respected in the Yi society. Women also made significant contributions in various fields such as literature, printing/publication, religion (especially Shamanism), and public health.[28]

Some Yi women, then, learned to utilize the roles imposed on them to develop their own talents and simultaneously adapt to social dictates.

Above all, women not only justified their conventional roles and status, but also seemed to have rationalized the consequences of performing their assigned roles. The rewards and punishments they received for their acts would have been known to all. By adapting to the social norms, they were guaranteed a certain degree of security, power, and authority in their particular domain. Being a mother, especially of son(s), elevated the status of women and secured their positions at home and in society.[29] Moreover, they gained compensation for their vicarious lives through the success of their husbands and children, especially their son(s). In general, women faithfully carried out their ascribed roles and, through them, received social recognition and fulfillment.

In sum, role-performance elevated the image of a woman's self. However, the self was other-oriented: a woman lived for men, children, and the family; she could not separate her own identity from those of their husbands and children. One could argue that their social selves became their subjective selves, their own "I"s, that they represented the patriarchy of the Yi society. Education, both formal and informal, both Confucian and early Christian, perpetuated women's traditional roles and status and helped develop their collective selves.

RELIGION

Religious distress is at the same time the expression of real distress and the protest against real distress. Religion is the sigh of the oppressed creature, the heart of a heartless world. . . .[30]

With this statement Karl Marx affirms that religion is a reflection of social reality as well as a reaction of people. Religious practices in the Yi dynasty reflect the social realities of that time and relate to women's suffering and distress as well as to their self-images.

Distinctions of gender role and status were apparent in religious practice. There were two major religions which critically affected the lives of men and women: Confucianism and Shamanism. Confucianism, the official religion of the dynasty, was the main religion of men. Ancestor worship, the major ritual of Confucianism, portrays the male as both dominant and supreme. The crux of ancestor worship from an anthropological view is that it reunites the ancestors with the living family members and thereby strengthens the identity of the family's lineage. Moreover, the ritual also reinforces family bonds, hierarchy, and sense of belongingness. The oldest man in the family, the first son, is customarily the ritual priest. All men, including male relatives and even young boys, participate in the ceremony. Rituals of ancestor worship exclude women's participation and serve to reinforce their marginality in relation to the matrimonial family and the greater society (they are also prohibited from participating in their natal family's rituals of ancestor worship): the rituals proceed only after the deliberate dismissal of women from the room or hall. Ancestor worship rituals remain a powerful social and spiritual force in contemporary Korean life, and women remain excluded.[31]

The only part women play in ancestor worship services is that of men's assistants. Women manage all the necessary preparations, such as cooking the food and setting up the ritual table. Food is an extremely important element in the ritual. It is a means of respect, communication, reconciliation, and sharing between the ancestors and the living males of the family. Women, therefore, have the significant responsibility of preparing properly the proper foods. However, they are not allowed to participate in the ceremony and may not even approach the ritual area while the ceremony is being held. The same custom still prevails in modern Korea. One woman pursuing her doctorate at Drew University Graduate School recalled the ancestor worship ceremonies of her childhood:

> I used to hate sitting outside the door after *chesa* (제사), the ancestor worship service. All the candles in the room were blown out, and the room was deadly quiet and dark. It was spooky and scary. After my eldest brother finished the ceremony, he told me to sit outside the door and make sure nobody, not even cats, went inside the room so that our ancestors' spirits might eat the food. One night, after the ceremony, I just ran away to my friend's house instead of sitting there alone in the dark. Later, my brother found out that I wasn't there. Boy, did he give me a hard time.[32]

Although she was ordered to act as a guard or doorman, she was never permitted to take part in the liturgical ceremony. This case vividly portrays the long-time tradition of female exclusion in ancestor worship in Korea.

After the ceremony, however, women would participate in the occasion more actively by rearranging the ritual food and table for the family feast. They would feed the family, relatives, and any guests who had attended. Women would also redistribute the leftover food to neighbors and relatives. By preparing, feeding, and sharing the ritual food with others, women would function as caretakers and nurturers as well as peacemakers among families, relatives, and neighbors. Without the fundamental assistance of women, ancestor worship would not be able to be performed. Ancestor worship, therefore, is a religious reflection of the sexual dichotomy that characterizes traditional Korean life, and it points to the ambivalence of woman's role as being at once a servant and a nurturing conciliator.

On the contrary, Shamanism, the indigenous Korean religion, was considered the religion of women in the Yi period, and it continues to be so regarded in modern Korea today. As mentioned earlier, the vocation of a shaman was socially and culturally reserved for lower-class women. In Korea, shamans have predominantly been (and are) women. The exact number of shamans during different periods has not been recorded; therefore, accurate data are not available. However, a census taken during the reign of King Sun-jo (1800–34) counted 1,519 female shamans.[33] This number accounted for two-thirds of the entire shaman population. Also, it is believed that, in order to evade taxes, a significant number of shamans did not report their profession. Yung-Chung Kim suggests that including unregistered shamans, the total number of male and female shamans could have been as high as 45,000. Accordingly, historically and traditionally, women and shamans have been closely aligned. Shamans also symbolize Korean women in terms of women's roles and status. Therefore, understanding the process of being a shaman, as well as the roles and functions of shamans, is important to understanding Korean women.

There are two types of shamans: *kangsin-mu* (강신무 : 降神巫: spirit-possessed shaman); *sesŭp-mu* (세습무: 世襲巫: hereditary shaman). The hereditary shamans are the skilled and trained religious professionals who have inherited the vocation through family lines. Both men and women can inherit the vocation.[34] *Kangsin-mu* is the spirit-possessed shaman who actually represents Korean women in terms of their roles and status. Therefore, in this book, only spirit-possessed shamans will be discussed for the purpose of understanding traditional Korean women.

In order to become a shaman, one must pass through two rites of passage: *sinpyŏng* (신병: 神病: spirit-possession sickness) and *naerim kut* (내림굿: 降神굿 : initiating ritual). Persons, mostly women, who are possessed by *sinbyŏng*, suffer various symptoms: loss of appetite and weight, weakness, depression, hallucination, headaches, heartache, thirst, insomnia, sweating during sleep, visionary dreaming, sleepwalking, speaking in tongues, taking off clothes, constant washing of hands or bathing, singing, dancing, shouting, crying, mumbling, silence, and other "strange" behaviors. Apart from being physical ailments, these symptoms also seem to be expressions of denial or rejection of the existential reality of the afflicted. Interestingly enough, these symptoms cannot be cured by medical treatment.[35] The only remedy is to accept the spirit(s) which possess(es) that person. While the symptoms of *sinbyŏng* may represent a type of rebellion against society's control of women, the illness itself may reflect women's unavoidable acceptance of their self-abnegation in that society.

Naerim kut is the ritual by which the spirit is accepted. At this ritual of initiation, the spirit(s) afflicting the person unite with her/him and become(s) her/his *momju* (몸주: body master/guardian spirit). *Naerim kut* is often interpreted as a conjugal ceremony, and the relationship between the *momju* and the possessed is that of husband and wife.[36] After *naerim kut*, the afflicted fully recovers from the sickness and becomes a new person, a shaman. Yet, a shaman is not autonomous; rather, she is the medium between spirits and human beings. She is the dwelling place of the spirit(s), who endow her with power and drive her will, and without which her function as shaman is impossible. The relationship between spirits and shamans resembles the relationship between men and women in the Yi society.

Theologically, this process of becoming a shaman can be interpreted as a woman's death and resurrection through marriage and through the observation of women's roles and status in that society. During the Yi dynasty, women belonged to men as shamans belong to the spirit(s). Marriage required a woman's self-sacrifice and self-abnegation for the sake of men and the family as *naerim kut* signified a shaman's own self-denial and acceptance of the spirit(s)' will. Marriage, in a sense, represented the death of a woman's own self. Yet marriage was viewed as the rebirth, or real birth, of a woman, just as a shaman is born as a new person by "marrying" the spirit(s).

It is interesting to note that this "divine marriage" and "resurrection" of a woman as a shaman had the effect of reversing gender roles in her personal life.[37] Instead of her husband acting as the main rice-winner and public figure in the household, the wife-shaman would take on that role. A husband had little choice in the matter, for this vocation was understood to be sanctioned by the spirits. It is not without reason that one of the main purposes of lower-class women's transformation of themselves into shamans was to increase the family income[38] (and, one could surmise, to reverse the oppressive gender roles). The shamans' husbands usually functioned as their wives' managers or assistants. From the standpoint of the conventional social norm, their husbands became emasculated. However, in the Confucian patriarchal family structure, even a shaman's home was represented by her emasculated husband, though the main power-holder was the shaman-wife. In my view, the role reversal of shamans within their own households represents the actual power women possess inside the home, which was inseparably linked to healing, nurturing, and sustaining the lives of the family members. In a sense, the shaman was and is a Confucian woman who has "come out of the closet." From this standpoint, the power and position of Korean men with regard to their household and family are merely symbolic.

Most shamans came from the *ch'ŏnmin* class, and the vocation itself was designated a *ch'ŏnmin* job. Therefore, being a shaman was considered a disgrace. Shamans and their families, even today, are considered social outcasts and must endure social discrimination and stigma.[39] Although *yangban* and the common people lived inside the city wall; *ch'ŏnmin*, such as butchers, artists, entertainers, and shamans, were exiled to specifically designated areas outside the city wall. *Ch'ŏnmin* could not mingle with the *yangban* and the *sangmin* (common class). In view of the fact that *ch'ŏnmin* were servants or slaves of one type or another and that most shamans were women, the status of a woman shaman was secured at the bottom of the social hierarchy. Nevertheless, shamans did play significant roles in various areas, particularly in directing family matters of villagers and healing the sick.[40] In this sense, shamans represented women in general, who were at the bottom of the social and family structure, and yet functioned as life supporters.

On the positive side, shamans' contribution to public welfare in the Yi period, particularly in the area of health, was significant. *Tongsŏ Hwalinsŏ* (동서활인서: East and West Medical Center) was established by King T'ae-jo, founder of the Yi Dynasty, in 1392 for public health care, particularly of the poor. Shamans were supposed to register in the *Tongsŏ Hwalinsŏ*, and the government appointed and controlled shamans were to be in charge of public medicine. At the end of the year, shamans who performed their duties well were exempted from paying taxes. The dynasty also employed shamans to initiate *kut*[41] and other religious rituals in order to protect the nation from war, infectious diseases, and natural disasters, such as famine, and to promote national wealth, power, and welfare. The Kings T'ae-jong, Se-jong, and Sŏng-jong, well-known Confucian worshippers and administrators, hired numerous shamans to pray for rain during seasons of drought.[42]

Throughout the history of the Yi dynasty, a number of famous shamans were employed by the royal court to ensure the well-being of the royal family. Those who officially served the royal court were called "*kuksa*" (국사: 國師). According to records in the reign of Yŏnsan-kun, *the Sŏng-suk-ch'ŏng* (성숙청: one of the government departments) was responsible for appointing the *kuksa*.[43] *Kuksa* not only cared for those who were ill but also functioned as advisors, counsellors, and prophets to royal families. In case of national crisis, kings discussed with and received advice from the *kuksa*. Shamans, therefore, were involved in critical decision-making processes of the kingdom and the fate of the nation;[44] they functioned not only as healers but also as counsellors and advisors behind the political scene. The role of *kuksa* may be symbolically understood as the women's role and power behind the scene in that society.

Above all, the *kut*, the major ritual of Korean Shamanism, demonstrates the shaman's various roles, particularly in relation to healing.[45] There are many different variations of *kut* according to the specific needs and purposes of the initiators. The nature of *kut* covers the whole realm of life and death.[46] For example, *samsin kut* (삼신굿: 三神굿) is offered to the "three-spirit grandmother" for childbirth, particularly for a male child. As mentioned earlier, male progeniture was one of woman's major functions because it secured not only patrimonial lineage and tradition of the family but also woman's position at home and in the society. *Chinogwi kut* (진오귀 굿) is held for the safe journey of the spirit of the dead to the other world. There are numerous *pyŏng kut* (병굿: 病굿) held for curing illness and disease. There are varieties of *chaesu kut* (재수굿: 財壽굿) for good luck, success, and well-being. Also, there are different forms of *kut* for rain and for fruitful harvests. Despite the varieties of *kut,* their central aim is healing—mental, physical, spiritual, relational, and cosmic.

The elements of *kut* consist of food, music, dance, and people. In particular, music and dance compose the major portions of *kut*: shamans sing and dance. Assistants play musical instruments such as the drum, flute, and gong. The spectators are also invited to dance and sing together.[47] Throughout its history, *kut* has been a culturally sanctioned form of social gathering and entertainment for women, for, in large part, it attracts and is performed by women. The sponsor, who is usually a woman, can invite her relatives, neighbors, and friends to participate in the ceremony. Therefore, in my view, the function of *kut* is not only to entertain but also to liberate women, albeit temporarily, from rigid social control and routine housekeeping chores, for the *kut* offers women a rare occasion to step outside the house and socialize with others.

Furthermore, a feast is characteristic of *kut*. Offering ritual food to the spirit(s) is a gesture of reconciliation between the spirit(s) who afflict and the victim(s) who are afflicted. After the *kut,* the food is offered to everyone—shamans and the spectators, friends and enemies, men and women, children and adults. It is an event of joy, of sharing and binding relationships between and among spirit(s) and people. It is an occasion for mending broken relationships, and women play the primary role in this healing process.

Along with *kut, chŏm* (점) is also a critical and vital part of Shamanistic practice. The purpose of *chŏm*, which can be described as a form of psychotherapy and prophecy, is to solve present problems or cure illness as well as to prevent evil intervening in the life of one's family. Unlike western psychotherapy, however, it is public in most cases. The shaman and the client(s), who are all women, sit together in a room. The clients express their views on the particular problem(s), sometimes supporting and sometimes contradicting one another. During the Yi dynasty, *chŏm*, in a sense, served as an outstanding, democratic way of working out human problems in a highly undemocratic society.

There are several ways for a shaman to conduct *chŏm*. The most popular method of performing *chŏm* is to throw rice on a small table: according to the patterns formed and the number of grains of rice which cling together, shamans tell the clients of their past and present and predict the future. It is significant that rice, the device used for *chŏm*, is the most common and essential material with which women deal in daily life; it is the life sustainer. Supplied with the prescriptions the shaman devises to manage a particular situation, women return to the home and carry out the instructions in order to protect their families from evil spirits.[48] In this way, women take upon the responsibility and authority of ensuring the family's welfare. Above all, *chŏm* is a way of fortune-telling about well-being, success, and prosperity, and, as such, it bestows upon a woman the spiritual and social power to manage her domicile to her liking. *Chŏm* remains very popular even among contemporary Korean women.[49]

The importance of these rituals to women in Yi society was considerable: just as shamans served as village priestesses, women in general functioned as household priestesses. The home was both the sanctuary of shamans and women, and each participated in the other's fate.[50] Although there were formal and informal sha-manistic sanctuaries, the *sŏnghwang-dang* (성황당) in villages and mountains (which still exist in Korean villages today), the home functioned as the main Shamanistic sanctuary, since Yi women were prohibited from going outside the home except at night.

Moreover, women, especially the oldest woman in the family, functioned as the household priestess and presided over the *kosa* (고사).[51] *Kosa* was a very common, age-old house ritual and re-mained popular during most of this century.[52] The success or failure of a family depended on the role of women as household priestesses. We shall see later how this role, which has been transmitted from the Yi period, influences the activities and identities of Christian immigrant women in the United States today.

In short, the religious practices in the Yi dynasty reinforced the dichotomy between gender role and status. Both Confucianism and Korean Shamanism served to legitimate and perpetuate the role of women as caretakers, servants, and healers. Confucianism commanded and Shamanism reinforced women's view of themselves as other-oriented and selfless beings, who lived vicariously. However, Shamanism offered women outlets through which to exercise their power within the home and guaranteed them legitimate authority to protect the household. Through Shamanistic rituals and observances, the average woman's self became identified with that of divinity, of the spirits. This kind of other-oriented "self-empowerment" molded the common woman into a "woman warrior,"[53] one who would by any and all means available stake out, defend, assert, and promote the well-being of her family. We will later see how such attitudes and behavior influenced the thinking and behavior of *ilse* Christian women in the United States.

Emile Durkheim asserts that religion not only shapes its members' consciousness and behavior but also perpetuates them through rituals.[54] According to him, a religion contains three essential elements: *(a)* a notion of the sacred and profane, *(b)* ritual, and *(c)* congregation. In particular, he affirms the role of congregation (church) in perpetuating religious ideas through congregational rituals. Although neither Confucianism nor Korean Shamanism had fixed congregations, both function, through rituals, to promote and reinforce women's roles as vicarious healers and family caretakers. Confucian rituals serve to exclude and marginalize women, whereas Shamanism serves to buttress women in roles of power within their marginalized spheres.

IDEAL WOMEN

From the Meadean point of view, the development of a full self means an individual's complete adaptation to the given social milieu. An individual who develops a full self not only represents but also resembles that social context, just as a cactus flourishes in the very desert it symbolizes. In this sense, the concept of the Meadean self is akin to Weber's "ideal type."[55] Weber points out that a specific social, political, and economic situation produces its ideal type of a person that is best suited to that condition. For example, Confucianism would produce its ideal person representing Confucian ideology. It is to be expected, then, that the Confucian Yi society would have produced an ideal type of Korean Confucian womanhood.

The ideal woman in Confucian Yi society was a nameless

woman.[56] Women were given names at birth but did not use them as such and were identified with their men. Before marriage, women were called "so and so's" daughter; after marriage, "so and so's" wife; after a child's (son's) birth, "so and so's" mother." Thus, women in the Yi dynasty did not have their own identities as individuals apart from their men. A girl's name was not even recorded in the official registry book of her natal family. It was considered an unofficial temporary name. When a woman married, her husband's full name was added to her natal family record, but only her surname was registered below her husband's name in his family book. Instead of calling a girl (or adult woman) by her given name, family members and friends addressed her by the particular function she performed in the family.[57] All of this bespeaks the fact that a woman was "nameless" in Confucian society; her existence was totally immersed in her men, and her own self was negated.[58]

Second, an "ideal woman" was also a self-sacrificing healer/ "warrior woman." The legend of *Pari kongju* (바리공주 : Princess Pali), who is considered one of the original shamans of Korean Shamanism,[59] is an another model of an "ideal woman." Princess Pali was the seventh daughter of a son-less king and queen. Angered by her birth, the king ordered Princess Pali to be thrown into the water. With heaven's help, she was rescued by a turtle and delivered to heaven. After many years had passed, the king and queen became old and ill and died. When Pali, who was in heaven, heard the news, she tried to rescue them from death. Through considerable toil and painful effort, she came down to earth and restored life to her dead parents. The king was very grateful to his once-abandoned daughter and invited her to stay with them in their palace and enjoy all its privileges. However, Princess Pali refused her father's benevolent offer, saying that she preferred to heal the sick and protect people from evil. This legend, which is considered to be one of the origins of Korean Shamanism and reflects woman's— particularly a shaman's—role as a "self-giving" healer and "warrior" for others.[60]

Women's sacrifice for men was very common, and Korean women even today do not have to look far into the past to see examples of the centrality of woman-as-healer/warrior in traditional Korean society. My mother's childhood story offers one such example. My mother, who was born shortly after the annexation of Yi Korea by Japan and died in Los Angeles in 1992, performed the role of self-giving woman-as-healer during her entire life. When she was seven or eight years old, her only brother (a man of the Yi society and the head of the family), who was more than ten years her senior, had been very ill. A shaman told the family that the only way for him to recover was for him to drink fresh water, drawn before sunrise, from a particular stream that was more than four miles from the house. Because my grandmother and my sick uncle could not trust any of the house servants with this important task (lest they draw water from a nearby stream at any time), they commanded my mother to go. For three years, my mother, then called *"sundungi"* (순둥이: good-natured creature), left her home at four o'clock each morning to draw water from the stream. My mother walked the miles with her servant, even on fiercely cold and snowy days. She went into the middle of the stream, faced the eastern sky, bowed her head three times, prayed for her brother, drew water, and immediately walked back to serve her brother— all in accordance with the shaman's instructions. When I asked her about this experience, she used to recall how her long braid would freeze in the morning cold and how her calves and heels would become cut, chapped, and frost-bitten. From the time of her first mission as female-*qua*-healer until the end of her life, my mother suffered from aching, chapped and bloody calves, especially in the winter. Until her death, my mother was the first to act as woman-as-healer, by preparing special medicinal brews and gruel (which require the greatest care and discipline to achieve an optimal health benefit) and by praying when any member of her family, even one of her sons-in-law, was ill.

Yi women not only devoted their lives to the service of their men and their families but also died for their nation. Yu Kwan-Soon is a monumental heroine in Korean history. Yu Kwan-Soon, a newly converted Christian student of *Ewha Haktang*, symbolizes the self-sacrificial "warrior woman" idealized by Confucian Korean society. She is famous as a martyr for Korean national independence from Japanese colonial rule. At the age of twelve, she led a throng of nationalist protesters during the historical *Samil Manse Sagon* (삼일만세사건: March 1 Independence Protest),[61] was arrested, horrendously tortured, and finally killed by the Japanese police. Her body was cut into many pieces as a deterrent to others who would follow in her footsteps, and her entire family was also tortured and killed by the Japanese. Yu Kwan-Soon remains the symbol of the ideal Korean woman of the Yi society, one who is at once a nameless servant of the men in her family as well as a "warrior woman" who does not hesitate to risk her own life for the life of the nation.

NEW WOMEN

Theory of Adjustment

There are various ways that human beings adjust in order to survive in a particular social environment. People mechanically and rationally assimilate with existing social situations, as women in the Yi dynasty adapted to their Confucian social context. Peter Berger's theory of "world construction"[62] offers a contrasting view of individual adjustment. He argues that human beings not only cooperate with, but also initiate changes and innovations in, their social environment in order to facilitate adjustment to it. For Mead, such innovation would involve the formation of one's subject self. However, both Mead's and Berger's view of adaptation to and innovation of the given situation is not universally applicable. Their theories are more pertinent to those who possess the power and authority to change and control their own lives as well as the context in which they live their lives, for example, in the West, White males. Women and minorities in most societies do not have access to such transformative and adaptive power; they find other means of adaptation and innovation, namely, transmigration and/or immigration.

Immigration or transmigration is another type of survival technique employed by individuals escaping from an unbearable reality. It is especially true of the powerless who cannot change their social environment. After the Civil War, waves of Black slaves migrated northward from the South with the hope of finding better social and political conditions. In recent times, the exodus of Russian Jews to Israel and of East Germans to West Germany (before unification) and of the Haitians to the United States after a military coup demonstrates the power of immigration or transmigration as a means of survival in a harsh reality. Likewise, immigration to America provided many Korean women who had found their social and economic situation in Yi Korea oppressive and suffocating with a new way of life,[63] affording them an opportunity for reconstruction of their social contexts and consequently for self-development.

In order to understand the self-development of contemporary Korean immigrant women, it is therefore important to understand the history of Korean immigration and the unique social experiences of the Korean immigrants.

Immigration to America: Emergence of New Women

The first 101 Korean immigrants arrived in Honolulu Bay in 1903. Some 7,226 people came to work in the sugarcane plantations of Hawaii between 1903 and 1905; among them were 637 women, most of whom were wives and daughters of the laborers. Only 222 more Koreans, mostly students and political exiles, came to the United States between 1906 and 1910; this group included only forty women and forty-three children.[64] Most of them worked in sugarcane fields, and their living and working conditions were intolerable. Sheltered in shabby huts, the men and women worked for more than ten hours a day, six days a week, under the fierce sun. Wages were sixty-five cents a day for men and fifty cents for women. Understandably, in the early 1900s, migration to the American mainland in search of better working situations became increasingly popular among Koreans in Hawaii. They went to such West Coast cities as San Francisco, Los Angeles, Riverside, Dinuba, Salt Lake City, Denver, and Seattle in the years between 1905 and 1910.

Why did Koreans immigrate to America? The major motive among these first groups (1903–10) was economic and political. At the turn of the century, there had been a widespread famine in Korea, especially in the northern part. Numerous people starved to death, and famine became a critical social problem. At the same time, the Hawaii Sugar Planters Association (HSPA) was experiencing an acute labor shortage, owing to the 1882 Chinese Exclusion Act, which banned Chinese immigrant-laborers from entering the United States. In order to solve the labor shortage problem, representatives of HSPA met with Horace N. Allen, who was the then Chief of the United States legation in Seoul and so had a congenial relationship with the then Yi king, Ko-jong.[65] King Ko-jong approved Korean immigration to Hawaii because it would help alleviate some of the effects of the famine as well as offer some relief to the HSPA.

However, the concept of immigration had been very foreign to Koreans. Koreans had always lived in a social structure based on inseparable blood kinship; therefore, for most Koreans, leaving the hometown or country meant literally cutting off their roots and blood-ties, or social and spiritual death. Despite their suffering (owing to famine) and sense of helplessness in the inflexible Confucian society, most Koreans were not attracted to the idea or prospect of moving far away to another land. At this point, the contribution of Christian missionaries, particularly Methodist missionaries, to Korean immigration to America was critical.

Christianity arrived in Korea in 1884 and appealed particularly to the poor and the powerless, especially those in the northern parts of Korea, who had long been ignored and excluded by the Yi dynastic governments. Through the sermons of such missionaries as the Reverend George Heber Jones, the image of America as a land of hope and opportunity—biblically speaking, the "land in which milk and honey overflowed"—was implanted in the minds of the new Korean converts. For those new Korean Christians, immigration offered promise and hope for a new life.

From the beginning of the history of Korean immigration to America, Christianity had an inseparable relationship with the immigrants and so became their main religion.[66] First, the fact that nearly half of the 101 immigrants on the first ship to the United States were from the Reverend Jones's Yongdong Church in Inchon, the first Korean Methodist Church, offers a clear indication of this missionary's impact on Korean immigration to America and the Christian influence in general on these Koreans. In addition, the majority of the first immigrants between 1903 and 1905 were north Koreans, the people who had first been Christianized in Korea. Moreover, practice of, Confucianism and Shamanism was not viable among the new immigrants, for both religions lacked a prerequisite for success in the new social context: strong ties between the extended-family social structure and the individual.

Besides the Christian missionaries in Korea, international tensions and eventual annexation of Korea by Japan influenced greatly Korean immigration to the United States. In 1910, with the Japanese announcement of the *Hanil Hapbang* (한일합방: the Treaty of Korea's Annexation to Japan), the Yi dynasty forfeited its sovereignty and officially ended. A wave of patriotism spread across Korea and, with it, the demand for the restoration of Korean sovereignty. However, under the oppressive surveillance of the Japanese imperialists, it became almost impossible to protest against Japan and to wage nationalist struggles to regain Korean autonomy. Some patriots escaped to China, established a "Korean Provisional Government" in Shanghai, and continued to work for Korean independence. Others came to America and sought U.S. support for Korean independence.

In addition to those who immigrated to the United States for economic and political reasons, a special immigrant group composed only of women crossed the Pacific in the 1920s. These were the Korean "picture brides"[67] of 1910–24. As the term *picture brides* indicates, women became brides of immigrant Korean men through the exchange of photographs. Women in Korea and men in Hawaii (and the mainland) exchanged their pictures and corresponded through letters. After the agreement to marry was established, the men would assume the responsibility of covering the cost of the women's travel expenses and would send the money to Korea. The legal process was handled by the cooperative efforts of the HSPA and the Korean government, and the women arrived in the United States to marry their prospective husbands.

As the figures cited above indicate, during the first waves of immigration (1903–05 and 1906–10), the ratio of men to women during the first waves exceeded 10:1. Most male immigrant laborers were single and eventually indulged in problematic social, moral, and hygienic behavior, including alcoholism, opium-smoking, gambling, and sex with (and rape of) the wives and daughters of their fellow Korean laborers. Suffering from loneliness, frustration, harsh working conditions, and racism,[68] such men became difficult to control as laborers. In order to protect the new immigrant women and to solve the problems of work and moral discipline, the HSPA and Korean worker-representatives adopted the "picture bride" system, which had originally been designed by the Japanese in Hawaii to solve their own problems of mate-less single laborers. Consequently, 1066 women were imported to the United States between 1910 and 1924 to serve as "picture brides." Unlike the laborers and political exiles, these women had a different motive in coming to America: the desire to escape from the oppression of females by the Yi dynasty.[69]

One seventy-eight-year-old woman whom the Sunwoos interviewed regarding her life as a "picture bride" succinctly described her decision to immigrate as a means of liberating herself from the oppressive social situation of her youth. In the 1975 interview, she recalled:

> When I was only fourteen years old, I recalled what I heard my older brother often repeat: "Our Korean women should have a chance to go abroad and not be content like frogs, just croaking inside a deep well and limited to knowing only that the heavens are high. They should learn about the breadth of society."[70]

She also remembered that when she had reached puberty, she was forbidden to move about, especially outside the house. She found such restrictions to be more and more intolerable, and when she first heard of the "picture bride" arrangements, she became very excited. She said:

> Ah, marriage! Then I could go to America! That land of freedom with streets paved of gold! . . . Since I became ten, I've been forbidden to step outside of my gates, just like all the rest of the girls of my days . . . becoming a picture bride, whatever that was, would be my answer and release.[71]

Such words vividly attest to the oppressive social context in which Yi women had to live and to the appeal of immigration as an alternative. Immigration, then, became a calculated and rational survival choice for such Yi women.

At the present time, reliable data on "picture brides" is lacking; therefore, it is difficult to cite accurate information about them. Moreover, the existing sources are confusing and contradictory. For example, Eun Sik Yang calls the "picture brides" "new women" because they were young (ranging in age from seventeen to twenty-five), and claims that they were relatively well educated.[72] However, in fact, most women in the Yi dynasty were not educated. Even in the 1930s, 90 percent of all women in Korea were illiterate.[73]

The "picture brides" whom I have known personally were relatively uneducated women yet strong in character and willpower.[74] They were assertive and decisive in domestic and public (church) matters. Above all, "picture brides" as a group were brave and ambitious: they chose a new life that brought them to America. They seem to have decided their own fate, since there is no evidence that their fathers (or brothers) sold them as "picture brides." In their bravery and autonomy, they were quite different from their traditional or "ideal woman" counterparts. The early immigrant women searched for a new way of life and decided to risk their oppressive past and present for an unknown but hopeful future. For this reason, they are called "new women" in this study.

Americanization of New Women

Immigration wrought great changes in the lives of the "new women." According to Eui-Young Yu, Koreans, particularly "picture brides," when compared with other Asian immigrants (Chinese and Japanese), showed the greatest ability to adapt to American life.[75] For example, in contrast to Chinese and Japanese, most of whom retained their traditional mode of dress, few early immigrant Koreans, particularly women, wore traditional Korean clothing. "Picture brides" also showed greater zeal in learning English and adapting to American-Hawaiian culture.[76] Above all, many of them chose English names such as Lucy, Etta, Mary, Rose, and so forth. In their outlook, they became very Americanized. One such acquaintance of mine in San Francisco always wore American-style clothes and spoke broken English along with broken Korean. She also called her husband by his first name and treated him as her equal. She made him cook and sometimes do laundry and go grocery shopping. She also rebuked him if he did not perform such chores well.

The early immigrant women were very different in their outlook and social manner from Korean immigrant women in America today. They were more intent on transforming their lives to reflect their new social context. For example, many elderly women today wear Korean dress, especially when attending church services. Maintenance of Korean culture and tradition is conspicuous in, particularly, woman's life. Since woman's leadership outside the home is not encouraged, most women, even younger ones, today withdraw themselves from active participation in the church/community especially decision-making matters. Contemporary women in this sense are more traditional than their foremothers.

Scholars like Wayne Patterson regard the rapid Americanization of the early immigrant women a direct result of their Christianization.[77] If that is so, contemporary immigrant women should be more Americanized, because an overwhelming majority of them practice Christianity and are better educated than earlier immigrants were. Yet these are the very women who struggle to retain their Korean culture and traditions more than the early immigrant women did. Another explanation, more plausible in my opinion, is that the early immigrant women's rapid Americanization was due to the very special "adaptation technique" they developed in to survive in the rigid social structure of the Yi dynasty. When they came to America and entered the not-yet-institutionalized Korean Christian church, they looked to a more well-defined American society at large. Because the church could not yet offer them strict guidelines on thought and behavior, the women may have been attracted to the already established mores of the American society. Unwittingly, they adapted their self-image to the American outlook while simultaneously using it to reject the identities imposed on them by Yi Korean society. In this way, American society served as the agent of developing both a new social self as well as the subjective self, "I."

The Early Immigrant Church and Women's Advancement   The church was very important for the new self-development of the early immigrant women. Within a decade after the first wave of immigration, Koreans had organized thirty-one churches and chapels in Hawaii and twelve churches in California. Altogether, the membership represented nearly two-thirds of the Korean immigrant population of that period. Korean communities developed around the churches, and, consequently, the churches became community centers.

Because of the lack of systematic studies and in-depth research in the area of early immigrant Korean churches, accurate information on the character, roles, and functions of these early churches is difficult to obtain. From the fragments available in the articles of Eun Sik Yang ("The Korean Women of America") and Alice Chai ("Korean Women in Hawaii, 1903–1945"), one may infer that the church had not yet been fully institutionalized, owing largely to the then relatively short history of Korean Christianity. Therefore, while the church did serve as the major social context of early immigrant Korean life, it had not yet established definitive doctrines, organizational structures, and systems of behavior necessary to incorporate itself as a concrete social and religious institution. In character, the Korean church was more like a movement than an institution. It was in the process of growing, together with its new immigrant converts, in a new land. Although the early churches—like contemporary ones—were dominated by men, the very fluidity of the church as a social structure enabled women to assume and carry out successfully important leadership roles in the churches.

The churches served as centers of education—of Korean as well as English, of American culture as well as biblical knowledge— and activism for the early immigrant women. Immigrant women served the Sunday School as teachers, managed the Korean language schools and boarding houses for school for Korean children, and raised scholarship funds for the youngsters' education. They also worked for the churches as deaconesses, stewardesses, and choir members. Accordingly, their eyes and minds were opened through the churches. Most important, they became involved in political activities through the churches, which then functioned as the center of the Korean independence movement (1910–45). Accordingly, women became educated about and sensitized to the world around them. They traded in their past lives of being blind, deaf, and mute for a new existence of awareness, activism, and assertiveness.

The Korean Nationalism of the Early Immigrant Women
Throughout the history of the Korean independence movement, the Korean churches in the United States played crucial roles as sources of financial support, movement organizers, spiritual leaders, charity, and pressure groups influencing United States and international policymakers. Christian women participated in the independence movement through various women's organizations formed for the purpose of supporting independence activities in Korea, China, and the United States. The *Hankuk Puin Hoe* (한국 부인회: Korean Women's Association) in San Francisco (1908) and the *Taehanin Puin Hoe* (대한인부인회: Korean Women's Society) established in Hawaii (1913) were two such groups. Although their leaders and members belonged to churches, the organizations themselves were formed independent of direct church influence. While it is not clear why these organizations were established apart from the church's control, one can surmise either that the immigrant church did not want to become directly involved in politics or that, as independent-minded women, the members did not want to be under the control of the men who dominated the church. Whatever the reason, the organizations' main purpose was to raise funds to assist in the education of Korean children and in the work of the Korean National Association, the men's organization of the independence movement in the United States. These two women's

organizations continued to play the traditional female role of men's assistants by fundraising for the men's movement as well as by providing financial and spiritual support to the patriots in Korea and China.

The "March First Movement" or "*Manse* Movement" surfaced in Korea in 1919 and proved to be the launching pad for women's self-actualization and for development of their new selves. Hundreds of thousands of women in Korea and America participated in this movement. During the same year, the Korean Women's Patriotic Society (한국여자애국단체) and the Korean Women's Relief Society of Hawaii (하와이한국여자구제회) were founded in California and Hawaii, respectively . These two organizations contributed at once to the independence movement and to the new self-formation of women by serving in the role of male-supporter (in this case financial contributions to the men's organizations) and by affording women the opportunity to act, with their own plans, independently from men in political and social affairs.

The Korean Women's Relief Society (한국여자구제회: *Taehan Puin Kujehoe*), headed by Maria Hwang, organized a spontaneous march in March 1919 in support of the *Manse* Movement. Dressed in Korean traditional clothes, women marched into downtown Honolulu singing patriotic songs. They also trained "emergency nurses" and sent them to Shanghai and Manchuria to care both for the patriots who were wounded in the course of their anti-Japanese activities and for their families. They sent money to needy nationalists and their families in Korea. They were also in the forefront of the anti-Japanese food embargo. The organizations' members made Korean soy sauce, rice cakes, and bean paste and promoted the anti-Japanese embargo under the slogan of "Don't Buy the Jap's Soy Sauce; We make better ones."[78] In order to sell their homemade goods, women, after having worked long, hard days, went from door to door carrying their babies on their backs and urging support of the independence movement. Even female children volunteered to work in the plantations to earn extra money in order to support the independence movement. Women did not merely imbibe Korean nationalistic ideology but eagerly assumed political action. The Society raised U.S.$200,000 for the independence fund, and until the actual liberation of Korea from Japanese rule in 1945, it functioned as a financial and spiritual pillar of the independence movement.

The Korean Women's Patriotic Society contributed to the independence movement in similar ways. The society not only raised funds and supplied money to the patriots in Korea, Manchuria, and the Shanghai provisional government but also supported the movement through political activities. For example, immediately after the Japanese army had seized Korean villages and massacred the inhabitants in Jilin, Manchuria, in 1920, the society publicized the barbarous act and collected funds to assist the victims. The society also sent a letter to Charles Hughes, then secretary of state, demanding, in the name of justice, U.S. political intervention.[79] Women who had once been "warriors" protecting their men and families within the home demonstrated their "warriorship" in the struggle to restore their nation. The politicization of these women meant that their men and their families no longer constituted the sole focus of their lives, that their loyalty to their nation came to play a much greater role than ever before in the past.

The representatives and leading members of these women's organizations were mostly "picture brides" and devout Christians. They powerfully demonstrated the tradition of women's self-sacrificial "warriorship," but this time, for their country. The church played a significant role in women's awareness of and participation in social and political realities. Through such activities, women's roles and status changed and new self-consciousness emerged. Women became assertive and chafed at the realization that they were still under the control of men, since their organizations were structurally under the umbrella of the Korean National Association.[80]

After the *Manse* event, the independence movement slowly waned. From this turning point onward, both women's organizations shifted their focus from the independence movement to women's self-actualization. The leaders realized the importance of women's education. In order to support more effectively Korean independence, they agreed that women should be aware of their responsibilities and rights within the family, church, community, and nation. The shift of women's interests and the society's goals were reflected in an article written by a picture bride that appeared under the title of "Women Should Work like Men," in the *Shinhan Minbo* (신한민보: The New Korean Peoples' News):

> The Korean women folk are partly responsible for the present Korean tragedy, because they have discarded their responsibility

and left it to the men who are only half the population. Sisters! Stop dreaming in a family which is actually an invisible prison. Stand up and unshackle our next generations from [traditional] constraints. Our utmost tasks are to free ourselves of bondage, to build our wealth, to enlist as soldiers, and to obtain an education. If we are prepared, there will be no discrimination against us women in political participation or legal activities. . . . Recently, magazines have spoken about women's liberation. We should educate ourselves so that we can gain equality with men [in the independence movement] and be second to no one in responding to our national duty.[81]

As this article illustrates, the "new women" in America showed tremendous independence in their thinking and action and demonstrated outside the home their formerly hidden power as "warriors." As individual persons, they also attempted to gain equality with men. In other words, the "new women" tried to create a new self-image. They had come out of their homes and worked for their country along with their men. Eventually, their roles and status would be greatly transformed. Korean women's nationalism meant that the center of their lives shifted from their men and family to their nation, Korea: they lived for and devoted themselves to Korea. From this point of view, the object of women's consecration and sacrifice was greatly expanded, although they were still placing something "other" at the center of the "self." In Hawaii and the United States, the churches and the culture of American political activism, rather than Confucianism and Shamanism, provided the social contexts for the shaping of these women's new self-image.

Women's Roles and Status in Family and Economic Arena

Though the public roles and status of the early immigrant women had been greatly expanded and improved, their work at home remained burdensome, and their contribution to the economic life of the family was enormous. Traditionally, women, except those of the lower class, did not work outside the home. However, the immigration forced most women to come out of their homes in order to supplement their husbands' income. Most early immigrant women worked in the sugarcane plantations alongside their men. The daughter of Maria Hwang[82] (the founder of the Korean Women's Relief Society) describes her bitter childhood memories about her mother's hard work:

My mother had many maids in Korea, but at Kipahulu plantation she worked in the canefields with my older brother and his
wife. I remembered her hands, so blistered and raw that she had
to wrap them in cloths. One morning she overslept and failed to
hear the work whistle. We were all asleep . . . my brother and his
wife, my older sister, and myself. I was seven years old at the
time. Suddenly the door swung open, and a big burly *luna* (over-
seer) burst in, screaming and cursing. "Get up, get to work." The
luna ran around the room, ripping off the covers, not caring
whether my family was dressed or not. I will never forget it.[83]

A personal acquaintance of mine in San Francisco, who had
been a "picture bride" and independence activist, spoke often of
her hardships as a new immigrant in Hawaii. When she came to
Hawaii as a "picture bride," her husband-to-be was already too
old and weak to work; therefore, she had to work like a horse on
a plantation in order to support the family. She used to work from
morning until night. She took her baby with her to the plantation
because there was no one to take care of him. The baby was left
alone in the field all day long while she worked; she was with him
only a few times a day in order to nurse him. At the end of the day,
when she went to her baby to take him home, he was too exhausted
even to respond to her. She said:

It was heart-breaking to see the baby lying like a rotten vegetable. I don't even know how much I cried. When finally, the
baby died, I hated my husband.[84]

This woman also spoke of many tragic occurrences among
"picture brides" in their relationships with their husbands. For
example, many young women arrived on Hawaiian shores to find
that they had been deceived by their prospective husbands. Many
laborers were illiterate, and so the letters that the women had received back in Korea had been written not by their prospective
husband but by someone the man had hired or befriended. Often
the descriptions of the prospective husband's personality, background, income, and savings differed greatly from reality. Moreover,
many of the men were much older than their photographs indicated;
a prospective groom might send a photograph of himself taken
years earlier, or even one of another young man entirely. When the
brides arrived, they found that many men were old and weak—
some from aging and others from hard work. Shocked and disappointed, some women ran away or were sent back to Korea because

they refused to marry. However, since Korean tradition considered it a disgrace for engaged women to return to their homes, many of the women found that they had no choice but to marry the men who had deceived them.

One picture bride interviewed by Sunwoo and Sunwoo described the painful experience of canceling her engagement. She had been engaged for two years in Korea and had waited for the travel money to arrive from her prospective husband. The man wrote that he was doing very poorly and could not save money for her travel expenses and that perhaps it would be better to cancel their engagement.

> "Cancel? Now I was really a doomed woman! Had I not already promised myself to him? This is more like a 'divorce'! Oh, now, my brazen 'marriage' and 'cancellation' must be revealed to my family! How can I survive the Hell I'm certain to face?" (She relates that she was as good as "murdered" by her narrow-minded family for she had) . . . ruined the entire family lineage, disgraced the family name so that none could hold up his or her head anywhere, etc.[85]

She was humiliated and physically and emotionally battered from morning to night by all members of her family. She could no longer endure the punishment, so she ran away from her home and went, luckily, to the home of her fiance. As this shows, most women had no place to go were they to cancel their engagements; therefore, they accepted reality, however harsh it was. Then, they plunged themselves into work in order to survive in a foreign land.

Women not only worked outside the home but also did extra domestic work for pay. Besides doing their own housework and child rearing, many women cooked and washed for single male laborers in order to supplement their incomes. The story of the Reverend Paik Sin-Kyu's wife communicates the importance of early immigrant women's economic contribution to the family through performance of additional domestic tasks. With three children, the Paik family had moved to Riverside, California, to pick oranges for a living. Setting up house in a former chicken coop, the entire family depended on Mrs. Paik's income, since Mr. Paik had virtually no job and income. One of the daughters recalled:

> Although there were about ten families, there were a lot of bachelors. About thirty of them. Since we were poor, father got the

idea that mother should cook for the bachelors. You know, that gives us food and a little money. So my poor mother had to cook for thirty to forty bachelors. Every morning she got up at three or four o'clock to cook for them on a makeshift stove. I always had to get up at three o'clock in the morning and help her pack the lunches.[86]

In this case, a mother and daughter together sustained the family by feeding and caring for men outside their own family.

The early immigrants' dreams were to save money, leave the plantation, become independent business owners and educate their children at university. With the woman's hard labor, such dreams came true for many of the immigrants and their families. According to my San Francisco acquaintance discussed above, many women ran boarding houses for bachelors and saved money. With the help of their women, men ran restaurants, laundry shops, shoe-repair shops, barber shops, and vegetable stands. Women also became their husbands' business partners and, less frequently, independent owners of small businesses. My acquaintance herself at different times owned a restaurant, laundry shop, and hotel. Women gained economic power and became equal to their men in work. Through that work, their roles and status had improved greatly as compared with those of their nonworking counterparts in Korea.

In accordance with the improved roles and status of these women, their voice and power within the marriage increased: men and women seemed to share a relatively equal division of family responsibilities and decision making and to respect each other. One of the picture brides recalled her participation in household decision making and her contentment with married life:

My husband always consulted with me before any family decision. He always did farm work outside and so did I. But later, when we had young children, I reared the children and did the housekeeping. He respected my opinion in running the house. We were a very happy family and had no trouble, except for a meager income.[87]

The case of early Korean immigrant women seems to confirm Blumberg's conclusion that the greater the contribution a wife makes to the family income, the louder her voice will be in family decision making.[88] The economic power of these women within their own homes seemed to have made them assertive and relatively autonomous.

Despite their newfound economic power, these early immigrant women did not neglect their traditional duties, such as cooking, cleaning, washing, and child rearing, especially financing their children's education. Most women worked very hard to send their children, particularly son(s), to school. In this sense, the roles and values of the Yi society still ruled the lives of these untraditional women. Maria Hwang, a very active new woman, was an example of a woman living with two cultural norms: the traditions of the Yi dynasty and the new social reality in America. Maria Hwang challenged the Yi oppression of women by leaving her husband (who had acquired a concubine) in Korea and immigrating to Hawaii with her two daughters, a son, and his wife. Before leaving Korea, she rebuked her husband, and implicitly, her society:

> I can no longer live under these circumstances with you. I am taking our children to America and will shame you in the future. These children shall become educated and I shall become a wonderful person. You can remain as you are.[89]

After immigrating to Hawaii, she, as well as her two daughters and daughter-in-law, worked very hard from dawn until late at night in order to prove to her estranged husband in Korea that her son would be educated to the "highest degree" (as one of her daughters recalled when speaking of her bitter plantation experience as cited above). One of Maria Hwang's daughters stated that the purpose of the women's hard work was to support the education of her younger brother.[90] Through the combined efforts and sacrifices of these four women for over a period of ten years, her brother was sent to the mainland to be educated and finally earned a doctoral degree in law at Hamilton Law College in Chicago. After ten years of hard work and support, his wife was able to join him for the first time in those ten years. Later, the son became a lawyer (though he couldn't practice) and the first president of the Korean National Association. The sacrifice and toil of four women made one man successful. Though Maria Hwang was progressive in thought and action, she maintained the traditional Korean woman's role of self-sacrificial mother and "warriorlike" caretaker.

In short, the new women were more expressive, assertive, active, and independent than their more traditional counterparts. Their roles became diverse, and their status became relatively more equal to that of their men. However, the new women still lived for others, mainly the family, and men continued to be the focus of their lives.

Nonetheless, the focus of women's concern within the family shifted from husbands to sons, while the objects of their self-sacrifice shifted from their family to Korea through political activities. The self-image of these new women seems to have been of a hybrid form developed through their specific socioeconomic-political situation. From this point of view, Mead's assertion that the self is a social product that cannot transcend its social context seems to be validated by the experience of the early immigrant Korean women.

Why and how did these women maintain the traditional women's self-image throughout the process of adapting to life in America? What was the role of the church in that process? While not providing answers to these questions, again, Mead's theory remains a reliable guide in linking the social experiences of immigrant Korean women, then and now, to their transformation or modification of traditional roles and development of self-identities.

In brief, the women of the Yi dynasty, the foremothers of the *ilse* women today, struggled not only to survive but also to create new selves in the midst of social changes. Throughout their struggles, religions—particularly Confucianism, Shamanism, and Christianity—played significant roles. The next chapter will explore the contemporary immigrant history of the *ilse* women and their socioreligious situations, which would affect on their lives in the United States.

CHAPTER 3

Women of Today (1945–Present): Immigrant *Ilse* Women in The United States

Contemporary *ilse* women are products of continuously changing social dynamics. In 1945, Korea was liberated from Japan and became an independent nation, though it was divided into the Republic of Korea in the south and the Democratic Peoples' Republic in the north. The United Nations and particularly the United States, played a significant role in the establishment of the South Korean government, and the U.S. impact was felt in all aspects of Korean society. In addition, as a result of the Korean War (1950–1953), Koreans had much more access to western culture through contacts with Americans in the military. As a consequence, old Korean values and norms began to recede, and new western lifestyles gained in popularity in the 1950s. These changes ushered in a period of confusion, ambiguity, and identity crisis for Koreans.

With increased economic, political, and social stability and national wealth in the mid-1960s, Koreans gained awareness of their identity problem and attempted to revive elements in their age-old culture. The traditional values and norms reemerged and powerfully influenced modern Korean society, with the result that the old and the new, the East and the West, coexisted as cultural forces.

The majority of Korean *ilse* women now in the United States lived through these social dynamics, and, without doubt, their contemporary self-images were affected by them. In the following section, I will review the pre-immigration social experiences of today's *ilse* women in order to compare them with experiences after immigration to the United States. The influence of these two differing social experiences will then be analyzed.

WOMEN IN MODERN EDUCATION AND RELIGION

Since 1945, the Korean government has interpreted women's liberation in terms of education and has accordingly expanded and
improved educational opportunities for women. After the achievement of national independence, free elementary school education
was made available to all children, regardless of sex, and the number
of women in high schools and universities increased steadily. In
1944, there were only 7,374 university graduates, 7,272 men and
102 women, in a national population of thirty million. 1980, 14.7
percent of the men and 7.9 percent of the women between the ages
of nineteen and twenty-four were attending colleges and universities.
Thirty percent of all college students were women.[1]

Participation in modern education, however, did not alter
women's roles and status; men continued to dominate modern
Korean society. According to a 1980 study,[2] the admission of women
to teacher's colleges was restricted because the parents of elementary school students feared that the presence of female teachers would
feminize the personality development of boys. Men occupied two-
thirds of all teaching positions and controlled the content and direc-
tion of education. Education's contribution to the modern Korean
society was still patriarchal, and consequently, gender hierarchy
continued to rule the life of Koreans. Lee Bong-Hee, a fifty-four-
year-old woman who received her undergraduate education in the
United States and currently works as an assistant editorial director
at an educational institution in New York, explained her motive for
immigrating to the United States as the desire to avoid gender discrimination in Korean education:

> I had always thought that I was very bright and intelligent.
> Throughout elementary and high schools I was a top honor
> student. One day, my high school class teacher, a woman,
> whom I had admired, said that women's greatest contribution
> to society would be to become housewives and mothers. Oh,
> at that moment when I heard her, I was so furious. I looked at
> her again. But I was also confused. Should I become a house-
> wife? In high school, I joined the choir of the American Eighth
> Army Chapel. We went to the chapel and sang all the time.
> The chaplain and the American soldiers treated us so well. I
> loved to go there. I also wanted to go to America and study
> there and become somebody, instead of becoming just a plain

housewife. That was my dream—it was in my senior year. My uncle, my father's younger brother, died and left his son. The son, my cousin-brother, was also a senior in high school. At that time I was busy applying to college. One day, my father told me to give up college because he had to send his nephew, his late brother's son, to college and could not afford my college expenses. He said that a woman did not need a college education. High school was enough, since a woman would become a housewife and should stay home and take care of the household anyway. Oh, I was so angry at him. But what could I do? I didn't sleep several nights and thought about what I should do. Then, I went to the chaplain and asked him to help me study in America. Boy, he was such a kind man. Through his help, I came to the States to study in 1957. I earned a B.A. in the States and later quit my graduate work to marry.[3]

As Lee Bong-Hee revealed through her testimony, modern Korean women were controlled by their fathers, who represented the patriarchy of the modern Korean society. There were definite limits to the education of women in such a social context, and the purpose of educating women was not to enhance their own potential but to serve as better homemakers and mothers.

Unlike Lee Bong-Hee, all of the women interviewed for this study went to university either in Korea or in the United States with the support and encouragement of their families, especially, their fathers. However, the patriarchal values continued to control women's academic choices, hence, their future. In the 1960s, when I pursued my undergraduate work at Ewha Womans University (the world's largest women's university), pharmacology and home economics were the two most popular majors. The former was regarded as one which would equip women to be the economic assistants of men. In other words, married women could run drug stores at home and help their husbands financially.[4]

Home economics was also considered the major which would produce the best housewives by equipping them with modern knowledge and appropriate skills. Kim Ai-Kyung, a fifty-one-year-old woman who has run a boutique for fourteen years in northern New Jersey, recalled the process of selecting her major and said:

I was scientifically minded. I was very good in math and science. I wanted to major in courses related to science. Biology? Chemistry? Physics? Accounting? Economics? They were all men's fields. The course most closely related to science which women could follow was home economics. My father told me that I would be able to pursue some scientific studies in home economics courses and at the same time learn how to be a good housewife—so, I majored in home economics.[5]

Modern education for women was geared to providing men with "better" housewives and (financial) supporters. Homemaking was considered the best and most important role for women, and, accordingly, education aimed to produce "modern housewives" who would combine modern knowledge with traditional values. As a result, education in the 1950s and 1960s did not generate any significant changes in women's roles and status. Most *ilse* women in the United States today are the social products of Korea's modern gender-hierarchical education.

Women's Destiny: Marriage

Woman and *marriage* have long been synonymous in Korean society. Marriage has been regarded as the ultimate goal and achievement in a woman's life not only during the Yi dynasty but also in modern Korea. In the 1930s, unmarried women or those who rejected traditional domestic life had nearly no alternative to staying home and being ridiculed, except becoming a Buddhist nun.[6] They were commonly called "Old Miss," a term that signified contempt and disgrace. I can recall the fearful image people had created of a middle-aged, unmarried female relative of mine. My entire family and neighbors and friends all treated her as a dangerous thing. Behind her back, every one called her "*chiral chaengi*" (지랄쟁이: hysteric/insane one). Because of the negative image of her implanted in me by my family when I was a small child, I was afraid to approach her, though she had always been kind to me.

Even in the 1960s, marriage was considered sacrosanct, an experience without which one's full humanity could not be fully established; marriage was performed even in death. It was common to marry the dead spirits of unmarried men and women through Shamanistic rituals. Shamanistic worldviews, which were deeply rooted in the Korean consciousness, held that marriage was a means to personal fulfillment. Persons who died unmarried would forever be full of *han* (한: 恨)[7] and harm the living. Therefore, their *han* was to be fulfilled even through "soul-marriage" in death. If we accept

Karl Marx's statement that "[t]he religious world is but the reflex of the real world,"[8] such Shamanistic "soul-marriages" reflected the indispensability of marriage in Korean society.

Although modern Korean society continued to impress upon men and women the essentiality and primacy of marriage in human life, it proved more flexible than the society of the Yi period in the choice of partners and form of courtship. In general, the father in modern Korean society permitted some room for daughters to select their partners. Many of the interviewees described their decision to marry their current spouse as a combination of traditional arrangements initiated by parents, relatives, and friends, in addition to their own will. Yang Byung-In, a fifty-one-year-old owner of a jewelry shop, recalled her marriage process and said:

> After graduating from university, I worked at the TT university library (in Seoul) until I married. Often, he [indicating her husband] came to do research, and we became closer. For about a year we dated. Then, he proposed to me. I told him that I should ask my mother for approval. My father, XXX whom you know of, was arrested by the Communists during the Korean War and was taken to the North. Since then, my mother managed everything. She was a great woman, and we [Mrs. Yang and her siblings] respected her.... Uhmm—He [her husband] didn't come from the same social class as mine, but he was bright and bold. My mother liked him and approved of our marriage. Even now, I often tell him, "If my mother had not approved of this marriage, I would never have married you—no way."[9]

During the Yi dynasty, when marriages were determined only by fathers, potential spouses never even saw each other's face until the wedding night. Thus dating, adopted from American culture, was certainly an innovation in the marriage process. Several interviewees had dating experiences to convey. Yet despite securing relatively increased freedom and greater voice in negotiating their marriage, women, for the most part, obeyed their parents. The parents, who represented the social norms, often had the last word. One interviewee, Chung Myung-Soon, a fifty-six-year-old restaurant owner, conveyed the power of her mother in determining her destiny. Mrs. Chung[10] married her current husband against the wishes of her mother, and now as fifty-six-year-old *ilse*, sees her life's sufferings as punishment for having disobeyed her mother. She believes that if she had done as her mother had willed and not married her present husband, her life would have been happier. Reminiscing about her past, she said:

> I met my husband in college. I loved him so much and wanted to marry him, but my mother opposed my marriage because he was the first son and I would have lots of responsibilities and burdens in taking care of his household. I knew my mother would never approve of the marriage, so I quit college and married him anyway. From the beginning of my marriage up to now, my life has been toilsome. After the marriage, I was involved in several small businesses, running gift-shops and restaurants with my husband until we came to America. He was working for the government when we were in Korea but made a meager salary. We couldn't live on his earnings. I had always had to work in order to help him. We immigrated to the United States in 1973 in order to improve our living conditions and to give our children better educational opportunities. After immigration, we started several businesses but failed at everything. My husband had a nervous breakdown and was hospitalized for a while. Now, he helps me run this restaurant but is not well and often causes lots of problems. I interpret my current fate as a consequence of having disobeyed my mother.[11]

Even if the process of choosing one's partner and getting to know him had changed to allow more flexibility, the purpose and content of marriage changed little from those of the Yi period. The primary purpose of marriage was to create male heirs and to nurture them and the entire family. Sarah Lim,[12] a fifty-one-year-old real estate broker recalled her mother's and later her own suffering in the service of her family:

> My mother gave birth to six daughters. I was the first one. Boy, she was so badly treated and oppressed by my father and his family as well as her own natal family. When her fourth daughter was born, my father named her *Chai-Nam*, which means "To be a Boy," hoping that the next baby would be a son. But again, my mother had two more daughters after her. Poor woman! I could see my mother's exploitation and suffering because she couldn't give birth to a male child. I decided that I would never marry. My mother died when I was sixteen, and I became a substitute mother and took care of my five younger sisters and my father. . . .

I was very active in high school. I demonstrated extraordinary leadership. I was always the class president and a good public speaker. I won many prizes and medals at speech contests, but my father, who believed in Shamanism and Confucianism, didn't let me go to college because I had to take care of him and my sisters.[13]

These examples illustrate the fact that despite changes in modern education and the marriage process, social consciousness regarding women's roles and status in marriage did not undergo significant change in the two decades following the establishment of a modern Korean society. Women's purpose was to serve men and families, and the center of a woman's life was to be others. Kil Young-Sook, a fifty-three-year-old housewife, spoke of the limitations placed on her self-development by the obligation to take care of her family:

After I graduated from Ewha Womans University in 1960, I went back home to Chŏlla-To [Chŏlla Province]. Later, my younger brothers began their college education in Seoul, so my father bought a house there, and I went back to Seoul with them. I stayed home and took care of them until I married in 1966.[14]

For most Korean women, except for those who were forced to work in order to support a family, work outside the home remained an alien concept and practice. Although several interviewees had employment experience before marriage, they considered their jobs merely as temporary ones with which to occupy their time until they married. Once married, most women became housewives and stayed home to take care of their husbands and households. The concept of a woman's career remained unfamiliar, for there was no notion of a woman's self apart from her husband and family. Women in modern Korea continued to form collective selves with their husbands. Park Jung-Ja, a fifty-six-year-old housewife who used to be a "warrior working-woman" but currently stays home because of health problems, reflected upon the collective nature of women's identities:

You know, I still believe a woman belongs to a man. My high school home economics class teacher, who was well respected, told us that women would become who they are according to what or who their husbands are. For instance, if you marry a soldier, you become a solder's wife. If you marry a scholar, you become a scholar's wife. If you marry a barber, you become a barber's wife. I think she is right. Women become who their husbands are.[15]

Mrs. Park's comments succinctly reflect the influence of Korean patriarchal values in forging modern Korean women's collective and dependent identities. Understood in terms of Mead's theory, such women could not transcend their social context to constitute an "I" that stands alone and apart from the collective. Homemaking, serving, and caring for men and family defined women's place in society and their image of themselves. As products of such a socializing process, most immigrant *ilse* women in the United States today have developed self-giving, collective self-identities through the convention of marriage.

Hidden Priestesses

As has already been described in chapter 2, Korean women's self-development has historically been linked with religion. In the Confucian Yi dynasty, women became self-sacrificial housekeepers, while Shamanism empowered them to act as "warrior-like" household priestesses. Outwardly, all women, except shamans, observed the social norms of passivity and dependence on men. Max Weber's thesis that religion shapes a believer's lifestyle (personality)[16] finds confirmation among Korean women. Their two religions made Korean women passive and serene in outlook yet assertive and strong as "warriors" in the domestic and religious arena.

From the turn of the century, Christianity, though with a small following, began to affect the consciousness and lifestyles of Koreans, particularly women. Missionaries established modern educational, social, and charitable institutions such as schools, hospitals, and orphanages. Christianity triggered the transformation from tradition to modernity in Korea and contributed to improving women's status through education. As research shows,[17] Christianity produced women leaders such as Kim Chom-Dong (who became well known by her American name, Esther Pak), the first woman from Korea to study in America. She became the first Korean female medical doctor in 1900. After returning to Korea, she contributed to the education of women and to the improvement of women's roles and status. Ha Nan-Sa, another pioneering woman, went to Ohio Wesleyan Women's College in 1896 and received a B.A. in English in 1900. After returning to Korea in 1906, she was active as a leader of newly formed women's societies (in Korea) and as a teacher at the aforementioned *Ewha Haktang*. Above all, Kim Hwal-Ran, well known as Dr. Helen Kim, the first Korean female president of Ewha Womans University (during the 1950s and 1960s), was a leader who had been strongly influenced by Christianity. Christian ideas, education, and the work of missionaries helped enlighten Korean women (and some men) and empowered them in various fields that had heretofore been off-limits to women.

However, women's roles and status within the institutional Christian church in modern Korea were similar to those they had been forced to assume (in Confucian rituals) in the Yi period. It was very rare for women to hold leadership positions within the church. The most widely and officially accepted position of leadership for church women in the 1960s was that of *chŏndo puin* (전도부인: 傳道婦人: "evangelizing woman"). In English, one may refer to them as "Bible women." These women had functions similar to those of Buddhist and Catholic nuns in administering education, maintaining the church, and caring for the ill and needy. Unlike Buddhist and Catholic nuns, the *chŏndo puin* were allowed to marry; however, many of them did not. Almost all of them, even in the 1960s, regardless of their age, were considered to be virgins or widows, that is, desexed and unsexed. They dressed in black traditional Korean women's dress but instead of wearing the full-length skirt, as was customary, had their skirts shortened to three-quarter length for convenience and modernization. They wore no makeup, and their straight hair was usually rolled up into a bun. They carried a black briefcase containing the Bible and other items, such as address books, pencils, notes, and some basic medicines, pertinent to their evangelical work. They visited their church members at home and in hospitals, led prayer meetings, and taught the Bible to women (most of the people who attended their informal meetings were women).

"Evangelizing women" served as the "hands and legs" of the official male ministers. They managed everything related to church life both inside and outside the church, with the exception of leading formal worship services. They were permitted neither to serve at the altar nor to preach. Nor could they administer the sacraments. They were also excluded from church administration and decision making, and their salaries were meager. A woman in her seventies who has been a life-time *chŏndo puin* in Korea and in a United

Methodist Church in Los Angeles remenisced about her past and said, crying:

> I can't believe how I was able to spend my whole life as a *chŏndo puin*. I also can't understand modern *chŏndo puins*. They are very spoiled. They are concerned too much about money. They always ask for salary increases. They also don't want to work doing nitty-gritty hard work, which I always did without complaining. Oh, you can't even imagine what kind of a life I had. My *Moksa-nim* (목사님: 牧師任: "Honorable Minister")[18] didn't treat me as a human being; I was treated as his servant. You know, church members also very much discriminated against me while they elevated the *Moksa-nim*, even though I worked harder than he, and the people really liked me. When I visited a member's house with *Moksa-nim*, people provided all kinds of good food and served us so generously. But if I visited them alone, they fed me whatever they had—left-over food. I was always so poor, but I never asked for an increase in pay. I worked very diligently because I was afraid of God who had chosen me for His work. If the wife of a *Moksa-nim* died, a *chŏndo puin*, if she was lucky, would be offered to serve him because she was a virgin. *Moksa-nim* is like God. He always marries a virgin.[19]

Women's leadership was not accepted in the Korean church during most of the twentieth century, and the roles women were allowed to play were those of assistants to men. Thus, women's roles and status in the church were akin to those they played within Confucianism and Yi society in general.

As described in chapter 2, Korean women have assumed with seriousness of purpose and a near-holy determination of will their role as "household priestesses." Their sense of religious duty and leadership was visible both inside and outside the home and nurtured and rewarded through Shamanism. However, in the modern Christian church, women became invisible, lacking positions of leadership both inside and outside the home. At church, all the priestly positions were filled by men, and women were allowed to serve only as invisible helpers behind the scene. At home, instead of being active warrior-priestesses, they became docile spiritual guardians, using the only tool permitted them: prayer. Forty-one-year-old Na In-Wha, who formerly worked as a registered nurse and is now a housewife, explained the role of her mother's prayers in determining her (Mrs. Na's) life:

As a nurse, I came to America in 1973. Through the arrangement of an alumna-sister [who was the wife of a pastor],[20] I met LLL *Moksa-nim* [her present husband]. I didn't want to marry him because he was planning on becoming a minister. At that time, he was in XX seminary preparing to be a minister. I didn't think I deserved to become a minister's wife. I was not good enough for that. Also, I didn't want to be the wife of a poor minister. I had seen so many poor ministers when I was younger. When I was a child, I used to take rice and other food to the minister's house because my mother told me to take food to his family. They were so poor. I hated their poverty. I called my mother in Korea and discussed my potential marriage with her. I told her that I did not want to marry him, but she commanded me to marry him. She told me that she had been praying for three years for me to become a minister's wife. She said that it would be God's answer to her prayers and God's will. Therefore, she told me to marry him. I had never disobeyed my mother—she has always been a woman of prayer. She always prayed for me and for her whole family, so I married him.[21]

In Confucian Korean culture, respect for older people in general, and one's parents in particular, is the most fundamental ethic to be observed. Obedience is considered to be a means and expression of respect. Therefore, Na In-Wha felt obliged to obey her mother's command concerning her future marriage and life. Moreover, her mother, as a woman of prayer, was regarded as God's medium; obedience to her mother was understood as obedience to God.

Despite lacking sanctioned space in which to wield spiritual power and authority, many Korean Christian women were involved in prayerful living and activities and had great impact on their children. All but three of my interviewees came from devout Christian families and had received their faith from their grandmothers and/or mothers. Min He-Yun, who came from an intellectually progressive, modern Korean family, said in her interview that her family had never practiced any religion. However, she did remember that her grandmother used to read the Bible and tell her Bible stories and that her grandmother used to pray in dark places. She also recalled attending church services, especially revival meetings, with her grandmother. Moreover, the influence of Christian mothers and grandmothers upon a woman's self-image was significant. Ahn Sung-Sim, a fifty-nine-year-old real estate broker, said:

My mother couldn't have a child after marriage. You know, if a woman couldn't get pregnant, her life would end. My mother said that she felt "strange eyes" [unbearable pressure] on her from all over, her in-laws and her natal family. She did everything so that she would become pregnant. She went to the Buddhist temple and prayed. She also did everything that the shamans instructed. Nothing worked. Then, someone told her to go to the church and pray; therefore, she began to go to church and prayed so hard. . . . Finally, she became pregnant, and had a baby girl though as a start. God answered her prayer. My mother became a dedicated Christian. You know, she is BBB, the famous female elder in RR Church. My father came from the family of a well-known Confucian scholar, ZZZ. But, influenced by my mother, he secretly practiced Christianity. Later our whole family became devout Christians. . . .

My mother had always wanted to live as a single person, being a *chŏndo puin,* and to serve the poor and the lonely. My mother's faith affected me so much. I promised God that I would be single and serve the poor and the abandoned on behalf of my mother. Early in my life, I decided to take care of the lepers and their families who were abandoned and isolated in *Sorok-do.*[22] I first went to the Methodist Seminary and worked at the Methodist Headquarters in Seoul until I came to America to study theology at HH Seminary. After completing my studies, I planned on going back to Korea to sacrifice my life for those poor and isolated lepers and their families. Later, I married; but I became a widow. I still think that I was punished by God because I broke my promise to God.[23]

As in the case of Ahn Sung-Sim, Christianity in Korea continued the traditional message of women's self-sacrifice in caring for and serving others. However, unlike the women in the Yi dynasty, Christian women broadened their sacrificial service from the domestic to the public arena, from inside the home to the outside world, just as the early immigrant women in Hawaii had shifted the focus of their service from husbands to children (sons) and nation.

Christian women, who formerly had acted as household priestesses in the Yi society, became invisible yet powerful household spiritual guards in modern Korean Christian life. Although they were relegated to work behind the scenes both at home and at church, they became a new kind of spiritual fighter as caretakers and men's helpers. When it came to subordinating women to men, the modern Korean church played a role much like that of the Confucianism of the Yi period. Most of the women who were interviewed, women who were descendants of devout Christian families, came from such a tradition. Women's obedience to men and sacrifice for the family have been crucial to women's place in the Korean Christian church. In sum, from a feminist perspective, Christian Korean society did not advance greatly beyond that of the Yi dynasty in its social treatment and placement of women. Modern women's social experiences were still very similar to those of their foremothers; in spite of the vast changes in the society at large, women's roles and status were not greatly changed. That is, women continued to exist for others. As a consequence, women's obedience and self-sacrifice remained important for their survival, and, accordingly, the self-image of most Korean immigrant *ilse* women was one of other-oriented self-sacrifice.

IMMIGRATION AND ILSE WOMEN'S NEW EXPERIENCE IN THE UNITED STATES

To understand the social experiences of contemporary *ilse* women in America, it is important to know their immigration history. The "picture brides" of 1924 comprised the last wave of Korean immigration to the United States until the 1950s. According to Hurh and Kim, immigration to the United States from 1910 to 1950 was banned by internal politics in Korea and U.S. immigration policies.[24] Therefore, for approximately four decades, new Korean immigrants were virtually invisible in American society.

However, contemporary immigration is, no doubt, inseparable with women because, unlike the early immigration, women take the major immigration force in terms of number. With the Korean War (1950–1953), a "breakthrough" occurred in Korean immigration: the United States reopened its doors to Koreans. The Korean War produced numerous "war brides," women who were married to American servicemen,[25] and orphans. Between 1950 and 1975, 28,205 war brides arrived in the United States. Although there are no accurate data indicating the exact number of the war orphans, records show that in 1950, 24,945 children were institutionalized in 215 orphanages in Korea.[26] Of these children, 6,293 arrived in the U.S. through international adoption (mostly through the Holt Adoption Agency) between 1955 and 1966, and female children outnumbered males.[27] The higher ratio of girls to boys arriving in

the United States is commonly viewed as a reflection of male preference in Korean society; in other words, male orphans were kept in
Korea, but females were offered for adoption by foreigners. From
1951 to 1964, these two categories, war brides and orphans, constituted 77 percent of the total Korean immigrants and the male-
female ratio was 3.5:1. Although these two groups of female Korean
immigrants prevailed in numbers until the 1970s, they have remained
all but invisible to the ethnic Korean communities, largely owing to
their pariah status among traditional Koreans (this is because war
brides have shared body and blood with foreign men, while orphans
have been uprooted from their family and lineage). War brides mainly
cluster around U.S. military bases and rarely participate in Korean
churches and communities. More to the point, they are not welcomed by most Korean churches. Orphan-women are scattered all
over the United States, depending on the location of their adoptive
families. Because of their isolation from the Korean community
(church) in the United States, this research excludes them. In this
paper, contemporary Korean immigrant *ilse* women in the United
States are from the following categories: women who came as students, women professionals and women who came with their families.

Women Students: Women Liberals

After World War II, between 1945 and 1965, six thousand Korean
students came to the United States[28]. Although few of these students
were women, they were unique in terms of their social status and
the impact of religion on their decision to come to the United States.
Many women of this group came from privileged families. In the
1950s, it was not easy to receive a passport from the Korean government and a visa from the U.S. Embassy, and studying in the U.S.
also meant a great financial burden for the family. At that time,
Korea, which had been newly liberated from Japan, was suffering
the shock and aftermath of the civil war. Socially and politically, the
nation was unstable, and poverty was rampant. In such conditions,
most Koreans were not in a position to send their children abroad,
especially to the United States, to study. Consequently, money and/
or political influence were needed for education abroad.

For women especially, coming alone to a foreign land was unthinkable. However, those whose fathers wielded wealth and power
were permitted the privilege of studying in the United States. Most

such women also benefitted from having fathers who had themselves received western education, many in the United States, and were therefore relatively progressive in their thinking and social outlook. I call these women "fortunate liberals" because they were relatively liberated from the limitations imposed on women by the Korean society, that is, from Confucian practices of *namjon yŏbi*. The "liberals" were also untraditional women. Among my interviewees, four of them came from the most privileged families in Korea and had fathers with extraordinary wealth and power in government. But the main characteristic of these "fortunate liberal women" was their lack of initiative in determining their own destiny. All were sent by their fathers, and many had older siblings who were already in the United States and were able to look after them financially and emotionally. Min He-Yun, the daughter of a once-wealthy businessman and politician, said of her coming to the United States in 1961:

> You know my father. I had no aspiration to study in the States. But my father attended a college in America, and my brother and sister were studying in the States. Before I graduated from my high school [which was the most prestigious girls' school in Korea at the time], my father had already arranged everything for my studies in America, so I came.[29]

Christianity played a significant role in producing another kind of "fortunate liberal" or untraditional woman. I interviewed three other women who had come to the United States for the purpose of studying. These women were not from privileged backgrounds. However, Christianity stimulated and encouraged them to start new ventures in this foreign land. Exposure to western culture and encounters with American missionaries had widened their vision and paved a new path for their future. Helen Choi, an educational consultant and programmer whose father was a Korean clergyman, said of her decision to go to America:

> From my early childhood, I had encountered American missionaries through my father. I had always dreamt about America and aspired to come to the States to study; so, after I graduated from my high school, I came to the U.S. and completed my B.A. and M.A. Of course, my father and the American missionaries arranged everything for my studies in America. I think my father was somewhat liberal. He didn't discriminate between boys and girls. I was raised in an egalitar-

ian family atmosphere. My elder brother went to a college in Korea, but I came to the States to study before him because he had to complete his military duty. Later, he also came to America to study.[30]

In terms of thinking and behavior, the "fortunate liberals," both from privileged and modest backgrounds, seem to have been rather courageous and advanced. For many of them, Christianity either catalyzed or sustained their educational efforts in this foreign land. After completing their higher degrees, most of these women married and stayed permanently in the United States. All of the American-educated women whom I interviewed have worked or currently work as professionals in mainstream American institutions. Grace Hurh, who works as an education director at a large preschool, said, "I am in charge of the whole educational program for two thousand children. Under me, there are eight supervisors and sixty-five teachers."[31] Like her, many of the women seem firmly established in their careers. To them, autonomy and independence appear crucial for making professional decisions and effectively performing their roles.

However, interestingly enough, all of my American-educated interviewees who had come to the United States in the 1950s and 1960s have been or currently are engaged mainly in education, nutrition, and medical technology, fields that have traditionally been populated by women. We may be able to attribute this pattern to the influence of their preimmigration social contexts on their professional choices. Moreover, we can also point to the lack of career choices for American women in general during the 1950s and 1960s as having influenced their decisions. Significantly, though, these *ilse* women, when compared with other Korean women, have developed somewhat autonomous and subjective selves in accordance with Mead's ideas. Did these women develop a personal center of their own in their lives? Are they different from the so-called traditional women? There is no simple answer to these important questions, because their responses to the interview questions were varied and complex. Nevertheless, most women of this group demonstrate assertiveness and competence both within their professional spheres and within their home. Their manners are highly Americanized and progressive. In many ways, their roles and status as Korean *ilse* women living in American social contexts seem to locate them as hybrids between the two cultures, the Korean and the American.

The Emergence of Professional and Semiprofessional Women:
Adventurous Challengers

The liberalization of U.S. immigration laws in 1965 ushered in the contemporary era of mass Korean immigration to the United States. This revised law accelerated the immigration of professionals and skilled persons, as well as family immigration based on invitation. According to Hurh and Kim,[32] 90 percent of the Korean immigrants living in the United States today arrived after 1965. The outstanding characteristic of this new immigration is that the majority of the new entrants were female and that most were young and adventurous female nurses and physicians. During the period 1966–78, female immigrants composed two-thirds of the total number of Korean immigrants entering the United States.[33] This female-male ratio contrasts sharply with that of the early immigration period, which was characterized by male predominance in numbers (the ratio of men to women was 10:1 during the period 1903–5).

Unlike the student group, the majority of these women (mainly nurses) came from socially less prominent and economically underprivileged classes. Confucian social mores had relegated caretaking and service-related professions to the lower classes; consequently, upper-class women looked down upon such jobs and avoided pursuing them in their own lives. Moreover, being a medical doctor, in general, had early on been designated a man's occupation in Korea and was regarded as an inappropriate field for women. Therefore, women in the upper class were discouraged from studying medicine. It was commonly said in Korea, "*Yŏja ka kongbu mani hamyŏn, p'alja ka seda*" (여자가공부많이하면팔자가세다: the life of a woman with much education will be filled with unhappiness). Therefore, for women working in the medical field in Korea, immigration to the United States offered them economic opportunity as well as a way to leave behind the social outcast status assigned them by their jobs. Chang Ok-Hee, who has worked as a registered nurse in the United States since 1970, reflected on this social situation, saying:

> My family was very poor, but I had lots of freedom. You know that in Korea, poor people have less social restrictions and more freedom in life. My father died when I was a child, and my mother remarried and worked. Therefore, I was raised by my grandmother. After high school, I couldn't go to college. I searched for a job but couldn't get one. Neither could I stay at home doing nothing. At that time, I heard that WW hospital,

which was run by American Presbyterian missionaries, were offering girls free nursing education and room and board, so I went there to study nursing and became a nurse. After training and obtaining a license, I worked in the same hospital as a nurse. But when American hospitals offered jobs for nurses, I took that chance and came to New York in 1970.[34]

After immigration, it was not easy for these professionals to adjust to the American working environment. For survival in their professions, they had to achieve the job requirements designed to meet American standards. Nurses had to qualify for their registered nurse license, and physicians had to pass their medical board examinations in order to be able to practice. Kang Jin-Sook recalled her bitter struggles to obtain a board license:

> I am not gifted in language. I used to hate learning English in high school. I was always an honor student, but English was always the lowest grade I received. English was really a problem for me. But in order to work in the hospital here, I had to get a Board license. How could I pass the exams which were written in English? I desperately needed to practice medicine in order to solve my financial problems. Above all, if I failed the tests, I would be humiliated and ashamed in front of my husband. My husband had passed the exams in Korea and was able to practice at a hospital when we got to the U.S. For one year, I went to English Language School and learned English. But I failed the exam. I was miserable. For the next two years, I studied so hard. You know, for those three years while preparing for the Board exam, my heart was always like a cloudy sky. I didn't feel joy or excitement. I had no social life at all. All I did was study and do housework. My two sons were so young, and they also had problems at school because they couldn't understand English. I had to supervise their homework. Can you imagine how I would have been able to do that, since I myself had problems with English and did not know much about America? Ugh, I lost a lot of weight. I prayed so hard. Finally, when I passed the exams, I couldn't believe it. I can't believe it even now. It was just a miracle. *Aigu* [oh my gosh], I don't even want to think about that time. My friend who had graduated *summa cum laude* from my medical school in Korea failed the Boards several times and gave up. She is now in New York, not practising medicine.[35]

Like Dr. Kang, professional women who had come to the United

States looking for better opportunities confronted numerous and daunting obstacles. Adjustment to life in this country often demanded extraordinary will-power and determination on their part. Most overcame hardships with their firm conviction in the possibility of a better life and their seemingly inexhaustible endurance capacity. These professional women established their careers in mainstream American institutions and have adjusted to life in America. For these women, autonomy is important. They are no longer men's helpers and subordinates in their professions. As Mead's theory would suggest, their social experiences have made them assertive and independent. Consequently, one might expect their roles and status as women to have changed considerably, but, as will be later shown, this has not been the case.

The Reappearance of Korean "Warrior Women" in the American Context

Family immigration to the United States has increased among Koreans since 1975, and the majority of the *ilse* women in the United States today came with their families. Most of these women were traditional housewives whose priority was homemaking and whose center in life was the family, that is, their husbands and children. Their motives for immigrating reflect their traditional roles and status. Park Jung-Ja, a fifty-six-year-old housewife, explained her reason for immigrating:

> My husband has such a gentle heart. He couldn't survive in the tough and competitive Korean society. After he graduated from college, he worked in a couple of firms. He was disappointed by the rotten business ethics, hypocrisy, and deceitfulness. You know, in order to survive, he would have had to do the same rotten things that his coworkers did, but he couldn't. He would also have had to bow down to those with power, but he didn't. Therefore, he was always a loser. Then, he worked as a translator in the American Eighth Army in Seoul. Through that job, we got the notion to immigrate—because my husband couldn't survive in Korea. My children would also be able to have better educational opportunities in the United States. I was an elementary school teacher before we moved to America. I loved young children and enjoyed teaching, but I resigned from the school and came here with my two children and husband for their sake.[36]

Like Park Jung-Ja, the majority of the contemporary *ilse* women came to the United States in order to improve their life conditions, particularly to advance their husbands' careers and to provide their children with a western education. From this point of view, they were not traditional, because they launched a new venture to change their lives; they were realistic and bold, as had been the early immigrant women of the 1900s. But unlike their foremothers, these immigrants of the 1970s were highly conventional: their motivation for change centered on the success of their husbands and children. Others remained the center of their lives.

However, starting a new life in America proved extremely difficult for these family-oriented women. After arriving in this country, most of them worked incessantly and supported their families while their husbands studied for advanced degrees, practiced their internship/residency as newly immigrated young physicians, or set up business. Work in the United States, for most of these women, was a shockingly new experience and made them aggressive, bold, and tough. Assertiveness and aggressiveness, traits which were discouraged for women in the Korean society they had left behind, became their "survival tools," not only for adjustment to their new life, but also for fulfillment within their new roles. Again, Park Jung-Ja, short and fragile in stature, who became a successful owner of several gasoline stations, recalled her tough "warrior-like" struggle in order to establish the business with her husband and to get "happily" settled as a family:

> After I came to America, I did everything. There's nothing that I didn't do. I had never worked so hard in Korea. I could never work like that again in my life. You know, I really don't understand why my husband had such bad luck in America. He failed at everything that he did. Failure. Failure. All failure. Finally, he became a taxi-driver. But what an unhappy man he was! One night, he was almost beaten to death by a customer. He drove a person to the place where he had wanted to go, and when my husband asked for the payment, instead of paying, the man beat my husband. I was shocked when he came home. His face was bloody all over. He couldn't even see because his eyes had been beaten too. I don't even know how he was able to drive home. I was fearful, angry, and cried furiously. After that, my husband became ill and couldn't function for a while. I thought that I had to do something, but I

didn't know what. Then, I attended night school and learned the computer and worked as a key-punch operator to support my family. I worked so hard and did all the overtime available, but my salary wasn't enough for my family. But after my husband's accident, I had decided to go into business, although we had no money at the time. I earnestly prayed for God's help. God really sent us an angel, a Jewish man who owned a gasoline station. He fervently wanted to retire from his business. After he heard of our successive failures and misfortunes in America, he handed over his business to us under unbelievably favorable conditions. We were so lucky. What a fortune God gave us! The business began booming unbelievably. We also expanded it to include truck and car rental service. Money just came in from all over. . . .

I would get up at five o'clock in the morning and go to the station. I worked from six in the morning to ten at night. I worked sixteen hours a day. There was no day off for me. I drove trucks and cars, did all the bookkeeping, pumped gas, and took care of the telephone calls. I did everything. But still, at lunch time, I ran home and cooked rice for my husband and brought his lunch to the station. At dinner time, I also dashed home to prepare supper for my kids and husband. . . .

My husband served as an elder and the chairperson of our church choir, so almost every Sunday I prepared food for the whole choir and invited the church people to my home and fed them. I couldn't go to church because I had no clothes to wear—though I had money. I just didn't have any time to shop for clothes anyway. Oh, I was so busy and slept only a few hours every day. But, it was fun to make money and to use it for the church, but *aigu*, it was tough. You know, women are so strong. Men are acutally too weak. Now, I am not afraid of anything. I can do anything and I can survive in any condition.[37]

The question must arise: "What did her husband do since Mrs. Park did everything?" That is a very legitimate question. But today most Korean women in the United States live as she did.

For *ilse* women work paradoxically has required sacrifice for men and competition against men. Many Korean women who had never before vied with men in public suddenly found themselves testing their own competence, confidence, and nerve at work. Oh Young-Ran, a forty-eight-year-old woman who is single and runs a successful travel agency in New York spoke of her struggles:

Moksa-nim! To do business is very tough. It is so competitive. Especially, in my business, I have to compete with shrewd Jewish men. You know, in business there is no man or woman. Just competition. If I fail in the competition, I die. To work is a matter of life and death for me. I have to be as strong and as tough as those Jewish men.[38]

Like Ms. Oh, many *ilse* women in the United States with small businesses, ranging from delicatessens and grocery stores to dry cleaning shops and boutiques, are engaged in fierce competition with other Koreans as well as non-Koreans. They find that their mettle is tested sometimes more than they would like and that the stress level is often unbearable.

According to Epstein's "work theory,"[39] a workplace is a powerful social institution which shapes an individual's self-image. We can then assume that immigrant *ilse* women who now work as shop owners and businesswomen have acquired good business sense, some degree of autonomy, and the ability to make sound business decisions. Because their work often requires them to be aggressive, the traditional Korean female virtues such as sacrifice for and submission to others and disinterest and passivity in things public would seem to be detrimental to their survival in America. In cases like that of Park Jung-Ja, "domestic warriors" have become "public fighters." Without a doubt, immigration has altered women's roles and status.

In short, the social, economic, and educational motives for immigrating to the United States differ among the *ilse* women interviewed for this study. Despite their diversity, there are basic similarities in their personalities: the women are adventurous, courageous, and relatively unconventional in that they were willing to uproot themselves from their homeland and risk whatever security they had had in Korea. Furthermore, because immigration pushed them out of their traditional roles into the public workplace, these women gained strength and competence in their work and in their self-image.

On January 13, 1991, at the East Rock Institute in Connecticut, I gave a talk based on this study and entitled "The Korean Immigrant Church's Impact on *Ilse* Women's Self-Development". A woman who was the successful owner and manager of a children's clothing shop in New Haven, responded to my presentation, speaking with newly found excitement at and pride in her work and life in America:

When I was in Korea, I knew nothing. I didn't even know how to control a housemaid at home. But now, I have five employees in my shop. All of them are White Americans—men and women. I have never thought that what I am doing is great. But through your presentation, I've come to realize that I am a great woman. *Ya, sinparam nanda!*(아, 신바람난다: "My 'spirit-wind' is blowing!") [I'm so excited and enthusiastic]. I've become somebody. What advancement I've made! *Kitpal nallynda!* (깃발 날린다: "My flag is waving high.").[40]

WOMEN AND THE KOREAN IMMIGRANT CHURCH IN THE UNITED STATES

For *ilse* women in the United States, there is another powerful social agent besides work and the family: the immigrant Korean church. For the most part, women's social experiences in the church sharply contrast those in the workplace. Oh Young-Ran, who previously spoke of relative gender equality in her business, in terms of severe competition, disclosed the dual worlds in which immigrant women live. She was interviewed in a Sunday School classroom after the Sunday worship service at Word Church on July 22, 1990. While I was setting up the tape recorder, she excused herself and disappeared for a few minutes. When she reentered the room, an entirely different person had appeared. She had been dressed in a formal, stylish outfit during the service and now was sporting blue jeans and a blouse. She seemed to be very comfortable and relaxed and said:

> Now, I feel much better. It is awfully stressful to come to church. One Sunday before coming to church, I was doing some oil painting, my hobby, and found out that there was no time to dress; so I came in my jeans and blouse. Gosh, people looked at me strangely. Later, one of the elders called me to him and told me to dress formally. You know, I am a good dresser—especially, when I come to the church—I am always very conscious about how I look and act and am cautious about my makeup and dress, my words and behavior. Lots of women have told me they do the same thing when they go to church. We go anywhere in jeans and blouse, but why not to church? Why can't the church be more flexible and leave women alone? Many women don't come to church because of these restrictions and requirement to lead double lives.[41]

Oh Young-Ran's case captures the dilemma many immigrant Korean women face in juggling work and church in their lives. As she indicated, such women are often stuck with the church's conventionalism, which necessitates a Janus-faced existence. It is logical to assume that their self-identities also become Janus-faced in the process of putting on the acceptable "face" at Korean church. Given the inconvenience and tensions that arise from such a dualistic life, why do *ilse* women bother to go to their ethnic church? In other words, what is the significance of the immigrant Korean church in their lives?

The Significance of the Church

Immigration can be understood as transplantation of human life from one environment to another. America has become the new soil, and American culture, values, and lifestyles the new environment to which the Korean immigrants must adapt if they and their offspring are to survive. Won Moo Hurh and Kwang Chung Kim have characterized Korean immigrants' adjustment to America as "adhesive adaptation and ethnic confinement."[42] What these sociologists stress is that the immigrants intermingle regardless of their educational backgrounds, jobs, and their length of residence in the United States. In other words, Korean immigrants form an ethnic subcommunity in the host society, America, and sustain their lives by centering them around that community. For Koreans, churches become the center of the Korean ethnic community. This holds true even for those Korean immigrants who have been educated in the United States and are relatively well adjusted to American public life, be it in the workplace or in civic organizations; they still make friends with Koreans and go to a Korean church.

Recent research shows that 70 to 80 percent of Korean immigrants are affiliated with Korean churches, and of them, roughly 40 percent became Christians after immigrating to the United States.[43] The church-participation rate of the Korean immigrants is phenomenal, when one considers that only slightly more than 20 percent of Koreans are affiliated with churches in Korea. The figure is also high when compared with that of any other ethnic group in the United States. For example, although approximately 85 percent of Filipino-Americans are Catholic, most of them attend American churches, while only 17 percent of them are affiliated with ethnic churches. Only 38 percent of Jewish-Americans are affiliated with synagogues. When juxtaposed to other ethnic religious organizations available to Korean immigrants, Korean churches seem to be not just the primary but the *only* social agent in their lives. It follows that the church plays a central role in the adaptation process of these immigrants and is without doubt personally significant in their lives. Based on the research[44] and my personal experience, I can surmise the four major sociological functions of the ethnic Korean church:

1. The church provides fellowship for Korean immigrants and serves as a social center for meeting people and making friends.

2. Churches provide social services and information to church members. Many churches provide health care programs. (Volunteer nurses and doctors examine church members' physical conditions, administer tests for liver functions and diabetes, measure blood pressure, etc.) People also exchange information about jobs, housing/apartments, business, and investments.

3. Churches confer social status and positions of leadership upon adult members. This function is highly important, especially for men. Most Korean men, except for those in prestigious professions such as medicine, law, and big business, find their social status has been denigrated after immigration; their traditional egos and pride become damaged. Korean churches help heal their psychological wounds by giving men recognition and power within the church leadership and bureaucracy through the position of lay-elder and lay-deacon, board member, and trustee. Most of the staff and administrative officers of ethnic Korean churches are men. In particular, being an elder grants prestige and power to a man: elders exercise tremendous power inside and outside the church, and almost all elders are men. Also, most of the celebrities in the Korean communities are the elders of their churches. In this sense, men still control the reins of power in Korean community. The church reflects traditional Confucian Korean cultural/social structure and system.

4. Churches strengthen the Korean identity of immigrants by maintaining Korean cultural traditions. It is very common to see women (particularly older women and children) wearing Korean costumes in churches, especially on Christian/American and Korean holidays. On New Year's Day, Korean Independence

Day (August 15th), and Korean Thanksgiving Day, churches often sponsor traditional games, sing Korean folk songs, and prepare Korean feasts. Moreover, as part of their Sunday School education, children are taught the Korean language and traditional Korean values, such as filial piety and obedience to and respect for one's elders.

Much of the above depiction of the Korean church's functions in the ethnic community suggest that the church is male-oriented and benefits one adult group, the men. Why, then, do women go to church? Women make up about two-thirds of the total Korean church membership, and they are the most passionate and devoted believers. Hurh and Kim do point out that the church may serve a psychological need of immigrant Korean women, that is, women go to Korean church in order to channel their anger, frustration, and depression.[45] Why are women frustrated and depressed? It is interesting to note that Korean male sociologists point out, particularly, women's psychological problems. At whom are they angry? Though Hurh and Kim do not elaborate on it, this is a significant issue. Surprisingly, some of my interviewees mentioned the psychological function of the church in their immigrant lives; they indicated that singing hymns allayed their sense of frustration, loneliness, and pain. Women seem to indicate their psychological problems as painted by Hurh and Kim.

Nevertheless, the purpose of Christian practice among *ilse* Korean women seems to go beyond social and psychological dimensions. Their attachment to the church is closely linked to an existential problem, that is, self-formation. When I asked the women, "Why do you go to church?" or "What do you like most in church life?" almost all of them emphasized the importance of the sermon. Women go to church in order to listen to sermons. They said that through the sermons they saw themselves, that sermons helped them know who they are and what they have to do in life. They emphasized that sermons reassure them and encourge them to be "Korean" women. Largely through the sermons, then, Korean churches function as the major social agent, inculcating values and norms by which the members, especially women, rationalize their conduct and interact with one another. In terms of Mead's theory, *ilse* women's selves are redeveloped through Christian rationalization and socialization. One of my interviewees convincingly illustrated the significance of the immigrant church in relation to her existence and selfhood. Min He-Yun, an intelligent and talented housewife, originally came from one of the most privileged, "liberal," and non-Christian families in Korea. She said:

I came to W College in Ohio in order to study chemistry in 1961. I was so lonely. You know, in the 1960s, sororities and fraternities, those kinds of things, were so popular with students. Everyone belonged to them, but I belonged nowhere. And so in America, I became a nobody. No one knew who I was and what kind of family I came from. I was totally lost. Then, in Old Testament class, my professor told us, "Life is not to be understood but to be meaningful." At that moment, my eyes and ears popped open. From then on, I searched for the meaning of life. I went to an American church with my Caucasian friends in order to seek life's meaning. There was no Korean church at all. . . .

After I married, we [her husband and two children] used to attend Anglo churches. But, we never participated in the church activities, except for the main worship service. We were always spectators, guests. My husband came from a devout Christian family, but he was not religious. He just accompanied me. . . . When my husband was transferred to New Jersey in 1979, again we went to an American church. But I always felt that something was missing in our religious life. Then, for the first time in 1981, we went to a Korean church, because my friend led us to her church. It was a liberal church. We enjoyed it, but the pastor had an extramarital affair, and the church was eventually closed. Then we came back to our American church—until we found another Korean church. Then, we tried my sister's church in Bergen county, but the pastor seemed like a theological school professor. He was too intellectual and lacked spirituality. I was not happy; therefore, we went back to our American church again. Meanwhile, we kept searching for other Korean churches. Then, we went to the church in Union. Gee—the pastor was too irresponsible and didn't treat us lay people well. Maybe he thought that we knew nothing. He didn't prepare for the Bible studies and repeated the same content for three weeks. You know, we could stand the pastor's negligence for a few weeks, but he was too much. Finally, we left. We felt so deprived and hurt. We were searching again and in the meantime went back to our American church. Ha, ha—that church seemed to be

our asylum because whenever we had problems with Korean
churches, we always went back there. . . .

And in my personal life, I was always unhappy. I had lots
of complaints about my husband. I was not satisfied at all
with my husband and my life. I always told my husband and
children "to do this and that." I complained a lot. I was miserable. Then, four years ago, we went to the Holiness Church
where we are now members. My friend, Mrs. P, introduced us
to it. First, we were so disappointed and bored by the pastor's
sermon. He is Pentecostal, as you know, and his sermon didn't
make sense at all. However, we tried for a while. Then, gradu-
ally we felt his sincere commitment to his faith and the Bible.
He seemed to be so peaceful and a good person. I forced myself
so hard to understand and accept his sermons. Finally, I found
out what my problem was: I had to accept myself as I was and
my situation, whatever it was. I had to stop complaining and
obey God. Also, I shouldn't analyze or criticize the pastor's
sermons and the Bible. I shouldn't use my reason. Religion is
not a matter of reasoning; it is the work of the Holy Spirit. . . .

I used to look down on my husband. He didn't come from
the same social class as I. I was so arrogant. But I realized
that I had to kill myself and make myself lower than he. You
know, actually I am much inferior to my husband. He is very
calm and rational, but I am very emotional. My pastor's
humbleness and his sermons changed my life. Now his sermon
is too sweet and in every way makes sense. Through him and
his sermon, I became myself, and now I am very happy. I used
to be full of regret and felt guilty about neglecting my children because I worked when they were young. And my husband and I used to fight a lot, but now, there is no fighting at
all, once I accepted my faults. . . .

It's been four years since I began attending this church.
From the beginning, my place in the church has been the kitchen.
When I go to church, I first go to the kitchen and work. I am
very happy. My life has meaning.[46]

Min He-Yun's comments point to several important issues regarding *ilse* women's motives for wanting to belong to a Korean
church. Among them, two in particular are closely related to her
existence as an immigrant in this country. First, although she was
educated in the United States and has resided here for over thirty
years, she is still a foreigner. At Anglo-American churches, to which
she kept returning, Mrs. Min felt like a guest or outsider. She was in

earnest need of a community to which she and her family could belong, one in which her identity as a Korean woman could be reinforced. The Korean church she currently attends gives her that sense of belonging and has served to sustain her life. Second, and perhaps more important for the purposes of this study, the Korean church helps her accept her life situation (discontentment in marriage, loneliness, guilt toward children) and supplies the rationalizing principles with which she can construct meaning and happiness in her life.

As in the case of Min He-Yun, the immigrant Korean church is important to many *ilse* women because it gives meaning to their immigrant existence and offers them an identity in an alien society. Women see themselves through the church. It seems, though, that although the Korean church helps women accept their present reality, it does not challenge them to reject and transform what they do not like in their lives. Instead, the church seems to foster a traditional self-image of women. From this point of view, immigrant Christian women may develop only social selves because they may not change or transcend women's conventional image. They subjectively rationalize their experiences and choose the social self for survival. Yet it is this very rationalization and choice which allows them to develop full selves, the subjective "I"s, with the church providing the bases for rationalization. Without a doubt, the church is significant and indispensable to their existence in the United States.

The Status of Women in the Immigrant Church

The impact of women's social experiences on their self-development can be studied in terms of women's status in an institution. As mentioned earlier, women's leadership in church life has never been accepted by Korean churches. However, of the forty-four ordained clergywomen in the U.S. United Methodist Church (UMC) in 1993, the majority are *ilse* women. Though the number is very small, it represents a revolution for Korean Christian women. These women are challenging the male-dominated traditions of the Korean church (and UMC in general) and contributing to the development of a new image of women in the Korean-American community.

Despite the years of educational and pastoral training among these Korean clergywomen, there is still no place for them in the more than 350 Korean United Methodist churches in the United States. Among them, only six churches have women as pastors. Two of the women work as copastors with their husbands, but their work is distinctly divided along gender lines. For example, one clergy-woman is only in charge of education in her church. Few of the *iljŏm ose* or *ise* women serve Korean churches. Most Korean-American clergywomen serve Anglo churches as solo or associate pastors. Yet many of these women express a desire to serve Korean ethnic churches.

The door to pastoral leadership in the Korean church in America is still closed to these women. This implies that the Korean church does not yet acknowledge or admit women's leadership, even though the United Methodist Church officially sanctions and supports clergywomen. All of these clergywomen, except a few, went to semi-naries in the United States. They studied with men and enhanced their knowledge and received the same training as men, yet their leadership role in the church is not only very minimal and limited but also often ignored. The traditional Confucian notion of women as properties of and assistants to men, based on gender hierarchy, rules in immigrant Korean churches today.

Something that happened to a Korean clergy couple in 1990 explains without further analysis the status of Korean clergywomen in the Korean immigrant church. The husband, having climbed the professional ladder, was transferred to a large and powerful Korean church in a large cosmopolitan city. However, the wife, a clergy-woman who had served an Anglo church, was forced to give up her ministry: the church hired the husband under the condition that his wife would serve the church as *samo-nim* (사모님: 師母任: pastor's wife) and not in any capacity as a clergymember.[47]

However, there has been some improvement in women's status in Korean churches. Although their number is still very small, some women do participate in church administration and decision making as members of committees, councils, and boards. Women are some-times appointed as chairpersons of committees. But by no means is their full potential tapped. Oh Young-Ran offers a clear example. Ms. Oh is not only a successful businesswoman but also an energetic person. She has money, time, enthusiasm, and interest in serving the church. She is also very sociable. A few years ago, she was appointed the chairperson of the Church and Society Committee at Word Church, but after a while she resigned. She described her experiences:

> *Moksa-nim* appointed me as the chairperson of the Church and Society Committee. But I have never been to one committee

meeting. Why? Because I was never informed of the meetings or invited to them. I was the chairperson, but men called the meetings on their own and decided everything without me. If anyone asked me about the work of the committee, I didn't know at all what was going on. It made me look so stupid. I looked like an irresponsible fool. If I am not given the means to do my work, why should I hold the position and responsibility? So, I resigned.[48]

Not only does the Korean church dismiss women's leadership, it implicitly encourages women's silence and submission to men in public life. Women are appointed and invited to board meetings; their physical presence may be welcome, but their presentations, or any other activity rendering them visible and heard, are discouraged. Suh Jai- Mi, a forty-six-year-old medical doctor, related her experience as a "leader" in church life:

> I was an administrative board member, but I resigned. You know, the church still wants women to be silent. A few times, I spoke up in the meetings. Gee, people looked at me fiercely. Their eyes seemed to be saying, "Woman! Shut up and sit down." For a while, I tried to be silent at the meetings, but sometimes I was frustrated and couldn't stand it. It was awfully hard just sitting like a statue, not expressing my ideas. But men don't want to listen to women. It was frustrating and also a waste of my time, sitting like a dumb person. Am I just a chair filling up empty space? Instead of sitting there like a dumb chair, I resigned.[49]

Given the large number of Korean women church members and their dedicated service, many Korean churches have been more attentive to women's need for participation in church leadership and worship services. Korean women now serve at the altar as liturgists, readers, and ushers, positions that had up to the 1970s been reserved mainly for men. In general, women are more visible than in the past in planning and leading the Sunday worship service. Sarah Lim, a real-estate broker and a wife of a pastor who had served Anglo-churches for many years, commented on the ascendance of women to the altar in the Korean church:

> In the [Korean] church, a great advancement of women's status occurred. Until two years ago, our church never had a women's dedication service at the main worship. Once a month, the

women would gather on their own and hold a dedication service at night. But now, once a month, we have an officially designated Women's Dedication Service at the main Sunday service, and women conduct the whole service. It represents tremendous progress. Yet, there is no change in content. The speaker is always our male pastor or another male speaker he invites from outside the church. He plans the entire liturgy. Though the liturgist is a woman, women only read the Bible and collect the offering. What is different from before? Same—hopeless. Also, the church exploits women. We do everything, as you know, but when something comes up for a decision, they [men] even wake up the sleeping elders [men] and decide, but never the women who are awake! Then, they order us to actualize the project that they had decided without our participation, like fund-raising and cooking.[50]

Her point is that women still act as men's assistants in religious ritual and are excluded from full participation in church life.

Emile Durkheim asserts that religion, through ritual, the embodiment of collective consciousness,[51] shapes the identity, or self, of a believer. As the visible and concrete actualization of religious ideas, ritual plays a critical role in the process of self-development. In Mead's terms, it serves as a means for communicating the norms and values of the religious community, the powerful social agent.

For instance, the sermon, as women pointed out earlier, is the most powerful means of conveying the ideas and values of the church that shapes the self-image of women in the Korean immigrant churches. For example, in these churches, the theme of Mother's Day sermons is commonly women's self-sacrificial devotion to family. Preachers exalt the self-abnegation of Korean women for children and others as akin to Jesus' death and resurrection. Most churches hold a special recognition program on Mother's Day, calling forth mothers over the age of sixty to the altar to face the congregation and receive gifts from the Women's Association (equivalent to United Methodist Women) or Sunday school for their lifelong, sacrificial devotion to the family. Through these rituals, churches implicitly and explicitly elevate women's sacrifice and portray other-oriented service as the priority in women's lives. In short, despite some changes and slight indications of improvement, the status of women in the Korean church, based on gender hierarchy, has not progressed much. Women continue to serve under men and are portrayed as their assistants.

The Role of Women in the Immigrant Church

Theologically and sociologically, the Christian church, especially the immigrant church, has been understood to be "inclusive" in its nature.[52] However, from the standpoint of *ilse* Korean women, the Korean immigrant churches are "exclusive." Korean churches in general are patriarchal institutions, based on a family-centered paradigm, and so directly affect the development of a woman's self-image. Single people or those without family may easily be ignored in the church. Again, Oh Young-Ran explains her solitary situation in the church:

> I have no friends at all in the church. Men do not greet or approach me because I am single and they are afraid of their wives. Women also do not approach me because I am "odd." I think they do not know how to deal with me. I feel as if people treat me like a dangerous thing. Coming to church makes me feel more lonely. But now, I don't care because I have only one reason for coming to church. That is to listen to the sermons. You see, I have no one to discuss things with my personal and business matters. But while I listen to the minister's sermon, my mind usually becomes clear, and I decide what I have to do. As long as this need is met, it is O.K. to come to the church. . .
>
> The church is too couple-oriented. I hope that the church will open up, so that singles can get along with other members. I have some requests to make to the Korean church. First, accept us [single people] as we are. Second, do not reject us, and don't look at us with strange eyes. Third, treat men and women equally as persons. Last, provide some programs for singles and include us in the church.[53]

As Ms. Oh points out, marriage is still the norm within the Korean church. Therefore, women who are not married usually become social outcasts. Matchmaking is an important peripheral function of Korean churches—pastors and church members commonly introduce singles to one another and arrange marriages. Moreover, churches reinforce the institution of marriage through Bible studies and marriage counseling.[54] The church's preference for married life and married people causes stress among some single women. Suh Jai-Mi, a divorced medical doctor, revealed her criticism of the church's bias against any lifestyle for a woman other than marriage:

I have been divorced for more than ten years. But until a few years ago, I was very confused. I was ashamed, depressed, sad, and guilty. I thought I was wrong and abnormal. But now, I am very sure that I am not abnormal. I think those who pretend to be happy housewives are abnormal. Most of them come to the church to show off their mink coats and their husbands' status. What do they do in the church? They only cook and wash dishes. They cook at home, and then they come to church to cook? Anyway, they feel sorry for me, but I feel sorry for them. They are so very concerned about my single status and push me to marry. Oh, I was so angry at Elder E. She always told me that I should marry and then introduced me to a widower, a drycleaner. Can you imagine? What does she think of me? Does she think that I am dying to get married? I do not discriminate against people or jobs, but I have gone through so many hardships and am well established in my career. So, at my age, now, I should become a drycleaner's wife and cook for him and wash his stinky socks? Is marriage that important? No, I will never exchange my career for an unbalanced marriage.[55]

Dr. Suh points out that marriage is still the normative lifestyle expected of women in the Korean immigrant church and that women's roles in the church are mostly related to traditional homemaking.

Several interviewees have been or presently are presidents of their churches' women's organizations, United Methodist Women (UMW). When they were asked, "What kinds of women's programs does your UMW have?" they mentioned various projects: fundraising; prayer meetings; visiting the sick and the deprived; sending money to poor churches in Korea; donating medicine, food, clothes, and money for missionaries abroad; providing their pastors' travel expenses for continuing education or attendance at conferences; sponsoring children's scholarships; and so forth. All of these categories cover women's traditional roles as caretakers, nurturers, and providers. Above all, cooking and preparing feasts were given undisputed priority. The case of Min He-Yun vividly portrays the role of women in the Korean churches in the United States today.

Min He-Yun is a woman whose undergraduate and graduate work was completed in the United States. An outgoing and active woman with extraordinary energy, she has gone through a long journey to search for the meaning of life. She said of her responsibilities in the church:

It has already been four years since I joined this church. Once, I served as the director of the Service Committee in our church UMW. The main task was to cook and wash dishes for the church's dinners. This is my second year serving the church as president of UMW. From the day I joined this church, my place has been the kitchen. You know, I wear only cotton clothes to church because I always get wet from cooking and washing in the church kitchen. Therefore, I buy all my clothes on sale from Laura Ashley twice a year. If I pay fifty or sixty dollars, I can buy a good one. But I am very attracted to color. I like colorful dresses, so my dresses are crazily colorful. Ho, ho, ho. But my children always complain—they say, "Mom, buy nice, stylish clothes and dress normally." But, I don't care. I am comfortable working in cotton clothes. Sometimes my legs become swollen. I can't walk or move around because I stand too long and work too hard in the kitchen. But, I am happy cooking and serving my church. . . .

My term will be over in November. Before the term, I have three big goals to fulfill. As you know, we have bought and just moved into this church. Our church will invite the town's mayor, influential citizens, officials, firemen and their families to a big feast. There will be a good two hundred people. We [UMW] will cook Korean food and serve them. We will also celebrate a huge open-church service. Our church will invite lots of people from other churches. There will be at least six to seven hundred of them. It will be a magnificent feast. The UMW will provide really good Korean food. And then, there will be a Thanksgiving feast. We have to cook for our church members and celebrate. Oh, I will be very busy, and I am excited. I actually enjoy all this work with other women. But after all these feasts, phew, I will be free to relax.[56]

As Mrs. Min reveals, the major task of Korean UMWs, the only women's organization in the churches, is cooking and serving. Women seem to receive recognition and fulfillment through cooking and serving. Women's roles in church today seem not to have transcended traditional homemaking roles.

As we have seen, the Korean immigrant churches are the indispensable social reality through which *ilse* women's lives in America are sustained. However, women in the churches, despite the diversity of their personal and social experiences and accomplishments, implicitly and explicitly are encouraged to maintain a monolithic lifestyle—the traditional homemaking. Therefore, no significant changes in women's lives, in terms of roles and status, have taken place in the immmigrant churches.No doubt there is validity to the assessment made by Pyong Gap Min, a male sociologist, depicting the Korean immigrant church as a prominently sexist institution.[57] The churches, women's major social context, seem to function as a mini-Korea, the extension of the "modern Yi society" in America. The following chapter will disclose how religious practice actually affects on women's everyday life in the United States.

CHAPTER 4

The Religious Factor in the Lives of Korean *Ilse* Immigrant Women in America

As discussed in the previous chapters, religion has played a central role in the lives of Korean women. How does present-day Christianity, the main religious influence on Korean *ilse* women in the United States, affect the lives of these women who now live in complex, multicultural social contexts? Do Christian beliefs help women adjust to life in the United States or hinder it? How has Christianity influenced the roles and status of these women? Have the roles and status changed from those experienced in Korea? How do these women perceive their lives? With these questions in mind, I shall explore the impact of today's Christianity on *ilse* women by analyzing their social experience in the domestic lives, particularly marriage and family, and their mode of adaptation to life in the U.S.

CHRISTIANITY IN WOMEN'S DAILY LIFE

Peter Berger argues that the conspicuous characteristic of modern religion, particularly in America, is secularism.[1] Berger's point is that secular knowledge affects religious interpretation, structure, and practice such that religion becomes diluted, or loses potency, in a secular world. Religion eventually loses its authority/power to shape modern people's daily life that it once had in premodern times, particularly in the medieval period. Moreover, Robert Bellah's paradigm of "religious evolution" supports Berger's view of the diminishment of religious impact on modern life in Europe.[2] According to Bellah,[3] religion in the modern era is the product of a five-stage evolution:

1. *Primitive religion*, which Bellah equates with folk religion, a union of religion and daily life. There was no distinction between

religious practice and everyday life, and religious community and society were synonymous.

2. *Archaic religion*, which Bellah chiefly characterizes as the development of religious myths and rituals. This stage involved the initial separation of the divine and the profane, yet religious ideas continued to serve as the normative guide in everyday life.

3. *Historical religion*, which Bellah analyzes as the period in which religious ideas and myths became concretized into historical revelation (as Jesus, in Christianity, became the incarnation of the mysterious Yahweh). Religious doctrines, rules, and rites became canonized, and religion was institutionalized. The members of the religious community came to believe in formalized sets of doctrines, and religious rules governed a believer's thinking and behavior. Simply put, religion became formalized and, consequently, impersonal.

4. *Early modern religion*, which Bellah describes as an attempt to bring impersonal or solely cultural religion back to a personal level. Religious leaders formed different religious groups, or sects, according to their own experiences and interpretations. Followers gathered around the leaders and practiced the religion formulated by the latter.

5. *Modern religion*, which Bellah hesitates to consider a religion at all because it is, he believes, very much polluted by the secular world. Its characteristic is secularism, and accompanying pluralism, which produces denominations, ecumenism, and new cult/religious movements. The beliefs and lifestyles of those who would be religious believers are more influenced by secular, rather than religious, worldviews.

What these White American male sociologists emphasize is the weakness of the impact of religion on modern people. In terms of Mead's theory, religious institutions as social agents lose their influences in modern life. Contemporary feminist scholars of religion offer a corrective insight into this male sociological analysis, one that accounts for the strength of the continuing hold of religion on some social groups, especially women, and in the case of Koreans, immigrant peoples.[4] Such feminist scholarship emphasizes the negative impact, that is, dis-empowerment, of contemporary institutionalized religion on women. However, this book seeks to modify that view, for my research has revealed the empowering impact of Korean Christianity on contemporary *ilse* women. The key is to redefine empowerment and assertion within the context of Korean women's lives in America.

Contrary to Berger's and Bellah's views, most immigrant Korean women who were interviewed are deeply immersed in the waters of Christianity and appear to be swimming in the religious archaic period of Bellah's scheme. Their daily lives are intimately tied to religious Christianity. Some women even prayed before their interviews began. Christian ornaments such as framed pictures of Jesus, printed or calligraphic Bible verses such as I Corinthians, chapter 13,[5] crosses, and various other Christian symbols usually decorate the walls of these women's homes and workplaces. An open Bible, underlined in red pen, along with detailed handwritten notes in the margins or on separate sheets of paper, is often conspicuously visible on the kitchen or living room table in most of these women's houses.

Visitors in the homes can see that the Bible is constantly read and that the women are well versed in its teachings. It is also very common to see *The Daily Bible Study*, Christian guides and magazines, testimonial novels, and various kinds of books related to Christian faith and spiritualism, as well as stacks of cassette tapes of hymns, gospel songs, and sermons. Their houses often not only resemble "mini-chapels" but actually seem to function as sanctuaries, very much as did the Shamanistic temples of the Yi dynasty.

Park Jung-Ja, the "warrior-like" contemporary homemaker, even remodelled her home and attached a house-chapel to it. Showing me her chapel, she said:

> It was my long-cherished dream to have a house-chapel. I have prayed for this for a long time. Oh, I am so blessed. It has just been finished. Now, I will furnish it with religious icons and make it a beautiful sanctuary. I have already used this chapel for praying and singing hymns. I also offered this chapel to our church and the ministers whom we [she and her husband] know. It will also be a good conference room and Bible Study classroom for our church.[6]

The religious impact on the life of the women interviewed for this study is deeper and more intense than that of any other influence. They make no distinction between religious and secular life: religious life itself is their daily life. Na In-Wha, a former registered nurse and present pastor's wife and homemaker, described her life as follows:

Our church has a daily six o'clock morning service, so I get up at five o'clock every morning. At five thirty we go to the sanctuary, and my husband and I pray until the morning prayer meeting at six. The worship lasts for about half an hour. After people leave, my husband and I stay and pray. Then, at seven, I come home and wake my children up. Then, I prepare breakfast for my husband and children. After the children leave, I tidy up the house. Until twelve thirty, the time is my own. I spend about one and a half hours in prayer. I even take the telephone off the hook, so that I cannot be bothered by phone calls. I read four chapters of the Bible every morning. Then at twelve thirty, I prepare lunch for my husband. Until three thirty, when the children come home from school, I do some housework. When I am very tired, I sometimes take a nap. When my children are home, I go over their homework with them. After that, I prepare supper. Even in the evening, I am very busy. I accompany my husband on visitations to our members' homes. Almost every night, we have some meetings, Bible Study, class meetings, and activities at the church. I try to attend most of them. Usually, I go to bed after one o'clock and I sleep only a few hours.[7]

Though Mrs. Na sounds as if she was extremely immersed in religion because of her role as a pastor's wife, the majority of the other interviewed housewives were as intimately caught up in religious life. Min He-Yun, an American educated intellectual housewife and the UMW president of Holiness Church, also revealed her deep involvement in religion:

I am so ashamed of myself for not attending the dawn service at my church every morning. Before, I used to join the worship every morning, but now maybe three or four times a week. You know, it is about forty miles from my home to the church. In order to attend the six o'clock service, I have to get up at four thirty in the morning. To get up then, I have to go to bed at least by ten at night, but I can't. I have lots of things to do at night. My husband comes home around seven or eight o'clock, and I have to feed my children and husband. I have to clean up the dishes and do lots of things. Also, at least three or four nights a week, I go to the church. For example, we have Tuesday night Evangelism Explosion Training, Wednesday Evening Service, Friday Night Bible Studies, amd committee meetings. Most of the time, I end up going to the church every night and come home around eleven o'clock, so I go to bed very late, around midnight. How can I get up at four thirty? While I am excusing myself, I feel shame. Many people who attend the night meetings still come to the morning service. They even go to work directly from the service. It is one of my prayer requests that God should give me more faith and strength so that I can attend the service every morning.[8]

Furthermore, she explained that her life begins with morning prayer before anyone else in the house is up. She then prepares breakfast for her high school children and husband. After they leave, she cleans up the house and spends the whole morning reading the Bible and praying. Also, every Wednesday morning she teaches the Bible at home to other Korean women in her neighborhood. Often, during the day she goes to the church to prepare food for the evening meetings or to run some errands for the church. Mrs. Min's whole existence is tied to Christian living and church life.

Because religion plays such a central role in the daily lives of the women who were interviewed, the church constitutes the major context of their socialization. It is their primary and main playground for social interaction and religious ideas serve as the rules and norms for their social lives. Ye Soon-Jong, a forty-three-year-old housewife and a member of Holiness Church, describes her social life:

I have two sisters in New York, but I don't have much contact with them because they don't understand me. They think I am insane about Jesus. We also have nothing to talk about. Once in a while we meet, but we feel so uncomfortable. I feel so sorry for them. I pity them. I worry about their souls and pray for them. . . .

I don't have many friends, but all my friends are good Christians. We very often meet together and study the Bible. We talk about our lives and always share our religious experiences and testimonies. We pray for one another and support one another. Oh, I love to be with them. I also spend lots of time on the phone, talking about religious things with these friends. I used to be very sociable, but after my deep involvement in the Holiness Church, I lost my contacts with non-Christian friends. Reading the Bible is too sweet. Talking together and sharing my life with my Christian friends make me so happy.[9]

Illustrating Bellah's category of "archaic religion," the lives of these Korean immigrant *ilse* homemakers are fully imbued with Christianity. Contrary to his view of the diminuation of religious intervention in modern life, the church and its religious ideals continue to dominate these *ilse* women's lives powerfully.

By contrast, in the daily routine of women who work outside the home as professionals or businesspersons, religion generates much confusion and contradiction. The reaction of these women to the involvement of religion in their lives is diverse. Many remain in the archaic religious mode of the aforementioned homemakers, but some seem to live in the midst of Bellah's historic and modern religious era, that is, in the mixed situations of the sacred and secular. However, the latter constitutes a minority; the larger portion of working *ilse* women seem to saturate their daily life with religion.

With the exception of American institutions where some of the interviewees work, most working environments, that is, offices and shops, regardless of contexts (American or Korean)—resemble "minichapels." It is very common to be greeted by tape-recorded gospel songs or sermons. The Bible and other religious books such as *The Daily Bible Study* are often found on the working tables or counters. Walls are decorated with crosses, church calendars, pictures of Jesus, or other icons. Most women say that they begin their days with prayer. Whenever they have free time, they read the Bible and religious books. All day long, they live in a religious atmosphere, listening to tape-recorded gospel songs, hymns, and sermons. Kang Jin-Sook, a fifty-one-year-old medical doctor, even purchased a house for religious investment. Showing me around her house, which is located in a heavily wooded area alongside a large, scenic lake in upstate New York, she explained her religious motive for purchasing and remodeling her house:

> Lots of people, especially my husband, objected to my buying this house because it had been a church's retreat center and would cost an enormous amount of money to reconstruct into a family house. Also, it is very isolated from the world. But I insisted and bought it. Some day, I hope in the near future, I want to use this house for God's service as a home for the elderly, or I will donate it to the church as a retreat home. Therefore, I didn't change much of this living room, which was a gymnasium before. We installed only necessary things, like a fire-place, but kept the stained-glass windows. It is quiet,

beautiful, and good for meditation. When I am home, I feel that I am living with God. I invited some ministers to come and meditate. You too are welcome. Come anytime, if you need to prepare a sermon or to meditate. My husband's medical clinics are not too far, but I must spend three or four hours to drive to work four days a week. Still, I don't mind. I really want to retire soon and work for God.[10]

As is apparent in her case, it is not uncommon for highly educated and American-trained professional women to fill their time with religion. To these women, religious ideals and values serve as major principles of social interaction and, consequently, organize the way they socialize. Grace Hurh, the successful professional educator who was educated in the United States since college and has been residing in this country for more than forty years said:

I came from a Christian family. My father was a devout Christian and always persuaded us to go to the church, but I never did. Oh boy, Christians seemed to be so stinky and hypocritical. I used to dislike them. I loved socializing with secular people. I loved dancing, drinking, and partying. Almost every weekend, we used to have parties with our friends. I enjoyed them so much . . .

But after my conversion experience four years ago, some time after I joined Holiness Church, I totally lost my secular interests. There's no fun or meaning in dancing or social gathering. I do not meet my old friends unless it is necessary. I lost touch with them. Reading the Bible, listening to hymns or a sermon makes me feel so peaceful. . .

On our last vacation, we [her husband and one other Christian couple] took the Bible, some religious books, and lots of cassette tapes of hymns and sermons with us to the countryside. We read and listened to them. We shared our religious experiences and discussed religion. Oh, it was the best vacation we have ever had . . .

You've heard the saying, "religion is an opiate." Sometimes, I wonder whether I am taking religion as an opiate. Well, to live a life means to be crazy in something. I'd rather be crazy in religion . . .

When I was upset or people irritated me at work, I used to be so angry at them before. But, since I became a Christian, I pity them. When they irritate me, I pray for them. Sometimes, it is very difficult to deal with non-Christians. But I try to be calm and to influence them through my Christian manner.[11]

Mrs. Hurh seemed to be creating her own version of monastic life, to which she retreats. She also demonstrated a saint-like self-image which allowed her to differentiate herself from ordinary secular people.

To many devout Christian women, homemakers and working women alike, religious ideals dominate their consciousness, conscience and behavior. The more religious the women are, the more they seemed to avoid the outside world and to retreat to religious havens, both physical and mental, akin to the lifestyles and organizational styles of sects.[12]

Nevertheless, some professional or working women, although a minority, practice Christianity more for purely ritualistic or social purposes. They may be those who practice modern religion as defined by Bellah. For these women, religion constitutes an element of stress in their socialization process. They either separate the two domains, the religious and the secular, or they seem to be confused about how much energy, time, and fervor to give to each world. Kim Ai-Kyung, an owner and manager of a boutique and the previous UMW president of Fellowship Church, is clearly ambivalent about her "two lives." She said:

> I have no time to read or study the Bible, so I carry around this Bible and *The Daily Bible Study* here and read them. I also listen to these sermons and hymns [pointing to the cassette tapes] while I work.[13]

Without a doubt, Mrs. Kim is highly involved in religion and church life, but the religious impact in her life is dualistic. She prefers old childhood friends to the unfamiliar church women and still keeps in contact with the former. She also enjoys playing tennis and golf with her husband's friends and their wives (some are Christians and some non-Christians). At social gatherings, she drinks and serves alcoholic beverages, which are viewed as an evil and prohibited in orthodox Korean Christian life, and her major socialization occurs in her husband's circles of acquaintance. However, she is firm about church attendance. She never misses Sunday worship except in case of emergency, and she attends almost all church meetings. She spends at least three evenings on church activities, such as attending Wednesday evening service, Bible study class, choir practice, and class meetings. Also, she emphasizes that she tries hard to be a good Christian woman, which to her means unconditionally believing and following all of the church's teachings and making friends with the church women. She manages to survive in two social contexts, the religious and secular, by developing dualistic values and attitudes while outwardly conforming to religious practice.

Unlike Kim Ai-Kyung, Helen Choi, a member of Word Church and an American-educated professional educator, exhibits another mode of adjustment. She expressed confusion and awkwardness in her attempt to survive in a dual social context.

> I am not that religious. I should be ashamed of my shallow faith. I very seldom read the Bible, and I participate in the church at a minimal level, attending only Sunday worship and Wednesday evening services sometimes. I don't get involved in any activities. But if there is a special service like a lecture, I try to attend. Oh, I don't like revival meetings. Why do Korean preachers shout all the time? And the content of the sermons? It bears no relation at all to our life here [on earth and in the United States]. Most speakers are invited from Korea. What do they know about our life here? Well, I shouldn't criticize too much. I should be more faithful. But, to tell you the truth, practicing Christianity doesn't mean much to me. It may be a habit because my father was a pastor and so I grew up in a parsonage . . .
>
> I like our minister's sermons, but in general, I am not comfortable with the church's overemphasis on the preservation of Korean culture. Since we live in America, Korean immigrants have to know English and must adjust to this culture. I often go to schools for teachers' workshops to introduce Korean culture. Oh, our children, especially the newly immigrated ones, have so many problems. Teachers do not know how to deal with them because of cultural differences. In Bergen County, Asian students are the majority of the minorities in the schools, and Korean students are the majority among all the Asians. But the problem is that the parents and the children are not familiar with the American educational system, values, and culture. Instead of insisting on Korean culture and values, the church should help and teach them to understand and adapt to life here in America. If they [the children] can't adjust, they cannot survive. I also do not agree in many ways with the church's old teachings and values. They are not relevant to our lives, especially to women's lives—you know what I mean? They are antiquated and worn-out . . .

In the church, I am very awkward in dealing with men. I really do not know how to behave. For example, should I shake hands with them or not? So, my hand stretches out halfway like this [she gestures with her hand a limp and reluctant handshake]—ha, ha, ha. . . .

Also, the church's administrative processes and structures are not democratic. It is too hierarchical and sometimes despotic. I sound like a bad Christian, but what I said is true. It is stressful to go to church.[14]

Helen Choi seems to be caught in the conflict between two cultures, the Korean and the American. Her immigrant church life seems to be the immediate cause of that conflict. She criticizes the church's defensive attitude toward Korean culture, which she believes hinders immigrants' adjustment to life in America. Furthermore, she renounces the church's patriarchal attitude toward women, many of whom are highly educated and function as independent individuals and, in some cases, leaders in nonchurch life.

As the words of Kim Ai-Kyung and Helen Choi reveal, religion, for some working women, may neither assist their socialization nor provide them with rules for social interaction. Rather, it causes confusion and tension and develops ambiguous and conflicting modes of adaptation. Understood in terms of Mead's theory, women of this category may develop schizophrenic selves in the process of adjusting to the complex sociocultural circumstances of church and society.

In sum, the more involved women are in the church, the more religious they seem to be. The more religious they are, the more they seem to avoid the world outside the church. In that case, the church may be detrimental to women's assimilation to the world outside the church. Also, for the "religious" *ilse* women (especially homemakers), Christianity serves as the major social institution and thus renders their lives coherent in terms of religious and social values. One could argue that their worldview is more insulated and their lives more intact than those of less religious women. But for some professionals and working women, professing Christian faith seems to be a cause for frustration and confusion, and these women tend to develop a dualistic and/or ambiguous adaptive mode in suspension between the religious and secular aspects of their daily lives. Their adaptation to neither the Korean church community nor the secular American society (including work) is complete or thorough.

The Operative View of God: Sexist Anthropomorphism

Emile Durkheim, who focuses upon the social function of religion, defines religion as follows:

> A religion is a unified system of beliefs and practices relative to sacred things, that is to say, things set apart and forbidden—beliefs and practices which unite into one single moral community called a Church, all those who adhere to them.[15]

Durkheim's point is that the essence of religion consists of notions of the sacred and the profane in informing the rites and regulations that shape a worshipping body's corporate self-identity, such that the congregation, with its rules and prohibitions, comes to play a critical role as an ultimate authority of convention, molding the believers' consciousness and lifestyle. From Mead's point of view, the notion of the Christian God as the "Sacred-Omnipotent Father" serves as the symbol of the Korean immigrant community that the church embodies and shapes the believer's self-understanding in the particular, Korean Christian mold.

Durkheim's definition of religion may not be universally applicable, because not all religions have these three elements (the sacred, ritual, congregation), although ritual is considered a universal element. For example, Buddhism does not seem to embrace any concept of the sacred, and Shamanism is practiced in order to meet the specific (usually practical) need of an individual and community; therefore, no organized congregation or systematic service of worship has developed in either one.[16] However, Durkheim's view of religion is important for understanding the functional impact of the belief in God for the self-development of women. Applied in terms of Durkheim's definition of religion, the Christian God as sacred entity symbolizes the unchallengeable authority and power necessary for the crystallization of religious ideas in the Korean Christian community. How does this God authorize and actualize immigrant women's self-image?

The God of *ilse* women is sexist-anthropomorphic. Most interviewees described God as an almighty male creator and proclaimed women's absolute obedience to him as unconditional, although some women imagined God as Helper, Judge, Protector, and Ruler. Only one woman, a real estate broker, visualized her God as Love, yet for her the loving God also is an omnipotent male. Their description of God raises an important issue: sexist anthropomorphism. The

Creator is a male and has almighty power over women. According to the interviews, the degree to which *ilse* women espouse sexist-anthropomorphic views of God correlates with their degree of religiosity and social orientation (Korean-Christian; secular-American; ambivalent about Korean and American, secular and religious). In other words, the more religious the women are and the more Korean their social context, the stronger they tend to affirm gender hierarchy and male supremacy. But, perhaps because they are withdrawn from the secular world, homemakers seem to believe in female inferiority more strongly than professionals or businesswomen do. Kil Young-Sook, a permanent homemaker and a devout Christian, was born into a Christian family in Korea and today is the wife of an influential elder of Fellowship Church. She said:

> I believe men are superior to women. If men and women are equal, there is always collision. Therefore, God made women inferior to men so that He prevents collision. Frankly speaking, my experience also proves it. I was the only girl among my three brothers. I was raised with my parents' special attention and love, so I was in a way spoiled and developed a bad temper. Gee, I had such a hard life after getting married. My husband and I fought so much during our twenty-five-year marriage, but I could never win. Oh, I was miserable. Now, I've given up. I realized that to win against a husband is not possible because God made men superior to women. You know, I was actually wrong to try to reverse God's order of creation. Men should rule over women. I decided to obey him [my husband] as I have to obey God. I am much more content since I gave up trying to become equal with him. You know, it also looks very bad to others [Koreans] if husband and wife are equal.[17]

God, for Mrs. Kil, appears to be the ultimate authority which demands her unconditional obedience (which is also to be offered to the husband), and, at the same time, people around her (the Korean community in general) are also a powerful social force who control her life. From the Meadean perspective, she may have developed a mere social self and represents a traditional Korean woman (who embodies social conventions), accepting her given roles and obeying her husband. For this kind of woman, the opinions of others are very important for defining herself, because she sees herself only through the eyes of the others. She must have developed a "looking-glass self,"[18] but not the Meadean "I."

Kil Young-Sook's comments express ideas characteristic of most devout Christian Korean homemakers, who demonstrate similar attitudes toward the relationship with their husbands and legitimate their inferior status as one ordained by God. Many women express their fear of a superior God. To them, God is far above and looks down at them at all times. The differentiation of power between God and women, with God above and women below, translates into male supremacy and female submission in daily domestic life.

However, just as Kil Young-Sook rationalizes her painful experiences, women also rationalize and decide to accept women's inferior position for the sake of personal survival and to legitimate their self-images. For religious women, especially housewives, their social selves must become their complete selves; that is to say, most women accept women's inferior status and adjust to their Korean-Christian social environment, which is ruled by age-old Confucian notions of gender hierarchy. In such cases, the Christian God legitimates female inferiority and shapes women's rationalization into a process of accepting the given social reality. This in turn inhibits any innovation in male-female relations.

White American feminists, such as Nelle Morton, affirm that Christian patriarchal concepts such as an anthropomorphic male God belittle and dis-empower women.[19] Viewed from such a feminist perspective, the Korean immigrant women in this research may appear powerless and dependent, lacking initiative. However true this may be in the political and public spheres, sexist anthropomorphism does not render these women incompetent and powerless in the family structure. To outward appearances, many are anything but incompetent social selves who only accept and justify their inferiority as part of God's order. In the domestic realm, however, one must measure their real power and competence by what they are able to achieve while having to defer to the male as the symbolic head of the household, while they turn the roles as wife and mother into tools of exercising their very real psychic/spiritual power and energy. For many *ilse* women, this almighty male God helps fortify the traditional "warrior-like" self-image of Korean women and to enhance their assertiveness and power. Park Jung-Ja, the "warrior housewife," without a doubt, is a model demonstrating the "hidden power" of Korean women through religious dedication in and justification of their lives.

As I said before, my husband was such an unlucky man after immigrating [to America]. He was a constant loser and a failure at everything he tried. He totally lost his confidence and faith as a man. He wanted to go back to Korea. You know, even though God made men stronger than and superior to women, in times of hardship, they become so weak. Can you imagine going back to Korea? First, we didn't have money to go back. But above all, how could we face our people [family and friends] there? Oh, God seemed to be so cruel to us. I had to help him gain his strength back and raise him up from the abyss of his life. But I did not know what to do. At that time [mid-1970s], I also had a terrible problem with my right arm. It was a nerve problem and so painful. I couldn't move and work at all for more than a year. But I had to do something for my husband and our family. In this impasse, I couldn't even cry. Finally, I decided to challenge the omnipotent God. I knew if God is willing, there is nothing that is impossible. The first thing that I had to do was to please Him, so I fasted for forty days as Jesus had done and did nothing but read the Bible day and night. On the fortieth day, I placed a bet with God. I promised God that I would donate $100,000 to our church-building project. If God accepts my offer, I would do anything for Him. It was my bluff to God. I had nothing. We lived in a one bedroom apartment with our two teenage children, a son and daughter. We [her husband and she] gave our bedroom to them, and my husband and I slept in the living room. One hundred thousand dollars fifteen years ago was an astronomical amount. Anyway, I was afraid of withdrawing my decision and becoming a chicken later, so I called our minister right away and announced my offering. You know, he said nothing. He might have thought I was insane. I didn't care what he thought. Then, I told my husband what I did and told him that we had to fulfill our commitment by all means and encouraged my husband. He didn't even seem to be shocked. He also might have thought I was crazy. . . .

I worked like an insane person to make money even with my disabled arm. I sometimes encouraged and sometimes chastised my husband with my utmost effort. Anyhow, we fulfilled my bet. In ten years, we paid off our whole offering, yet we were still able to buy this beautiful house and become loaded. Thank God![20]

Contrary to the common expectations of the passivity of Korean women, in view of some White American feminist theories, for example Morton's theory of women's disempowerment by patriarchal symbols (male God) of Christianity. Yet, the main point is that this woman's strength was geared to fulfilling the traditional woman's role as caretaker and helper and not to making innovations or developing her personal life. To many devout Christian Korean women, especially homemakers, God, the ultimate Christian symbol, justifies and empowers Korean women's traditional self-image as leaders or warriors in caring for and strengthening others.

Working women, on the other hand, exhibit a much more complex attitude in their theological anthropomorphism, as Lee Bong-Hee, an American-educated professional, illustrates. She calls herself a "born-again Christian," yet she rarely reads the Bible and maintains minimal contacts with the church. She attends only Sunday worship and hardly participates in any other church activities. Nonetheless, she accepts the male Creator-God and wavers between God-sanctioned male omnipotence and male-female equality:

> I don't think women are inferior. I think men and women are created equal. I think the church made women inferior to men. You knew my deceased husband. He was very critical about the church, yet he was a devout Christian. He was also very liberal and progressive in many ways. Yet, he was also so male-chauvinistic. I once read his diary before we married, and I was shocked. It was like this: "We will marry soon. Then, I have to be prepared to control her as her boss." I told him that I would marry him only under certain conditions. One of them was equality. During my marriage, we often argued because of his bias against women. You know, Christian men think that they are gods in relation to their wives, and they try to justify their superiority by identifying men with God. But, frankly speaking, I am sometimes confused. I came from a conservative tradition. I sometimes wonder whether God really made men and women equal. I mean, does God really approve women's ordination?[21]

Differences between what she has learned about the biblical male God of might and the daily life she experiences as an intelligent, educated, and independent individual seem to confuse Lee Bong-Hee. In other words, the church justifies female inferiority through the biblical God, while Mrs. Lee justifies human equality through her education and career experience. She seems to be in conflict between the two social practices in the church and the world outside the church.

Like Lee Bong-Hee, many Christian women seem to be confused and puzzled about women's existence in the United States and their status vis-à-vis Korean men. Chang Ok-Hee, a registered nurse, is another woman who demonstrated *ilse* women's confused and ambivalent self-image and understanding of gender power:

> I am sure God made women much superior to men. Don't you know that God made women out of Adam's rib? It means that God made men as tests or practice before He made women. God recognized His mistake, so in his next effort He made woman perfect. But I think God cares for order. In order to keep the world in order, God put women under men as God rules the whole world, but it is through women that God perfects men. I think women should be lower than men for the sake of peace and order in the family, even though they are much superior to men.[22]

Ana-Maria Rizzuto asserts that the image of a personal God is the product of a person's childhood experience with intimate people, especially with parents.[23] Chang Ok-Hee described herself as coming from the socially and economically deprived classes in Korea; she came from a very strong matriarchal tradition, one in which the mother always worked and supported the family as the rice-winner. Consequently, she developed a strong matriarchal understanding of human relations. However, when trying to abide by the patriarchal Christian traditions, she became confused. Since there was no other figure of authority or principle available to her for legitimating her position, she used God to rationalize her contradictory views of male and female power and superiority. Most of the interviewed working women seemed to be confused or uncertain about their anthropomorphic views of God, because the image drawn by the Korean immigrant church and their own reality as strong working women were not in accord. Their anthropomorphism was ambiguous, and their attitude ambivalent.

In short, these Korean women, regardless of professional or religious background, generally subscribe to a sexist anthropomorphic understanding of God. They try to live their Christianity in accordance with the elements of Korean culture which dictate that women are, or should be, inferior to men by nature and social function. Christian women, especially homemakers, use God in order to help them accept and legitimate their patriarchal social and religious realities. These housewives demonstrate a certain assertiveness and initiative even as they accept and justify gender hierarchy and inferior status through religion, while working women exhibit more ambivalent and confused responses.

Jesus, the Selfless Savior, as Women's Role Model

Without Jesus, Christianity would not exist. Jesus represents Christianity and symbolizes the invisible yet almighty Christian God. As indicated above, faith in the omnipotent and invisible Christian God is an extraordinary source of control and self-identity in the lives of Korean immigrant women. How, then, does the "visible God," Jesus, affect *ilse* women's lives?

The image of Jesus held by *ilse* women is generally ambiguous and abstract—and rather complicated—though its impact on women's lives, especially on the lives of "religiously pious women," is powerful. The more religious the woman, whether homemaker or working woman, the more Jesus was described as the Son of God, Savior, and "the very God." Many women defined Jesus as Savior without hesitation. As if reciting lines from a script, they were quick to proclaim the basic Christian creed: "Jesus is the Son of God. He obeyed God until death. He is free from sin, yet he died for our sins and saved us from death." Na In-Wha, a pastor's wife, added further, "Jesus is God Himself, but he did not claim his equality with God. He obeyed God and died for God's Will to save us" (Phil.2:6–7). These women sounded like taped recordings of Christian doctrines regarding Jesus, but the emphasis was on Jesus' obedience to God and his sacrifice for "saving humanity."

However, most of these women failed to articulate a personal relationship with Jesus or to describe Jesus' saving acts as significant in their own lives. Rather, Jesus seemed to be significant to the *ilse* women's self-development mainly as a role model of self-sacrifice. Grace Hurh, an American-educated and devout Christian professional, explained the impact of Jesus on her self-development in this way:

> Jesus is my savior and role model. Whenever I am not sure of how to decide something or how to behave, I always ask myself, "What would Jesus do in this situation?" Then, I think about his obedience to God and death for us. Most of the time, he clears up my uncertainty and makes me clear as to what I must do as his follower.[24]

For most *ilse* women, Jesus is indispensably identified with their vision of their role as obedient and sacrificial lambs for the service and glory of God. Their conceptualization and language in describing their image of and relationship to Jesus are akin to those used by Grace Hurh. For example, Ha Yul-Nyu, a dedicated Christian medical doctor, described Jesus' impact on her life:

> Jesus is my life-guide and Savior. He also watches over my shoulder twenty-four hours a day. Sometimes, he is very burdensome, and I am so scared of him. But I am thankful for him because he saved our family from our life crisis. Several years ago, my husband had an extramarital affair. He lived with a woman outside the home and asked me for a divorce. I felt betrayed and was utterly devastated. I seriously thought about divorce and seriously discussed this problem with my two sons. At that time, my first son was a senior and the second a sophomore in high school. My first son adamantly opposed my divorce, but the second was very supportive. I decided to divorce my husband. But, during the period of that turmoil, my second son did very poorly at school, and his academic performance dropped sharply. Therefore, I reconsidered my decision to get a divorce. . . .
>
> Frankly speaking, I wanted to divorce my husband and to start my life anew. I have been the main rice-winner in my family—even now—throughout my marriage, and I was not happy in my marriage. I felt oppression and no fulfillment. But in this case, what could I do? Should I divorce for my own sake? Should I endure this humility and pain for my sons? It was so painful to decide my life and future. I really did not know what to do. Then, I thought about Jesus' sacrifice for us. Jesus knew no sin, but he died in order to save us. It must have been very painful and shameful for him, but he endured his pain and shame in order to obey God and to consummate His Will. Then, I thought, why can't I endure this pain? Why can't I die as Jesus died? I have been a Christian since I was a child. If I do not sacrifice myself for the family as Jesus sacrificed for us, how can I be a Christian? Also, I realized that being in this painful situation is my fate. Why can't I accept it as Jesus obeyed God, accepting his painful death? Therefore, instead of divorcing my husband, I decided to kill my "ego" for the sake of my family, especially my sons. I tried to forgive my husband and accept him. After that incident, I was totally reborn. I decided to dedicate my life to helping others. I do

not have much hope or joy in this life. I consider my medical profession as God's calling. I try to help people with my best efforts through my vocation. I want to dedicate myself as God's servant and follow Jesus' footsteps as his disciple.[25]

Dr. Ha's image of Jesus served as a model of sacrifice for her and helped her accept her pain and unhappiness and preserve her marriage by maintaining her role as a sacrificial mother and wife instead of changing her situation. Moreover, traditional roles of Korean women require self-sacrifice for the family good. In accordance with tradition, Dr. Ha gave up her own personal development and happiness and decided to sacrifice her life for the family. Her image of Jesus was critical to her acceptance of the role as sacrificial female. Since her two sons left home for college almost ten years ago, she has been active in the Korean YWCA and Family Counselling Center in northern New Jersey, and her financial and moral contribution to the Korean community has been sizable. Also, beyond her public service, she devotes a good deal of her personal life to helping her clients and their families as their counsellor. Her sacrificial service extends from living for her sons, to helping others, to serving God.

However, Dr. Ha does not seem to be enjoying the sacrificial role she has chosen to perform. Having given up her joy or hope in life, she sounds rather pessimistic and sad. The glory that was afforded Jesus for fulfilling his role as sacrificial lamb seems not to be a glory or honor offered to Dr. Ha for her sacrifices.

Like Dr. Ha, many of the interviewees depicted their role as that of vicarious sacrificial lamb, or Jesus. Kang Jin-Sook, a fifty-one-year-old devout Christian medical doctor, also expressed her zeal about sacrificing her life for others and for God:

Big Sister[26]! Nothing interests me in this world. I have accomplished almost everything. I have a good family and promising sons. Both my sons are in dental and medical schools. My husband is doing well in his medical practice. They don't need me as much as they did before. I have also a very good job. But, I feel no satisfaction or fulfillment. If I work five more years, I am eligible to take early retirement benefits. I plan to retire early and spend the rest of my life serving God. I want to go to underdeveloped countries such as Africa and work as a missionary. Even if my husband doesn't want to go with me, I want to go alone. But, I am not sure yet. Also, I have no desire to live long. I will serve God, and then I want to die as God's servant rather young in age. You know, Jesus also died young, but he really served only God.[27]

Dr. Kang did not appear to experience joy or fulfillment in her career or in her personal life, as she once had done when rearing and caring for her sons and family. She genuinely expressed her desire to sacrifice her life in the service of others and, ultimately, God. Like Dr. Ha, she sounded depressed. Does sacrifice or vicarious living contribute to these women's depression? Future studies on the psychology of sacrifice by women, especially, Asian women, may help answer this question.

Sacrifice has been deemed and lived as the core of Korean women's virtue since the Yi dynasty. Women in the Yi dynasty sacrificed their lives for men (father, husband, son), and the early immigrant women in America in the 1900s shifted their object of sacrifice from husbands and sons to the nation, namely, Korea. Similarly, Christian Korean women living in the United States today, seem to be extending the object of their sacrifice from husbands and children to God. The "others" are still the focus of *ilse* Christian women, and God becomes the center of these women's sacrifice, a center more abstract than family and nation. In lieu of Confucian doctrines and mores and patriotism, Jesus serves as the model and justifying symbol for the sacrificial life of these women.

Again from a Meadean point of view, these women are incomplete persons, because the "others" as the centers of their lives control them. However, women do reflect upon and rationalize their sacrifice and select Jesus as their legitimating principle. From this perspective, with the help of their image of Jesus, these women have developed rational processes and have become "complete selves" within their traditional, collectivistic cultural mindset and context.

Nevertheless, these women, in general, no longer seem to be content with or completely unquestioning of their sacrificial roles— despite their religious identification with Jesus. From these interviews, one senses in many of these devout Christian women, homemakers as well as professionals, a pessimism and otherworldly escapism, rather than enthusiasm or celebration. Interestingly enough, the more religiously involved the women are, the more is their "meaning in life" centered around "others" and God, the more their sacrifice is justified by identifying with Jesus' obedience and sacrificial death, and more severe their pessimism. For example, forty-eight-year-old, Min He-Yun, a pious Christian homemaker, expressed the same pessimistic and otherworldly attitude in relation to her sacrificial role:

> Serving God, as Jesus did, is the goal of my life. If I do nothing but serve God, I will be very happy. You know, I have no ambition or interests in this world. Before I was deeply involved in the church, I used to have lots of aspirations. Once I thought about going back to school to study medicine or law and to become a medical doctor or a lawyer. But no more. What's so good about living like that? I want to live like Jesus and go to Heaven for eternal rest. To tell you the truth, if I die now, it will be a great honor for me because I will meet Jesus and God in Heaven. I am very sure that I will go to Heaven after I die. Even thinking about this, "serving God in this world and meeting Jesus and God in Heaven," makes me feel exhilarated. But, sometimes, I worry about my family. Who will take care of them after I die? But then again, I am sure that God will take care of them.[28]

For Mrs. Min, as for the others who spoke above, her image of Jesus legitimates her acceptance of this world as undesirable and meaningless, rather than encouraging her to improve her situation, and it directs her energy toward serving God in this "temporary" world.

The image of Jesus as a selfless and sacrificial servant informs the self-image of these Christian women in very definite but limited ways. In other words, what they do not see in Jesus is his revolutionary or transforming (H. Richard Niebuhr's term) power.[29] The role of Jesus as an obedient and selfless savior hinders change in or innovation of women's self-image. Yet, Jesus, women's rationalizing self, is undoubtedly related to *ilse* women's self-development and their legitimation and acceptance of their traditional roles as selfless and self-giving caretaker.

On the other hand, among the "less religious" working women, the image of Jesus as a sacrificial savior seems to create anxiety, rather than calm acceptance. Oh Young-Ran, a single and competent entrepreneur, explains her anxiety and confusion caused by Jesus:

> I may not be a religious person. I came from a Confucian family, and my father was a strict Confucian. After I came to America, I was too lonely. Therefore, my roommate, who was a Christian, led me to church in 1975. Since that time, I have

professed Christianity, but I still have too many unanswered questions. Jesus is one of my unresolved questions. *Moksanim*! [Pastor!] I believe in God, but I cannot believe that Jesus is God and my Savior. Also, I cannot understand his sacrificial death for me. The Church says that Jesus died in order to save me from sin. Actually, I don't think I committed lots of sins. I think I am an honest and good person. However, I respect him as a great person, maybe a prophet. But, as a Christian, I have to believe him as my savior and God. It creates anxiety. I don't know what to do with him. It bothers me a lot.[30]

First, as a single woman, Ms. Oh has no immediate object of sacrifice, such as a husband or children. Second, as a competent businesswoman, she has absorbed the contemporary American (secular), existential mindset and work ethic which discourage other-oriented sacrifice in an individualistic and competitive life. Therefore, Jesus' sacrifice is not relevant to her life and, instead of providing assurance and acceptance of the status quo, contributes to uncertainty and anxiety.

Helen Choi, a former minister's daughter and professional, also expressed her confusion and said:

I am ashamed of not being very religious. I believe Jesus as the Son of God and our Savior, but I cannot believe the Immaculate Conception. I try to believe his Resurrection and Second Coming, but I can't. I wish I could believe everything that the Church teaches us—-maybe because I have such a shallow faith. But, actually, I don't think about him very much.[31]

Like Ms. Oh, Helen Choi does not have any objects of sacrifice at home. Her two sons are grown up and are independent. Her husband also was educated in America and is largely assimilated into American life; one would describe him as rather progressive and "liberated" from Confucian conventions. Therefore, the old cultural value of self-sacrifice does not speak to her, and the self-sacrificial role of Jesus is confusing in her mind and life. For these women, Helen Choi and Oh Young-Ran, Jesus' impact is not as critical as it is on the "religious women," and the value of his sacrificial image not so clear-cut. The interesting point is that, unlike the "religious women," none of the latter viewed self-sacrifice as the primary requirement of being a virtuous woman; none demonstrated pessimism or otherworldly escapism.

WOMEN IN MARRIAGE AND FAMILY

The Puritan wanted to work in a calling; we are forced to do so. For when asceticism was carried out of monastic cells into everyday life, and began to dominate worldly morality, it did its part in building the tremendous *cosmos* of the modern economic order. This order is now bound to the technical and economic conditions of machine production which to-day determine the lives of all the individuals who are born into this mechanism, . . . Perhaps it will so determine them until the last ton of fossilized coal is burnt. In Baxter's view the care for external goods should only lie on the shoulders of the "saint like a light cloak, which can be thrown aside at any moment." But fate decreed that the cloak should become an *iron cage*. (Emphasis added in italics)[32]

With this statement, Max Weber asserts that the religious idea of asceticism shapes the believer's specific lifestyle and through it the modern economic system, that is, bureaucratic capitalism, in which people are fatally imprisoned. Here, Weber suggests that the believer's world order and structure are replicas of her or his religious ideas and that people become locked into the socioeconomic and political framework they construct. This Weberian connection between religion and social structure illuminates my research in the sphere of marriage and family as well as the way that, for Korean immigrant women, the Christian God structures the domestic world.

Marriage and family continue to occupy a central place in the lives of most *ilse* women, and because one refers to the other, references to them are made interchangeably in this book. For many women, life begins and ends with marriage. Marriage is still viewed by many Koreans, men and women alike, as a woman's holy mission. Like the women in the Yi dynasty, fulfilling one's womanhood implies fulfilling one's marriage responsibilities and establishing a family. When the question "What message do you want to leave to your daughter(s) at your last moment?" was posed to each interviewee, most women (housewives and career women) replied, "Marry, have children, and be happy." Chang Ok- Hee, an earnest Christian and registered nurse, reminisced about the urgency of marriage in her younger years:

When I came to America in 1970, I was twenty-eight years old. I was already an "Old Miss." Ha, ha, ha. I had so much pressure from people in the church. Whenever people asked me when I would marry, first, I was so embarrassed and later, I became offended and even depressed. People told me that I should marry. I knew that. I wanted to marry, but it was not easy to get a Korean man at that time. People said that they prayed so that I would marry and told me to pray earnestly for that. To tell you the truth, I prayed so hard. Above all, I couldn't stand my mother's pressure. You know, she treated me as a retarded daughter. Finally, in 1972, I went back to Korea to get married. My brother-in-law, who was a pastor in my home town, arranged my marriage. I met this man [pointing to her husband] in July and married in November.[33]

Her experience vividly conveys the significance of marriage in the Korean community. Moreover, Korean women and the immigrant church reinforce the expectation and pressure on unwed women to marry. Even the second-generation American-born Koreans in the States today are not exempt from this cultural pressure, and neither are divorced and widowed women in their forties and fifties.

Interestingly, the emphasis on marriage correlates with the level of religiosity these women exhibit. The more religious the woman, the more important she regards marriage to be, and the more intense her efforts to justify marriage with religious reasoning. Park Jung-Ja, the "warrior" housewife, says, "God said, multiply and prosper; therefore, women should marry and bear children." As she explains, many women consider marriage as God's mandate to and blessing upon women and childbearing and childrearing as the sole manifested justification for marriage. The basis for that justification, though, is God, or rather, submission to God's will. However, a noteworthy paradox surfaced during this study. Although religious women strongly advocate the institution of marriage, the image of marriage they portrayed is rather gloomy. In other words, marriage is considered a burdensome responsibility and the source of self-sacrifice. Yang Byung-In, a religious businesswoman, said:

Women should marry; however, there is one condition—that they expect to fulfill "women's sacrifice." Without women's sacrifice, marriage is not feasible. Women should serve and care for their husbands as they did their fathers and/or younger brothers. Having children and rearing them well are the best contributions women can make to society and God.[34]

Such thoughts and fervent defence of the institution of marriage by the devout women echo the Yi dynasty's emphasis on marriage and womanhood.

These women's view of divorce resembles that of their foremothers—it is forbidden territory, condemnation, shame—yet their premise is Christian and not Confucian. As discussed in chapter 2, maintaining and fulfilling one's marital responsibilities in traditional Korea was a means by which women could secure status/position and power at home and in society. This remains true for *ilse* women in the contemporary Korean community—the immigrant church— in the United States. Women continue to be recognized and treated as persons mainly according to their marital status.

To many devout *ilse* women, divorce is now viewed not only as a violation of Korean customs and a failure to fulfill one's womanhood, but also as a violation of God's order and betrayal of one's commitment to the Almighty Father. Park Jung-Ja, a pious housewife, protested against divorce with the use of Scriptural injunctions:

> Marriage is sanctioned by God. God said that no one can separate husband and wife because God joined them as a couple (Mark 10:7–9). Therefore, by all means, divorce is not justified. No matter what kind of hardship a woman has, she has to hold her marriage together unless her husband abandons her or has an affair with another woman.[35]

"Religious" women adamantly defended and struggled to preserve Korean traditional views of marriage and justify their stance with their interpretation of the Bible. Moreover, they insisted that a woman's fate was defined by her husband's. In other words, men have the right to break up a marriage, but women must endure and preserve it. Therefore, marriage continues to be considered by such women as the ultimate lifestyle and goal of women.

However, interestingly enough, these very devout women expressed considerable flexibility and openness toward remarriage. Many of them support remarriage. Their reasons seemed quite practical, not religious: emotional stability, economic safety, avoidance of loneliness, companionship in old age, and so on. Yet, underneath the surface of the pragmatic notions, it was apparent that these women viewed remarriage as an opportunity to (re)establish a successful conventional marriage. In other words, remarriage would provide the means of being reaccepted into, and readjusting to, the tradition.

However, some working women, particularly those who are single, demonstrated ambivalent attitudes toward marriage. They admitted the importance of marriage, but their justification of marriage was practical and realistic rather than religious and ideological. In these cases, Weber's view of the primacy of religion in people's daily life seems less relevant. Chung Myung-Soon, a devout Christian and a restauranteur in New York City, who depicted her marriage as a painful path of thorns, advocated marriage but rationalized it with conventional common sense rather than with religious conviction:

> I had lots of rainbowlike dreams and hopes in my youth. I wanted to be a great woman. But all my ideals have gone away since my marriage. Life seems to be a continuum of painful struggle. But, I have seen the misery of single women. Even though some of my single friends have become successful in their careers, they seem to be so lonely and miserable. I hope Cho-Yun [her daughter] will marry a good man and have children. I think, though marriage is painful, it is still much better than single life.[36]

Unlike Chung Myung-Soon, Lee Bong-Hee, who is a widow and has two grown daughters pursuing graduate studies, expressed a different view. She did not deny the importance of marriage but also accepted "single life" as one of several acceptable lifestyles in modern society. She said, "If my daughters choose a single life, it is O.K. with me. They should be happy with whatever they decide." This may be a reflection of her reality as a widow and working woman with two unmarried daughters. For her, religious ideas of marriage and traditional Korean customs do little to justify her situation. Moreover, having been educated in the United States and having lived here for over thirty years with eyes and ears close to academia (her husband was an academic and her two daughters are academically oriented), Mrs. Lee is aware of feminist ideas and the choices available to women in American society today.

In addition, Oh Young-Ran, a single woman with a business, expressed desire for change away from Korean Christian emphasis on marriage. She said:

> The Church is too family-centered. Single people feel alienated. Many women, single or divorced, stop coming to the church. I know someone who is divorced but is very religious and attends

only the early morning service so that she can avoid people. Being single may be one's fate. I respect women who are so proud of and happy with homemaking. But I wish these religious people would understand us single women and also respect our lifestyles and treat us like human beings.[37]

As these working women demonstrate, some Korean women do have choices to marry or to stay single. They do not look not to religion but rather to their personal inclinations and professional priorities to define their feelings toward marital status. For them, being married is not necessarily a requirement for being a good Christian or for fulfilling one's womanhood. Further, a considerable number of working women, regardless of their religiosity, expressed openness toward divorce and remarriage. They seemed to be more influenced by pragmatic considerations and less by religious concerns.

In brief, most of the women who were interviewed believe that despite some changes in their views of marriage and divorce, marriage still remains the ultimate life-goal of *ilse* women. The more religious the women are, the more strongly do they defend traditional marriage and the importance of women's sacrifice and childbearing duties with religious reasoning. Religious women still view themselves as sacrificial objects in the service of their men and the family. Even some who do not defend the idea of women's sacrifice enthusiastically still subscribe to it religiously. The idea of women's sacrifice remains a powerful one throughout Korean families in America. Those women whose lives are absorbed in religion become the most traditional wives and mothers. Those who are less absorbed in religion also adhere less to traditional views of marriage, womanhood, and fulfillment. The church seems to stand with the first group of women, by justifying their stance with religious ideas, and apart from the latter group. In short, one could argue that the Korean immigrant church helps most Korean *ilse* women maintain tradition rather than change or modify their life situations in accordance with changes in the greater American society.

Male Preference in Families

According to a 1980 survey,[38] more than 90 percent of women in Korea still prefer sons over daughters. Male preference and significance in a Christian family also does not seem to have changed much after immigration to the United States.

One Korean male pastor I have known for many years sees himself as a sacrificial lamb in the process of preserving the age-old patrilineal tradition. He grew up in a devout Christian family. He is the middle sibling among his three brothers, none of whom have sons. While on her deathbed, his mother called her three sons together and lay down her last command: one of the sons must give birth to a son(s) in order to carry out the Lee family name. Rev. Lee's two brothers, who were in the process of immigrating to the United States, refused to try to have any more children. Therefore, my pastor-friend, who was then in his late forties, promised his mother and tried to have a baby in order to obey and fulfill her will. He said:

> How could I ignore my mother's will? As a Christian, especially as a pastor, I couldn't disobey her. Since my two brothers did not want to try again, I had to try. Therefore, I promised my mother that I would try. As you know, I have three daughters, and my first daughter is in college already, but this little boy (two years old) is really a burden. I am already in my fifties. I have to be healthy and live long for him. Whenever I see him, I just feel the burden of my responsibilities. Many times, I really regret having had him. Also, I feel that he is not my son. He is my mother's son; further, he is the son of our whole Lee family.[39]

As Rev. Lee confessed his predicament, it became apparent that the traditional preference for males among Koreans victimizes men as well as women. Furthermore, within this tradition, women such as Rev. Lee's mother, who deem it their ultimate responsibility to provide sons to a family, perpetuate male priority for their own survival (without sons, they and their lineage lack immortality and status). Coupled with the Christian teaching of obedience to God, which many Koreans translate into obedience to Korean culture and traditions, male preference among Koreans in the United States today continues to have critical impact on the lives of Korean women; change in self-image and behavior as insurers of male progeny does not seem to be taking place.

One young woman in her early thirties, a longtime acquaintance of mine, fiercely challenges the traditional role as the insurer of male progeny imposed on her by her religiously pious husband and mother-in-law. She is an American-educated *iljŏm ose* and is married to a young Korean pastor. During the six years she has been married, she has borne five children. Her husband is an only son; therefore, he and his mother desperately want male children. Because she first gave birth to three daughters, she was under severe pressure to have a male child. Though she gave birth to a son as her fourth child, her husband and mother-in-law demanded more sons. After having given birth to her second son (her fifth child), she telephoned me and cried out, "Am I a child-bearing machine?"[40]

The traditionally Korean insistence on and Christian rationalization of male preference also seems to ignore the woman's age and health when pressuring them to bear sons. Mrs. Han Jini, a Korean Christian woman whom I have known for more than thirteen years, is presently fifty years old. She has one daughter in her early twenties and another, twelve years old who has Down's syndrome. Mrs. Han has struggled financially, physically, and emotionally for the past twelve years to care for her mentally retarded daughter. Yet her mother-in-law, a pious Christian who lives with Mrs. Han and her family, insists that the daughter-in-law should try again, even at her late age, to bear a son. Although he does not often verbally echo his mother's wish, Mr. Han does express his desire for a son. The mother-in-law has been praying for the last twenty years for a grandson with which to continue the Han family name and glorify God. Once, when asked by her then-eighteen-year-old granddaughter, "Grandma, if you have a choice between having a drug-addicted delinquent grandson and a Harvard-attending granddaughter, which would you choose?" Mrs. Han's mother-in-law immediately replied, a drug-addicted grandson. The mother-in-law, like many Korean Christian women, both young and old, interprets a lack of male (sons/grandsons) as God's punishment for one's sins. In the Protestant tradition of garnering material remuneration as a sign of election (cf., *The Protestant Ethic and the Spirit of Capitalism*), male progeny, for Korean Protestants, is a sign of election: By giving birth to males, a woman absolves herself and her family from God's wrath and disfavor and wins God's blessings for herself and the entire family.

As is apparent in the three aforementioned cases, "more religious" often means "more traditionally Korean." In this sense, the religious environment in which many Korean women find themselves in the United States does not seem to be very different from that of their preimmigration social and cultural contexts in Korea. Rather, "religious women" live in a "mini-Korea" within the United

States, with respect to preference and esteem for males. Gender hierarchy and inequality in Korean families in America today generally flourish as if these Koreans were living in their native country.

However, women who have work experience, regardless of their religious piety, generally exhibited flexibility and open-mindedness toward rethinking gender valuation and, particularly, male preference. Sa Mi-Ja, an ex-nurse and businesswoman who is the mother of two daughters, expressed her contentment with them. Park Jung-Ja, who had worked nearly all of her adult life and is now a pious housewife, expressed equal support for her children—both her son and her daughter—morally and financially, although she at times seemed to reveal psychological preference for her son over her daughter. She said that she had always wanted her son to become a medical doctor but that he could not fulfill her wish. Therefore, her daughter carried out the parents' wish and became a medical doctor. Throughout her daughter's medical education and training, Mrs. Park worked hard to support her daughter. Though Park Jung-Ja is a religiously "hot" fundamentalist, her work experience as a "warrior woman" seems to have helped her transcend traditional Korean norms regarding the value of women and women's ability and place in the public (professional) world.

Despite some openings toward rethinking and re-evaluating male/female competence, roles, and status, the majority of women, even explicitly, expressed their preference for sons to daughters. In general, male preference is still dominant in Korean Christian families in the United States today.

Women's Role and Status in the Family Structure

Applying Durkheim's insight that human beings are symbol-making creatures,[41] one can see language as a symbolic form through which communication and social interaction occur. Since the self is a product of socialization through symbols, observation of daily language is another way of examining women's selfhood in the Christian family structure. Hence, an examination of women's language will illumine their notions of status, roles, and family order.

The Korean language is highly hierarchical. Unlike most cases in English, one word cannot be applied to all situations and people. For example, *you* in English is universal, applicable to everyone, regardless of sex, age, socioeconomic class, and status. However, in Korean, the same *you* cannot be applied to everyone. There is no counterpart in modern English, but the distinction in French between *vous* and *tu* and in German between *sie* and *du*, is comparable. The respectful language, such as *thou* in English, is commonly called *chondae-ŏ/mal* (존대어/말: 尊對語: language of respect) and is used to address one's elders and persons in socially higher positions. In contrast, *pan-ŏ/mal* (반어/말: 半語: half-word) can be used when speaking to people who are of the same age or younger, as well as to persons in the same or lower socio-economic class. These linguistic norms embody and perpetuate the age-old Confucian, hierarchical social morality. As a consequence, it is the custom for Korean women to use *chondae-ŏ/mal* (존대어/말: 尊對語), such as *thou*, instead of the egalitarian *you*, when addressing their husbands. An interesting discovery that emerges from these interviews is that the form of language used by these interviewees correlates with their religiosity, education, social roles and status.

The religiously pious women tend to consistently use *chondae-ŏ/mal*, calling their husbands *thou*, and reinforcing through their language a domestic status that is inferior to that of their men. Their social roles generally remain that of the traditional caretaker, and the family structure is hierarchical. Also, Korean-educated "religiously hot" women more insistently and consistently use the *thou* form and are more likely to show their strong adherence to Korean traditionalism than the American-educated, less pious women.

Even though Ha Yul-Nyu holds professional status as a physician, she offers a good example of those women who employ "linguistic respect" toward their husbands. Dr. Ha, who was educated in Korea and is a devout Christian, has a husband who is her own age and inferior to her in education and social status (he has been a store-owner and intermittently unemployed). Yet, in every manner and use of language during the interview (and on other occasions throughout our acquaintance), she demonstrated her determination to show respect for her husband and speak to him using the *chondae-ŏ*. During the interview, when I referred to her as "Dr. Ha" (her maiden name) in accordance with Korean custom,[42] she hurriedly corrected me and called herself "Mrs. Whang," using her husband's last name—an American social pattern she has adopted. Since her husband is not a "Dr.," it may be that she intentionally lowers her status by referring to herself as "Mrs. Whang," an appendix to him.

The interviews reveal that the *thou* users, those educated in

Korea in particular, justify their speaking behavior through their hierarchical understanding of Christianity. Many women, homemakers as well as professionals, expressed the view that men should be the head of the family, just as Christ is the head of the Church, for the sake of family order and in accordance with God's hierarchical scheme of creation;[43] therefore, women must render unto their men respect in language and manner.

Na In-Wha, a pastor's wife, not only strictly uses "*thou* language" to her husband but also compares a home to heaven and defends patriarchal family order. In her interview, she said,

> God is the ruler in Heaven; a house is a paradigm on earth of the Heavenly Kingdom. Therefore, a husband has to rule the family as God rules the heavenly world.[44]

Na In-Wha's family view and order can be easily understood as part of her status and role as a pastor's wife: she must maintain traditional social and moral norms in order for her husband to maintain his immigrant church successfully.

H. Richard Niebuhr classified Christianity in relation to culture through his five famous typologies: Christ against Culture; Christ of Culture; Christ above Culture; Christ and Culture in Paradox; Christ the Transformer of Culture.[45] One can argue that Korean Christian beliefs function to legitimate women's adherence to the traditional Korean culture. In other words, Korean-educated Christian women are most likely highly traditional in terms of their familial roles and status. In this respect, the Christianity of the Korean immigrant women in the United States today is an agent of "culture maintenance," and language functions to keep Korean immigrant women who are Protestant Christians in Niebuhr's second category, Christ of (with) culture.

Apart from the verbal form of "linguistic respect," Korean-educated *ilse* women live out their ideas about patriarchy and hierarchy in other ways. Even those who do not engage in regular use of *chondae-ŏ* with a male partner advocate patriarchal order within the home. One interviewee of this group is Suh Jai-Mi, a Korean-educated divorcee, physician, and relatively radical critic of the Korean immigrant church. However, unlike the "religiously hot" Korean-educated women, Dr. Suh's religious justification lacked conviction and revealed a mixture of pragmatism and confusion about gender roles and status within the family. She said:

A man should be the head of the family. It is the same principle that a ship must have only one captain. If there are two
captains, there will be confusion, and the ship will not know
where to go. Similarly, man should rule over a woman at home.
I think God made it that way—but, if a man cannot function
as a rice-winner or as the head of the household, . . . then
maybe a woman has to be. . . .[46]

Usually a highly articulate woman (in my other interactions with
her), Dr. Suh was inarticulate in her interview about her thoughts
and failed to complete her last sentence. She mumbled her last words
and hesitated, as if to cover up the contradictions in her response.
Dr. Suh's beliefs about the primacy of the male in the governance of
a household blended what she believes to be religiously sanctioned
with functional considerations. Yet her religious beliefs did not seem
to legitimate her position as head of the house, a position that she,
as a divorced woman with one young son, assumed by choice and
necessity. Being a rice-winner and "master" of the house seemed to
reinforce her "abnormal" status as a husband-less, independent
woman, a deviance from the traditional Korean norm that is a source
of shame and embarrassment in the immigrant Korean community
even today. In the traditional Korean view, only women without
privilege, such as poor women of the lower classes or widows, work
and become heads of households.

In most Christian families in the United States, men continue to
be authority figures and heads of families, but their image is rather
symbolic, as it was during the Yi dynasty. However, unlike the women
of the Yi dynasty, who were legally forced to humiliate and subordinate themselves to men, Christian Korean women in America seem
to denigrate their status intentionally as a means of survival within
Korean contexts, that is, Korean communities and churches.

Kil Young-Sook is a mother of three grown-up daughters, two
who are attending Yale University and one who is in high school.
Her language toward and regarding her husband, her elevation of
him as the (symbolic) head of the family hierarchy, and her deliberate
denigration of herself in the same hierarchy reflect family patterns
in traditional Korean culture. During her interview, she justified her
hierarchical reality with her religious convictions. She explained:

The household order in my home? Of course, my husband is
the boss. He is always absolutely right and perfect. You know,
we [she and her three daughters] treat him like God. Whenever

he says anything, we always say "yes." There is no objection. But we know he is not always right and perfect. However, if we say "no," there will be big problems—arguments and fights. Ultimately, he always wins. Otherwise, our family peace, especially order, is broken; therefore, we always say "yes" to him. Then, behind his back, we [she and her daughters] sometimes laugh. But I believe God is Order. A house has to be in—reflect and embody—God's order. Therefore, I have always taught my daughters to obey their father now and their husbands after they marry. Whatever they become, and no matter how successful their careers may be outside the home, it doesn't matter. They must be lower than their husbands and serve their husbands inside the home in order to maintain the family order. I am very lucky, for my daughters are very obedient to their father and they are very good.[47]

These women, Mrs. Kil and her daughters, seem to have developed dual selves, one which justifies male superiority for the sake of obedience to God and the maintenance of family stability and one which realistically differentiates the pretense of male infallibility and superiority from the truth. The pretense is necessary to maintain the family, whereas the truth can obstruct family peace. It is the women's job to construct that peace, while the authority figure of the husband and father enjoys the fruits of their work. Consequently, the entire family receives God's approval and blessings for having abided by His order of creation.

The piously Christian Korean women who constitute the majority of my primary sources in this study seem to work hard to make themselves inferior beings in the traditional Korean way, and the religious systems in which they live lend themselves to the perpetuation of these women's inferiority. Religion for them legitimates women's subordinate place in the Korean community in America. If not perpetuating or legitimating women's inferiority, interpretations of Korean Christianity as maintaining family order, even if functional rather than ideological in intent, seem to confuse women's gender consciousness and identity, as in the case of Dr. Suh. In sum, Korean Christianity in the United States functions to maintain and encourage patriarchal family structures of *ilse* life. Women remain subordinate to men as the age-old Confucian Korean tradition has dictated.

What, then, are women's current domestic roles in this patriarchal family structure? Have there been any changes in roles compared to those of the Yi period or the immediate preimmigration period? Based on these interviews, it is difficult to discern many changes in the domestic roles of the Korean-educated Christian women, housewives as well as professionals. Caring for the family and molding and developing the husband/children are the major tasks of the immigrant women in America. As a result, these women also develop collective selves, as their foremothers did during the Yi dynasty.

Na In-Wha may serve as a typical model. She worked for many years as a registered nurse in order to support her husband during his seminary studies. After her husband entered the ministry, she resigned from her profession and became his unpaid full-time assistant. When asked about her role in the family, she described her special role as her husband's assistant:

> My husband has a great responsibility to care for his congregants, God's children, and to lead them to Heaven. If he fails in his job, he will be punished by God on Judgement Day. I have to help him fulfill his job; therefore, I quit nursing and now devote myself to helping him in his ministry. . . .
>
> Listening to sermons is the focal part of my religious life, but I cannot listen to my husband's sermons during worship periods. Why? Because I am too busy and nervous while my husband preaches. You see, I worry about him a lot—whether he'll forget what he should say next or mumble during his preaching; whether he is thirsty or seems like he's going to faint; whether he perspires a lot; whether his suit is buttoned right and the clerical gown is properly put on, and all those kinds of things. I have to observe his gestures and facial expressions. We have two Sunday morning services, one at nine o'clock and the other at eleven o'clock. My husband preaches the same sermon at both services. Therefore, after the first service, I run to his office and tell him about every detail of his sermon—his gestures, inflections, expressions, content, examples, etc. He listens to me and corrects what he did wrong the first time when he preaches at the second service. When my husband completes a service without mistakes, I usually feel so fulfilled. Phew, it's a relief. You know, I do not preach to the congregation, but I think I am more exhausted than my husband. . . .
>
> My husband also does not know anything about our house. I keep from him anything that is not church related. I do everything. I don't even let him put a nail in the wall. He spends all of his time just for church matters. But of course, my children

complain about their father—that they never get to spend time with him. I also think it is not good for a father not to know about what's going on in his children's lives, so I've told him to spend about half an hour with our children each day after they come home from school. But this doesn't seem to work well.[48]

Na In-Wha sounds as if she exists solely for her husband and his ministry, and at the same time, she expresses contentment and fulfillment through him and his work. Having given up her profession and having immersed herself into her husband's life, she not only takes care of her husband but also develops him. She resembles those women in the Yi dynasty who carried their younger husbands on their backs and raised them as their mothers. Absolutely denying her own self, Mrs. Na has developed a collective self with that of her husband. Although she is not visible in his ministry as anything other than "the minister's wife," she is the person empowering her husband and his work behind the scenes. Through him and his successes, she empowers herself and in turn exercises her power over him and his ministry. Though unwittingly, Mrs. Na portrays her husband as a symbolic figure not only in the home but also in his ministry. It is she who does most of the work and he who presents it to others.

Despite these continuities in traditional role-playing, the center of life for many women seems to have shifted somewhat away from their husbands and more to their children, as compared with the husband/man-centered women of the Yi era. The interviewees told remarkable stories of their dedication to and sacrifice for their children. Park Jung-Ja, the "warrior-woman," expressed her sacrificial devotion to her children in this way:

We [my husband and I] endured much turmoil and numerous hardships for the success of our children. I've always wanted my children to be highly educated and successful in America so that they do not have to go through the pain of struggle that my husband and I have. For my son's admission into Bronx High School of Science, I fasted for two years and prayed. At that time, I worked like an insane woman for sixteen hours each day. But I never ate anything until twelve noon. For lunch, I only drank a cup of water and had a bowl of soup for dinner. After my son got into Bronx Science, I again fasted for a whole year for my daughter's admission to the same school. Both of them graduated from Bronx Science and went to good colleges. I am proud of them, but do you know what I got from that sacrifice? Ulcer. I suffer this terrible ulcer even now from those days of fasting.[49]

After the interview, she invited me to dinner at her home. However, she could not eat most of the foods she had prepared because of her ulcer problem. She is proud of her sacrifice, though she suffers tremendously, because sacrifice is still Korean women's supreme virtue and honor.

The roles of Korean-educated *ilse* women as caretakers, nurturers, and life-savers today in the United States resemble those of the women in the Yi dynasty. However, previously in Korea, such sacrifice was justified and rewarded by Confucian ideology. Today in America, *ilse* Christian women's sacrifice is equated with that of Jesus and is legitimated by notions of Christian virtue.

What is the situation of the American-educated *ilse* women? Do they use the "*thou* language"? Are their roles and status and family structure different from those of the Korean-educated women? What is the impact of religion on their domestic lives? It is very difficult to define clearly the answers to these questions because the interviews with the American-educated women reveal much contradiction, confusion, and ambiguity regarding religiousness and "linguistic respect" as well as regarding religion and domestic gender hierarchy.

The American-educated women stated that they seldom use *chondae-ŏ* to address their husbands but refer to them either as "you" (instead of "thou"), or as "Mr. So-and-So" (instead of "Sir So-and-So"). However, these women expressed some awkwardness and discomfort with using either the Korean or the American forms of addressing one's husband—the Korean formalistic *thou* is too hierarchical and burdensome, and the universal English *you* too informal and levelling. Interestingly enough, none of these call their husbands by their first names, as did the early immigrant Korean women of Hawaii.

Though the language the American-educated women use with their husbands may not be as overtly sexist as that used by Korean-educated religious women, the Christian beliefs to which the former subscribe still justify a sexist family structure. Min He-Yun, a housewife, and Grace Hurh, an educator (both of whom belong in the "religiously hot" category), hold the opinion that a man has to be the head of the family for the sake of maintaining order, just as God rules the world with order. However, the actual interactions of the husband and wife are not rigidly hierarchical; these people seem to treat each other as equals. The family structure of these two women falls somewhere between the traditional hierarchy of Korean patriarchy and the relatively egalitarian partnership orientation of contemporary (younger generation's) American family structures.

Furthermore, in Helen Choi's home, her husband often prepares dinner, not only because she works late, but also because he enjoys cooking. In general, in the American-educated *ilse* Korean family, there seems to be no rigid division of domestic roles or hierarchical demarcation of status between husband and wife. However, the overwhelming majority of *ilse* Korean men in America take no part in performing housekeeping chores, such as cooking, dishwashing, and washing clothes. According to recent research,[50] Korean women in the United States still do 95 percent of the cooking and more than 90 percent of the dishwashing.

Many factors may affect the relatively untraditional domestic arrangement of the American-educated first-generation Korean families. Among them, the educational context and social experiences of each spouse may be the main determinants. All of the American-educated interviewees were married to Korean men who had also been educated in the United States. These men have been relatively Americanized in thought, manners, and lifestyle. However, it is also commonly acknowledged that the more involved in the Korean church, the more those "liberal" husbands tend to become traditional in manner, that is, "Koreanized." In other words, those "Americanized" husbands avoid helping their women or doing "women's work," when surrounded by Koreans or in a public setting such as church.

In addition, unlike the majority of Korean female immigrants to the United States who had arrived as fully developed adult selves, that is, after the completion of their education in Korea at least in their late twenties, most of the American-educated women had come to the United States in their late teens or early twenties. Their adulthood developed in American educational, cultural, and social settings. Therefore, the traditional religious beliefs promulgated in the Korean immigrant churches do not accord with their American education and social experiences. In other words, Korean Christianity is not the sole principle guiding and rationalizing their thoughts and behavior.

These women, in line with Peter Berger's view of modernity as pluralism, seem to have multiple principles justifying their views of family life and domestic roles. Consequently, there appears to be some contradiction between these women's religious conceptions of women's domestic role and status and their actual familial arrangements. Many of the American-educated women agreed to hierarchical family structure as a religious principle for the purpose of preserving family order, but they seemed to live out a rather egalitarian family life based on practicality. Their interviews reveal ambiguity and complexity in both their notions and their realities of "household order." For these American-educated women, Christianity seems inadequate as a legitimator of adherence to traditional Korean culture, and American education and workplace more helpful as adaptive agents in living American lives as Koreans.

In the main, their language, domestic roles/status, and family structure all reflect a midway situation of the two cultures, the Korean and the American; American-educated Korean women are "cultural hybrids." From the Meadean point of view, both social environments, the Korean and the American, seem to be at work in these women's lives.

However, in terms of role performance, the American-educated women still consider nurturing, caring and self-sacrifice for the family to be the major domestic tasks of women. Grace Hurh, a professional educator, reflected upon her past and said:

> I feel very sorry toward my children. You know, child-rearing is a woman's most important task. But, when I was young, I didn't realize that. I took my children to the baby-sitters because I worked. Now, I really regret what I did. If I had young children now, I would never work. I would fully devote myself to the children.[51]

Saying this, Grace Hurh advocated women's sacrificial duties to the family, especially children. Like her, the majority of the American-educated women continue to value women's traditional, familial role of nurturer and sacrificer and in that way remain attached to Confucian Korean tradition.

As affirmed by Jean Baker Miller on women in general, the tradition of women's self-sacrifice for the development of others remains a primary domestic task of *ilse* Christian Korean women, regardless of their educational context and working status. However, unlike their foremothers, these women make sacrifices that have expanded from and transcended the gender boundary: their self-sacrifice is not limited to men (husband and sons) but also extends to their daughters. They sacrifice for the family *in toto*, regardless of the family member's gender, place in the hierarchy, and familial role. In this sense, their self-sacrifice for others has shed its traditional sexism.

In sum, Korean-educated Christian women seem to adhere to their given tradition and culture. Their family structure is sexist and hierarchical, and women occupy a subordinate position and perform traditional roles in the family. In order to adhere to their traditional culture, these women justify their roles and status with their religious beliefs. However, the family structure and domestic roles and status of the American-educated women, including those who work, appear more complicated and less coherent than those of the former because their Korean Christian beliefs do not accord with their bicultural experiences. The two social realities serve as conflicting legitimating principles. Some of these women seem to be confused and uncomfortable with the apparent contradictions, yet they manage their lives by building dual social structures and adopting multiple forms of rationalization. They maintain relatively traditional family structures, yet their roles and status are mixtures of American and Korean cultural patterns.

Therefore, Weber's view that religion shapes the behavior and lifestyles of its believers and constructs on their cosmos helps interpret the relationship between the religious beliefs and the family structures/interactions of the Korean-educated *ilse* women—who adhere to a single rationalizing (religious) principle—but not to the American-educated Christian women, whose rationalizing principles and processes are multiple. Yet, it is clear for both types of Korean women that Korean immigrant Christianity maintains and legitimates the Korean culture and women's traditional roles and status in the face of modern American secular culture along the lines of Niebuhr's "Christ of Culture" paradigm.

Self-Denial and Self-Assertion

Obedience and self-sacrifice have been synonymous for Korean women and have directly affected the development of the image of the "selfless woman." The Yi dynasty produced "selfless women," and self-abnegation, for most *ilse* women in the United States— particularly "religious women"—remains essential to their gaining recognition and status in the Korean community. But unlike the Yi women, they live with no law forcing self-abnegation upon them. How, then, do these *ilse* women not only take on but perpetuate the image of the "selfless woman"?

A major finding in this research is that prayer seems to be inseparably related to the process of women's self-denial and functions as a means of gaining the self-discipline needed to attain that goal. Many women begin and end their days with prayer. Chung Myung-Soon, a restaurant owner, described her prayer-filled life:

> I don't have specific or special times set aside for prayer because I am too busy and have no time. Therefore, I pray while driving a car coming to work and going home. I pray while in a bathroom. Whenever time is available, I pray. I don't care what time or place. I just pray all the time. Without prayer, I cannot sustain my life. Physically, emotionally, and financially, I am exhausted. As I said before, I run this restaurant, and my sick husband causes lots of tension and problems, even though he tries to help. I still have lots of debts to pay because I opened this business with loans. In fact, I have tremendous responsibility for my home and business. My shoulders are too heavy. I am a mother, father, owner, servant—everything. Sometimes, I just want to run away from all these burdens. Perhaps I am too selfish for just thinking about myself. I just earnestly pray in order to deny myself so that I may pay off all the debts and fulfill my duties. I look forward to the day when I am freed from all these burdens and can serve only God.[52]

Chung Myung-Soon uses prayer as a means of discipline in order to deny her personal needs and to accept her harsh reality. In this way, she supports her daily existence.

As in Mrs. Chung's case, prayer, for most *ilse* women, is a powerful instrument of self-denial. When using it as a self-disciplinary tool, most women develop very systematic and structured prayers. Min He-Yun, who had majored in Religion at a Methodist university in the United States, illustrates her life of systematic prayer:

> I live on prayer, and my days begin and end with prayer. Without prayer, I cannot manage my life. I also pray in a very systematic manner. My prayer starts with thanksgiving and then goes on to adoration, confession, and supplication. First, I pray for my husband and his business and my children; then,

I pray for my pastor and the church; then, for my family members—my parents and siblings—in Korea and here in America; then, for my church members and friends or any others whom I care for or consider; and the last is "myself."[53]

Though none of the other women are as clear about the order of their prayers as Min He-Yun, most of them do set aside a special time for prayer and do it regularly. Also, like Min He-Yun, they structure the contents and order of their prayers significantly. The objects of prayer are the immediate family (husband and children), the church and its members, relatives, and others. However, unlike Min He-Yun, many women are reluctant or uneasy about including themselves in their prayers. Some say that they do not pray for themselves; others express guilt about praying for themselves. Oh Young-Ran, a single business woman, commented:

I am all alone in America and am a self-supporter; therefore, I mainly pray for myself and my business. If I am sick or in trouble, no one will help me. Also, if my business is not going well, I cannot pay my employees. I have a tremendous responsibility to myself and to my employees. However, when I pray for myself and my business, I feel so guilty. I mean, I feel so selfish—I should pray for others. Therefore, forcefully and hastily, I try to pray for others, such as my relatives in Korea—and others.[54]

Because Korean women have always considered themselves and have been considered by others as selfless caretakers, women still consider praying for themselves, that is, focusing on their own lives, to be a "selfish" act. Even those women like Min He-Yun who include themselves in their prayers, treat the inclusion as a mere appendix to the "main" prayer. Furthermore, the content of their prayer for themselves is absolute self-denial. Women unanimously said that they pray to God for him to kill their own selves and to fulfill their duties as wives and mothers by freely obeying his will. Interviewees' comments on prayer indicate that the more "religious" the woman, the more fervently she prays for self-denial and the more she avoids any decision making: by refusing to make decisions, she demonstrates self-denial and unconditional obedience to God. Therefore, women's prayer as a means of self-denial is closely linked with (non)decision making. Consequently, those women who are homemakers and religious fundamentalists avoid intellectual rationalization and tend to justify and interpret any causality in their life experience as God's will. In this vein, Ye Soon-Jong, a housewife and a member of Holiness Church, explained how the selection of her son's college was made:

> My son was accepted by several prestigious colleges, and we couldn't decide on one. Therefore, I prayed very hard to find out what God's will for my son's schooling is. Before making a decision, we [her family] made a tour-trip to those colleges. When we arrived at Johns Hopkins, we were greeted by an evangelical group of Korean Christian students. Oh, they were on fire with religion! We prayed and sang hymns together. I told my son and my husband that this group of Christians is God's answer to my prayers and His Revelation to us. It is the school that God chose for him. Then, we immediately decided on that college. Since that time, my son has become very active in that prayer group, and we are very happy.[55]

The family does not seem to have used any intellectual standards for the important decision about a son's college education because Mrs. Ye acted as prophet and "conveyed God's will" to her family.

Another woman, Min He-Yun, who is also a member of Holiness Church, projected her avoidance of decision making and her acceptance of all causality through prayer. Before her husband began his new business venture three years ago, he had worked as a section chief of the engineering department of a large multinational firm in the United States. After having reached this stage, he was faced with the realization of having reached his peak in this organization. He apparently had before him three relatively unappealing options, including resignation, and the couple could not decide what path he should take. Therefore, the interviewee prayed day and night for God's guidance:

> You know, it is so strange. After my fervent prayers, among the three choices, two of them gradually became useless by themselves. The one choice left to my husband was resignation and to start his own business. At that time, we didn't have the money to begin a new firm. But, it's really strange—out of the blue, partners appeared and offered their financial investment because my husband already had experience and technological knowledge. However, still, my husband hesitated; so I pushed him to resign and accept their offer. I was sure that God sent those partners and arranged all this work. Therefore, my

husband began his new business, and the company is doing well so far. You know, we never decide anything with our reason; instead, I always pray so hard before making any decision. God always shows His Will for us. How do I know it's God's Will? Well, you have to see how things are going, and then you accept the thing. That is God's Will.[56]

Speaking thus, Min He-Yun little sounded like a woman with American bachelor's and master's degrees. Further, she revealed that she does not even use her common sense or logic for planning family vacations. Once, she and her family went skiing without praying about it beforehand. Throughout the vacation, she was very restless and anxious because she feared that something might happen to her home: the house might be on fire or it might be robbed. Since that experience, she has not attempted anything without prayer. She has repudiated her intellectual and rational faculties for unconditional surrender to faith and has trained herself to accept a given situation, whatever it may be, instead of changing or modifying it to her liking. As Min He-Yun and Ye Soon-Jong demonstrate, most "religious homemakers" decide domestic and extra-domestic matters through prayer. Their decision making is generally an acceptance of a given situation rather than an active construction of a new reality based on reason and sense of adventure.

Yet, these women cannot be viewed entirely as being passive in their acceptance of given situations. An important phenomenon that surfaced from the interviews is the self-assertion of these women through their self-denial in prayer. Although the "religiously hot," self-denying women use prayer as a means of self-discipline with the goal of denying the self, the same women ultimately interpret and actualize "God's will" in the lives of their family and themselves. At critical moments, these women are the ones who admonish their families to accept given realities as the work of "God's providence." Somehow, they seem to have appropriated the authority to translate God's will into language that the whole family can understand and act upon; even their husbands, who are the ultimate authority figures in nearly every other aspect of family life, seem to accept and abide by the "holy knowledge" of their "prophetic" wives. In this sense, such "pious Korean women" call to mind the role of "house priestess," or medium between the spirits and family, that traditional, Shamanistic Korean wives and mothers held. However, paradoxically, these women do not identify themselves with the power or authority they create through their priestly or prophetic role. Instead, they negate themselves while applying their power to their "decision making by default" and, consequently, to controlling their men and families. Women's self-abnegation through prayer can actually amount to women's self-affirmation and unknowing self-empowerment. Power, however, is rationalized by them as being "other-directed."

For some interviewees, prayer is not the sole method of decision making. The majority of the businesswomen, though very religious, employ mixed methods of decision making that include prayer and discussion or consultation with their husbands. For the most part, these women use prayer as a means to self-denial (they pray to "kill" the self, to be obedient to God, to be a dutiful wife and mother) but use consultation with their husbands to manage business matters. For example, Yang Byung-In, a businesswoman, employs prayer to assist her in self-denial and consummation of her conventional role as selfless mother and wife. However, for business decisions, she uses both prayer and conversation (i.e., reason) with her husband. In most cases, the businesswomen accept the advice or decisions of their husbands in matters of business. Although they do apply their rational faculties, the outcome is usually dictated by the husband. From this perspective, one can argue that the religious housewives who pray for decisions assert the self in matters of family importance more definitively than do the "rational" businesswomen. As the sole interpreters of God's message, the former enjoy great authority in their homes. However, the religious businesswomen, as practitioners of traditional self-denial through prayer and as receivers of their husbands' decisions, seem to have reduced opportunity for and intensity of self-assertion in decision making. For these religious businesswomen, prayer appears significant as a form of self-discipline in the service of performing traditional women's roles and insignificant as a form of self-assertion and self-affirmation.

In contrast, other working women, especially those who are single and American educated, use prayer as means of self-affirmation and self-empowerment. They stand directly in contrast to the "religiously pious" women, particularly homemakers, whose prayer is a disciplinary tool for their self-abnegation. Helen Choi, an American-educated professional educator said that she meditates—

when she has time—for self-perfection and spiritual tranquility. She hardly prays about decision-making tasks but decides things through discussion with her husband. Like Mrs. Choi, most working professionals decide things by consulting with their husbands. For the majority of these women, their husbands function as "mini-Gods." In this sense, they share a common attitude and practice with the religious businesswomen.

During the interviews, another important fact surfaced in relation to decision-making: the majority of the women, homemakers, businesswomen and professionals, rarely discuss problems with their pastors. Moreover, they express reluctance or skepticism toward revealing their problems to male pastors. For example, Dr. Suh Jai-Mi stated:

> Just a couple of times, I went to see our pastor in order to discuss my son's teen-age problems. After that, I never discuss anything with pastors. First, I don't trust them. They are human beings, and there is no confidentiality. Above all, what do they know about women? They don't understand women and our problems.[57]

Like Dr. Suh, most of the interviewees seem to avoid discussing their problems, especially problems related to women's lives (e.g., marriage, divorce, husband's infidelity, wife beating), with their male pastors; therefore, the husband becomes the most available and reliable person, besides God, with whom a woman may discuss her problems. Yet, it is difficult to discuss family problems with one's husband, the man who is a major part of those problems. This situation leaves women with hardly anyone to turn to for advice on such matters.

In general, the women who were interviewed confessed a need for and lack of discussion partners in the United States; they said that they are lonely. In Korea, women have traditionally shared and discussed their problems with other women—such as mothers, grandmothers, aunts, friends, and neighbors. But most of the interviewees live in nuclear families, so the members of the unit family become the major agents of discussion. Therefore, the scope, persons, and roles that may allow for discussion of the problem are severely limited. Furthermore, many of them complained of the limitations in communicating with their daughters, owing to language and cultural barriers (most of their children speak English and are Americanized in terms of culture and values). Moreover, most of them pointed out that they are busy in their jobs and do not have time to explore their problems with others. The problem seems to deepen for single women who have no family members around them.

To summarize, prayer reflects the social reality of *ilse* women's roles and status. These women remain in their own eyes "anti-existential," that is, they want to be selfless beings and to be subordinate to men. Their prayers for self-denial symbolize anti-self-development. Only a few, mostly American-educated professionals, pray for their self-empowerment in their personal and public lives. For most of these women, regardless of their background and religiosity, prayer is a tool with which to nurture women's traditional consciousness (as selfless caretaker) and help them fulfill their wifely and motherly roles. In other words, prayer disciplines women, especially religious homemakers, to be other-focused. Yet, paradoxically, they assume, through prayer, the role of God's interpreter during periods of crucial family decision making and use their power to control their men and families. In this way, women's prayer for self-denial provide occasion for self-assertion. Nevertheless, this religious process of self-denial and self-assertion contributes to the perpetuation of women's traditional role as a selfless caretaker and a nurturer of others, for the focus of prayer in women's lives is primarily the good of others.

Some women, particularly single women and professionals, also use prayer for self-improvement and self-perfection, although prayer is much less significant for them than for the "religious homemakers." In other words, they also use prayer as a disciplinary means of self-assertion. However, the majority of these women suffer from guilt and tension emanating from their awareness of conventional Korean Christian perspectives on women's praying. Women of this category are less likely to use prayer as a means of decision making. Human agency—such as that expressed in comments from their spouses, or in their own power of reasoning—is more likely to affect their decision making.

Consequently, the role and impact of prayer (Christian discipline), in *ilse* Korean women's lives is diverse. Whether prayer is used for the purpose of self-denial or self-perfection, prayer is an indispensable, and often powerful, survival mechanism for *ilse* women.

New Self-Cultivation

Traditionally, the Korean society programmed women to live for others, especially for their men and families. This was achieved directly, by law and force, during the Yi dynasty and implicitly, by custom, in modern Korea. As a result, the selfhood of women emerged as a "collective self," bound up with their men and family. For women, separating themselves from their family amounted to suicide. As a consequence, the notion of women's individual worth and the development of women's potential other than in homemaking have been discouraged. However, *ilse* women in the United States live in relation to a very different social and cultural milieu, one that espouses and encourages individuality. In addition, feminism in America has become a powerful impulse for generating the self-cultivation and self-fulfillment of women. How has this new social and cultural force affected the life of Korean immigrant *ilse* women? How do Korean Christian women in the United States cultivate and fulfill their own lives?

Most of the interviewed women, whether they work outside the home or remain at home as housewives, seem to be too busy to develop a new conception of self. Moreover, the majority of the interviewees play double roles, housekeeping and rice-winning, and therefore find little time and energy to focus on self-cultivation through hobbies or participation in civic activities. In one case, I had to interview a woman at 9 A.M. on Sunday because she had no other time when she could talk freely. When I arrived at the home of Yang Byung-In, a jeweler and member of Fellowship Church, it was 8:45 A.M. Mrs. Yang was already nicely dressed and welcomed me. The house was sparklingly clean and orderly. There were a couple of pots on the stove, as she was preparing *komt'ang* (곰탕: Korean-style beef broth) and some other dishes for lunch and dinner. On one side of the sink, there were bunches of *paech'u* (배추: Chinese cabbage) soaked in salted water for making *kimch'i* (김치 : traditional, Korean pickled vegetables).[58] Serving me a cup of hot coffee and *ttŏk*, she described her schedule:

> I got up at five o'clock this morning, because my husband goes golfing very early on Sunday morning. I had to help him dress and make breakfast for him. You know, marriage is a woman's most fulfilling contribution, but there is one unconditional presupposition: women's sacrifice. Without a woman's

sacrifice, a marriage is not going to work. Well, I have been working since five o'clock this morning. My husband comes home around eleven o'clock and then we [she and her adult son, who lives with her] will have lunch with him and go to church [her church service begins at 2:00 P.M.]. Therefore, while he is away, during the only time I have for myself, I have to prepare some food for dinner and make *kimch'i.* Whenever I have free time, it is spent catching up on my housework because I work from morning until late evening every Monday through Saturday. Also, during the weekday evenings, we often go out on errands, or to a social gathering, or to church meetings and services, a Bible class, choir practice, sometimes a revival meeting. So Sunday morning is the only time I have for myself. That is why I asked you to come for the interview this early—I am very sorry about that. Oh! Life is too busy. But I am so happy doing all this work . . .

But, He-Young [her daughter, who works and lives away from Mrs. Yang] always tells me that I should enjoy my own life. She said, "Mom, don't you know how to live your own life? Why don't you enjoy your life instead of working all the time at home for daddy and us? If we are hungry, we will get food and eat. We can cook. Also, let daddy and Tae-In [her brother] get their own food if they are hungry. Don't baby them. Go out golfing or meet friends and go to a movie with them. Oh, you are boring and helpless. I will never live like you." You know, my daughter favors feminism, but I am not interested in it. I may still be traditional, as she said. But these young women today seem to be too egoistic. In my opinion, American individualism and feminism make these young [American-born] women quite different from us. To me, they are very selfish.[59]

Here the two cultures, the Korean and the American, collide. The mutual criticism of each woman's lifestyles, the mother's and the daughter's, reflects the cultural and generational differences between contemporary Korean and American values. The daughter's American-feminist values and behavioral context prompt her to reject her mother's traditional role performance. For the daughter, living one's *own* life and cultivating it seem more valid than sacrificing one's time and energy for others, especially those who can fend for themselves. However, from the mother's point of view, her daughter's individualistic and feminist attitudes seem not only alien but also offensive to her, even though she, as a longtime U.S. resident, has adopted many aspects of American lifestyle and contributes significantly to her family income.

Like Yang Byung-In, most women are very busy playing double roles—traditional homemaker and rice-winner—and do not seem to have time or energy for self-cultivation. Another example is Kim Ai-Kyung, a member of Fellowship Church, who has run a boutique for more than thirteen years. She said that she has not visited her family in Korea for more than sixteen years because she could not leave her husband and children alone:

> I want to visit my parents and relatives in Korea. I also want to see my friends over there, but I hesitate to visit them. When my children [two sons] were young, I couldn't leave them here alone because there was no one to take care of them. Also, I had my business to take care of. Now, both of them are grown up—the older boy is in medical school, and the younger one is working at a bank in New York City. But, when they come home, they still don't even open the refrigerator to get their own food or drink. I always serve them. And my husband—he does not know anything about the house. He doesn't even know how to make *ramyŏn* (라면: Oriental-style instant noodle soup). If I went to Korea, he would starve to death. How can I leave him alone and go visit my family in Korea? It would be very selfish of me. As a Christian, I should be a model fulfilling my duty as a faithful wife and a mother.[60]

Like Yang Byung-In and Kim Ai-Kyung, even working women do not seem to heed their own need to fulfill certain personal desires, such as visiting one's family, and to cultivate their personal potential outside the traditional role of housekeeping. They maintain their traditional female roles while simultaneously taking on the new role of economic provider and use their Korean Christian faith for justification.

For career homemakers, individualistic fulfillment is an even more remote possibility. When I visited Kil Young-Sook, the wife of a physician and a devout member of Fellowship Church, she had just returned from a golf lesson and shared her thoughts on self-cultivation:

> I am sorry for not serving you with home-made Korean food. I have just returned from my golf lesson. Oh, it is so hard. I really do not enjoy it at all. It is rather burdensome. You know,

I am not an athletic person at all. When I was in high school, I used to hate physical education. But, I have to learn golf. Otherwise, I will be so isolated. I don't have friends, and my social life is made through my husband. His friends, mostly medical doctors and their wives, all play golf so well. Whenever I am with them, I am left out; therefore, I try very hard to learn golf, but it is really a pain . . .

How do I use my own time? Well, I don't have my own time. My time is only for my husband, my daughters, and my home. My husband comes home from the hospital around three o'clock in the afternoon. When he is home, I have to be with him. When he has a day off, I do not plan anything for myself. I move according to his schedule. He loves to sit down and rest at the stream running through our back yard. If he sits there, I have to be with him. You know, sometimes just sitting beside him and doing nothing annoys me because I don't enjoy it—I have lots of things to do in the house. So, I go inside and do my house work. I can never leave the house while he is at home; therefore, I do not have my own time or my own life. I don't even know what I like to do, I mean, my hobby.[61]

As is apparent from her comments, Kil Young-Sook is a typical example of a woman who is absolutely controlled through and shaped in the process of self-immersion in her husband and family around her. She seemed to have no sense of her own self. In order to fit herself into her husband's social circle for survival, she must ignore her own interests and potential. Judging by her words and behavior, she appears to be not an appendage to, but completely immersed in, her husband.

According to this research, the overwhelming majority of Christian *ilse* women, homemakers as well as working women, do not allow themselves to develop a self-image or to cultivate personal interests and hobbies other than those pertaining to their traditional role performance. From the Meadean perspective, Christian *ilse* women maintain "social selves" produced through the objective adjustment to the external environment.

On the other hand, mainly American-educated professionals and single women (who are viewed as outcasts from traditional Korean norms) speak of various ways through which they experience personal development and fulfillment. Helen Choi, an American-educated professional whose children are mature and independent, said that she fills her free hours by playing tennis, listening to music, or meditating. Oh Young-Ran, a single entrepreneur, spends her leisure time painting. Sarah Lim, a real estate broker and wife of a minister, said that she is beginning to learn to cultivate her hobby because her two sons are in graduate school and her husband often goes away on pastoral trips. It is interesting that these working women who develop their own interests and talents label themselves as "less, or not, religious." These women are conspicuously far less involved in their churches than the "religious women" and so may be considered "spectators" from the viewpoint of traditional Korean Christians in the United States. In addition, these more self-cultivating women are relatively free of traditional obligations such as homemaking. Therefore, the relatively less religious and more unconventional women tend to develop their own lifestyles and to cultivate their own potential for personal fulfillment.

In sum, the Korean immigrant church may help the "religious women," particularly homemakers, legitimate the traditional women's self-image and so inhibit their development of a new self aimed at non-other-oriented, or nonvicarious, personal fulfillment. On the other hand, women whose lives are less immersed in Korean Christianity seem relatively liberated from traditional expectations of selfless nurturer and allow themselves more time, freedom, and ease for self-enrichment.

Other-Worldliness and This-Worldliness

Most Christian women whom I interviewed, like their traditional foremothers of the Yi dynasty, still focus their lives on others, namely, their husbands and children. However, unlike Yi women, who received compensation for their sacrificial performance in the form of respect and care in old age from their children, and ancestor worship in death, *ilse* women do not necessarily receive rewards for self-sacrifice today. Nor do they expect them.

Korean newspapers in the United States frequently print articles exposing the problems of the elderly, such as exploitation of their unpaid labor (as, for example, babysitters or storekeepers), loneliness, abandonment, poverty, and psychological stress. Moreover, more and more elderly Koreans are leading a lifestyle that was unheard of in the Yi period and still is condemned in Korea today: independent and solitary living.[62] To let one's parents and other elderly relatives fend for themselves alone during their old age has always been considered an egregious sin in the Confucian tradition. Yet many elderly people, even those who had been living with their sons' or daughters' families, find their own homes or apartments to escape family tensions, feelings of rejection, excessive house maintenance and babysitting chores, and/or a sense of imprisonment (in the case of suburban dwellers whose children do not have time to take them on errands or outings). In old age, dependence on one's children, as a natural, honestly earned reward for self-sacrifice as a mother, is no longer guaranteed.

A recent incident drawn from the experiences of one of my relatives vividly portrays an *ilse* woman's unrequited sacrifice for the family. My aunt, Kim Mi-He, has always been a traditional Korean woman, ceaselessly sacrificing herself for her family. She has spent her entire life serving her husband and raising her five children—four daughters and one son. After her husband's death ten years ago, she was immediately rejected by her only son, whom she had always regarded as her "mini-God." Since then, she has been living in the United States and has helped rear five of her grandchildren, the children of two of her daughters, along with housework for these two daughters while they were away at work.

Last year, at the age of 77, Aunt Mi-He underwent surgery for cancer. Though she had been in America for more than ten years, she longed desperately to return to Korea in order to spend her last days there and be buried next to her husband's tomb.[63] However, her son would not allow her to return to his house, and her daughter in Korea also hesitated to receive her because of the latter's insistence upon her position as *ch'ulga woein* (출가외인: 出家外人: stranger after marriage)[64] and thereby exonerated herself from responsibilities to her natal family.

One of her daughters in America, whose children Aunt Mi-He had reared, hesitated to accept her into her home, owing to a busy work schedule and in consideration of her husband's feelings on the matter. Although two other daughters offered their homes to her, Aunt Mi-He was reluctant to accept because these two daughters live alone and have no "man of the house" upon whom Aunt Mi-He could lean psychologically. This example discloses multiple facets of the problems afflicting contemporary *ilse* Korean women in the United States, from persistent psychological dependence on men (although this aunt has lived as a typical "warrior woman" for the empowerment of her husband and children) to homelessness (even if psychological) and sense of abandonment, that is, uncompensated sacrifice.

When I visited Aunt Mi-He after her surgery, she was on her deathbed and reminisced about her past in the following manner:

> I am full of *han*. I was so gifted in art, especially singing and oriental painting. When I was a student of Sookmyung High School [in Korea], I was a tennis champion representing the school, and won numerous medals. I also received prestigious prizes, such as the National Art Prize, from various art contests. I was very good in painting. My dream was to become an artist; therefore, after I graduated from that high school, I tried to go to Japan and study Oriental Painting, but I couldn't fulfill my dream because my family told me I must marry. I still have the desire to paint, but it is too late now. I really regret not having had the guts to develop my talent. Look at me now—I've spent all of my energy on my husband and children, but what do I get now? I don't even have a place to rest in my old age. I have become homeless. None of my children want me because I am sick and because I will be a burden . . .
>
> Where is God? What does God do for me in this misery? Is this my reward after all my sacrifice? If so, God is not fair at all . . .
>
> I am seriously thinking about going back to Korea and living in a nursing home. But I worry that will cause shame and problems for my children. I don't know what to do. I regret my sacrifice. Life is empty, empty. If I am reborn, I will do what I want to do; I will live my life as I want. Ai Ra! Don't sacrifice your life for anyone else, even your children. Do what you want to do! Develop and cultivate your gifts. Live your own life. Don't care about what people say. I was too stupid to follow the convention. I looked to everybody else but me to see how I should live. I never expressed what I felt and thought. I just wanted to please everyone, especially my husband and children. But it is useless. I realized my mistake now, but it is too late. Now I am old and sick, waiting for the day to meet my husband in the otherworld. I just pray that the day I lie down next to my husband comes soon. But I doubt whether he will recognize me. Is there another world besides this? I think life will end at the moment of death, but I still want to believe that there is another world in which my sacrifice will be rewarded. If not, I will be too miserable. Oh, I am too full of *han* because I didn't live my real life.[65]

Aunt Mi-He's message on her deathbed powerfully and painfully raises serious existential, social, and theological problems regarding Korean Christian women in America. She conveys the contemporary consequences of a traditional woman's life, a typical "social self:" homelessness, unwantedness, regret. Her words and predicament reflect the changing nature of elderly Korean immigrant women's social situation and status. The old Confucian system of justice no longer applies in the United States, and the new Christian promise of salvation and otherworldly compensation seem dubious. To Aunt Mi-He, regardless of what God may offer her in an afterlife, her earthly life amounts to an exercise in futility.

In Korea, living in a nursing home in one's old age is still regarded as the worst misery and disgrace one can experience, making one an "unfulfilled person."[66] Also, sending one's parents to a nursing home is still considered sinful. However, this shame-ridden reality becomes an inevitable lifestyle for many elderly Korean women in America who are not rewarded for their this-worldly self-sacrifice.

As in the case of Aunt Mi-He, Korean immigrant women in the United States live in a social milieu unlike that of traditional and contemporary Korea. Most interviewees in this research seem not to expect rewards for the sacrifices they made on their children's behalf. Park Jung-Ja, a "warriorlike" sacrificial housewife and a member of Word Church, said:

> As you know, my son has just married. When Lynn [her daughter] is married, I will be free from my responsibility. I firmly told them many times that I will not take care of their children. I raised them [her children] and sent them to good schools and have seen them marry. I have done everything that I was obligated to do. From now on, they have to be responsible for their lives and their children. I really want Lynn to marry a good Christian man. After that, I will prepare for my old age. I don't want to depend on them. After Lynn gets married, I will fully dedicate myself to serving God and will rest in Heaven after I die.[67]

Like Park Jung-Ja, many "religious women," homemakers as well as professionals, place their ultimate goal of life in serving God and seem to expect a heavenly reward.

Therefore, the degree of women's religiosity and their attitudes toward the world seem to be correlated. The more religious the woman, the less she tends to consider her rewards and meaning of life in terms of this world. Such women take on an otherworldly orientation in their daily thought processes and in justification of their behavior (particularly, domestic self-sacrifice).

Ye Soon-Jong is a pious fundamentalist and member of Holiness Church. I had known her for more than ten years when we both attended Fellowship Church. I had always remembered her to be a highly outgoing, energetic, active, and social person and had recalled how beautifully she had decorated and maintained her house in an exclusive area in northern New Jersey. My impression of her home and life were of brightness and vitality.

After she transferred to Holiness Church, she became more pious. She still lives in the same house, but my impression of her home and of her lifestyle, when I visited her for the interview, was radically different from that of the past. The interior of her house was gloomy, the general atmosphere was sullen and closed. The former vitality and brightness had vanished. The furniture was the same as before—nothing new had been added—but the window shades were pulled down, and sunlight had not entered the rooms for some time. The house resembled an old museum with dusty objects on display. The only apparent new feature was the open Bible on every table in the house; this gave the house the feeling of an abandoned chapel and seemed to reflect her disengagement from this world. She said:

> I still have young children to care of. My last daughter is a fifth-grader. After she goes to college, I really want to devote myself fully to serving God. I have no expectations of my children, except that they become good Christians and offer their lives to God's service. I also have no interest in worldly things. Jesus said, "Store your treasures in Heaven, where there is no moth nor thief to steal your treasures in Heaven" [Matt. 6:19–20]. My hope is in Heaven.[68]

From the interviews, one can generalize that most religiously pious women tend to develop a sectarian attitude that draws them out of engagement with the world[69] and turns their attention toward the "other world" as their destination. Though these women still sacrifice for their family, they seemed neither to experience joy in living vicariously nor to expect this-worldly compensation.

In terms of women's fulfillment or reward through sacrifice, the so-called less pious women also do not seem to expect any earthly reward from their sacrificial role performance. However, their attitude toward the world seems relatively positive and active. For example, Helen Choi, an educator, said:

> My two sons are all grown up. The first one, who is a lawyer, is married and doing fine. The second is an artist. Though he does not make good money, he is O.K. I think I did my duty all right, but I do not expect them to take care of me in my old age. As long as they are happy, it is O.K. with me. Until now, I did not really contribute to the society because I spent most of my time and energy raising children and taking care of my family. Now, I am ready to serve the Korean community. As you know, I have lots of experience in the educational field. I have also witnessed many problems related to immigrant life, such as the culture shock of the new immigrant children and their parents, juvenile delinquency, the problems of youth gangsters, and communication gap between generations, and even between *ilse* and *ise* . . .
>
> You know, the Korean community really has tremendous problems. Who should be the most accessible and effective agent to deal with these problems? Of course, the church, given that almost all Koreans in America go to church. But, the church is not really doing anything. You know, most immigrants attend church—Sunday is the only day for the whole family to get together and go to the church. It is a perfect day for family education, for the immigrant Koreans to learn about American culture, for example, the public school system, American values and manners, etc. I really want to help those who want to adjust to life here in America. Why can't the church provide lectures or seminars to help people to adjust to American life instead of insisting on Korean culture? Why doesn't the church invite experts to help our people? I am willing; I now have time and experience. I really want to share my experience and knowledge with those who need it, but the church never uses me. Seeing those problems and the church's indifference about the community problems makes me frustrated.[70]

For Helen Choi, "this world," especially the immigrant Korean community, demands her serious and earnest attention and efforts. After having fulfilled her traditional roles as nurturer of the family, she feels ready to use what she has gained in terms of her own immigrant and professional experience to help others adjust to life in the United States. Given her educational and professional training, she feels she is an important asset to her ethnic community, but an asset that is going ignored because she is a woman and an "Americanized" Korean.

Though the less pious women no longer expect direct or worldly reward for their sacrifice, service for others remains important in their lives. Like Helen Choi, professional (and usually American-educated) women expressed their readiness and willingness to serve their community, Korean as well as the greater American society, but are frustrated about the church's lack of initiative in using them as resources. Dr. Suh, a member of Holiness Church and self-labelled as a "nonreligious" Christian stated:

> Do I expect to be taken care of in my old age by John [her son]? No, no. Rearing him well was my duty, and I did it. Now, he is at Harvard and interested in majoring in business. I am still responsible to him until he finishes his education. After that, he has to take care of himself and later on his own family. That is his business, and I hope he will do it well. That is all I want. I don't expect him to take care of me . . .
>
> I am now ready to share my American experiences gained through my profession and the education of my child with new immigrants. So many families in the church have problems. You know, Koreans are so narrow minded and short sighted. They are only concerned about making money and the *ilse* Korean community. To our children, America is their country. They cannot be confined to the Korean community solely. The [Korean] community has to produce politicians, law-makers, lobbyists, and artists. Look at our children. Most parents still urge their children to go to medical school and law school or engineering college so that they can make money. No, our children should enter the main stream of American society. They have to work not only for the Korean community but also for the American society in general. Why can't the church open its doors and provide educational programs and career counselling? Why can't the church expand the vision of our [first] generation and that of our children? As a single parent, I have struggled to raise my son and, at the same time, to establish my career. But, now, I have more time to serve the community. I am willing to help people if the church asks me to serve—but I won't cook or wash dishes. No way.[71]

The "less religious" women like Mrs. Choi and Dr. Suh do not place their hopes on, nor do they expect any reward from, their children or their husbands in terms of "paying them (the women) back" in their old age. However, service to others, either to God or to people, remains important to Korean *ilse* women. For the "more religious" women, the object of service is God. Their reward is expected in the afterlife, while the object of service for the "less religious" is community and/or society. Their expected reward seems to come from their inclusion in and recognition by the Korean church and community as community builders. However, these churchgoing women who are interested in worldly affairs and fulfillment suffer from frustration, because their kind of service is not properly recognized, encouraged, and channeled by Korean institutions in America.

ILSE WOMEN IN TRANSITION

Based on Mead's assertion that an individual, as a social member, cannot transcend the social context, I have proposed the hypothesis that specific role models are products, or manifestations, of the specific social embodiment. Among the several social agents and institutions that form a social matrix for the self, this study is particularly interested in the Korean immigrant church. To study the role models of women produced by the church is to study women's selfhood in that social morale. The Yi dynasty produced its unique role model for women: the obedient and self-sacrificial wife/mother. What is the contemporary role model for the Korean Christian immigrant women in the United Sstates?

Although most Korean immigrant church women espouse similar attitudes toward Christianity, it is difficult to propose a definitive role model for them because they are affiliated with different denominations. As *the ilse* women have demonstrated different attitudes toward their world and role performance, it is to be expected their role model(s) in different denominations will be diverse, that is, closely linked to their religious context. As Max Weber has articulated the difference in the understanding and application of the same doctrine of theodicy among Protestant denominations,[72] each denomination, as a social context, produces its members' unique behavior and, with that, its own ideal type of believer. This research explores the women's role models produced by the three United Methodist churches selected for the project.

This study finds that most women do not claim a role model that is separate from their church affiliation and that, for the most part, they lack any consciously selected role models to speak of. When I posed the question, "Would you tell me about your role model, if any?" most women showed embarrassment or hesitation. Many of them answered the question with, "Let me think about it," or, "Can I tell you later?" or "Well, I don't have any." Most women seemed to have difficulty in thinking about women whom they emulate. This can be interpreted as indicating that the old Confucian "ideal woman" may no longer function as Korean immigrant *ilse* women's paradigm. Only a small minority of the interviewees presented role models which explicitly represent the nature or context of their churches.

The role models for the women of Holiness Church are biblical women: Sarah, Hannah, and Ruth. All of these women were described as women of obedience and prayer. One interviewee explained that Sarah obeyed God's will and, as a reward, gave birth to her son Isaac in her old age. Also, Hannah's supplication to bear a son was granted by God; and she dedicated her son Samuel to God, just as she had promised. Therefore, Sarah and Hannah were portrayed as women of prayer, commitment, and obedience. Na In-Wha, the wife of the pastor of that church, emphasized the obedience of Ruth and explained her reason for selecting Ruth as her role model:

> Ruth is my role model. When Naomi, her mother-in-law, was about to return to her hometown, she advised her two widow-daughters-in-law to go back to their own homes because they were pagans. However, Ruth insisted on following her mother-in-law and taking care of her. Because of her loyalty and obedience to Naomi, Ruth was very blessed later and became the great-great-grand-mother of Jesus. You know that story . . .
>
> A few months ago, we had to give a new name, an American name, to our daughter. She is in the fourth grade. The children and teachers sometimes have problems pronouncing her Korean name. I wanted to name her "Ruth" because I want her to be an obedient woman as Ruth was, so I suggested the name Ruth and explained why I liked that name. But my daughter wanted to be called Rebecca and said, "Mommy, I don't want to be an obedient woman like you or Ruth. You have no freedom at all. You don't even wear the clothes that you want to wear. You are always concerned about what the

church people think about your clothes or your behavior. You obey Daddy and other people too much. I want freedom. I want to be Rebecca because she is the mother of Jacob, the Israelites. I want to be a mother of the people in this world." So, we granted it, and her new name is Rebecca. You know, the children today are very different from us.[73]

As Na In-Wha's case indicates, being a mother is still important, even to *ise* female children. However, obedience to a more traditional image of women may no longer be critical to many *ise* girls and women as women's roles and role models in America change.

Interestingly, all of the women who named biblical women as their role models are homemakers whose major social context is the church, whereas none of the working or professional women of Holiness Church suggested any role models, biblical or secular. The more revealing fact with respect to role models is the correlation between women's religious context and their role model(s). The Holiness Church, known as the most fundamentalist and pentecostal United Methodist church among the three in this study, seems to mold women into traditional homemakers for whom the old norms of obedience and sacrifice still are the primary values. For women of this church, the changing values, images, and role models facing women of contemporary America are less likely to affect their self-image and sense of womanly enterprise. At the same time, it appears likely that the religious impact on formulating/adopting role models for the working women of this church (and in general) is rather weak, since these women suggested no clear, and certainly not religious, role models in their lives.

In contrast to the women of Holiness Church who were interviewed, the women of Fellowship Church, homemakers as well as working women, could not name definitive role models. Nevertheless, several of them expressed their admiration for a mother, an aunt, or mother-in-law. Ahn Sung-Sim, a real estate broker, expressed her respect for her mother as a woman of deep Christian faith and spoke highly of her devotion to her family and church. Yang Byung-In, a businesswoman, also spoke of her veneration of her mother. She described her mother as a woman of devotion and service to her family and others. Since her mother had been widowed in her early thirties, she raised her four children by herself and at the same time provided financial support to several students (outside her family) who were in need, without letting her family or any one else know of her deeds. She also portrayed her mother as a woman who lived out her commitment to her Christian faith and service.

Sa Mi-Ja particularly lauded her mother-in-law for her spirit of independence and her sacrificial devotion to her children. As a refugee during the Korean War, her mother-in-law moved to South Korea from the North and worked very hard in various occupations in order to raise and educate her four sons. With her sacrificial support, all of her sons graduated from the most prestigious university in Korea, Seoul National University, and have become well established in their careers. Now in her old age, the mother-in-law is not dependent on any of her children and lives independently with her husband. Sa Mi-Ja describes her mother-in-law as a woman of Christian faith and will-power and respects her as a woman of independence.

Despite offering these admirable portraits, none of the women of Fellowship Church use the term role model to refer to a respected mother or mother-in-law. These women, like those of Holiness Church, revere women's sacrifice for and devotion to the family, but the objects of their veneration are not biblical; rather, they are ordinary women. They know directly and intimately the older women they respect. Also, the women who express their admiration for these ordinary women are all working women, while the women of Holiness Church, who propose biblical models, are all homemakers. The focus of the working women of Fellowship Church is on women's activities based on faith and a sense of women's independence. This may reflect their very real situation of playing double roles, traditional housekeeping and rice-winning. In contrast, the homemakers of Holiness Church view as their ideal type those women who perform the traditional role of obedient and sacrificial wife and mother.

Again, there is a close relationship between the social nature of the church and women's role models. The essence of Fellowship Church is one of socializing its members as members of the Korean community in the northern New Jersey/New York City area; many of its members, both men and women, are financial, intellectual, and social leaders of this region's Korean community. Its emphasis is more on this-worldliness, as compared to the other-worldliness of Holiness Church. Further, the changes in women's lives emanating from their interaction with multiple social members as businesswomen and professionals correspond with changes in their consciousness and behavior as women. Though these women still highly revere women's sacrificial service, their religious views do not seem to support the traditional role models as much as those of Holiness Church homemakers.

Additionally, none of the women of Word Church, homemakers, businesswomen, and professionals alike, suggested any role models. The fundamentalistic Holiness Church stresses the supremacy of obedient biblical women as role models, and Fellowship Church, whose uniqueness consists in providing an enjoyable and meaning-ful social environment, produces practical, socially active (in family and community) women as role models. Why does Word Church, then, whose missionary emphasis focuses mainly on preaching, not produce any role models for women? This is still a puzzle, but I would surmise at this juncture that although members of Word Church focus on the weekly sermons as the main drawing point, they lack church activities through which to play out and absorb the religious ideas they hear on Sunday. In other words, there is not much occasion to witness, adopt, or test an ideal type or model. Second, the preaching style of the minister is neither indoctrinating nor inspirational; rather, it is quite rational and explorative—he tells things in an "objective" manner without imposing his inter-pretations on his congregants. It is possible that these two factors have some effect on the Word Church interviewees' lack of role models.

Despite the different role models and revered women produced by two of the congregations, it is important to note that none of the interviewees named as role models their own mothers, most of whom had faithfully played the traditional roles expected of them in Korean society—obedient and self-sacrificial wives and mothers. One can interpret these findings reflecting a break or gap in the formation of role models of Korean women in America. In other words, the old models of the ideal Korean woman are in question or are fading away, either because their inherent flaws are recognized or because their merits are difficult to realize in an immigrant setting. It is also possible that a new role model is in the process of being developed or that the immigrant church, the major social context, is itself changing and thereby has no clear identity upon which to base its ideal types of Christian Korean women. On the other hand, one can also surmise that the secular knowledge and experiences of these immigrant women are complicating their ideas of ideal womanhood in immigrant America. There is no one answer to this question of why there is no role model, but without a doubt, Korean immigrant *ilse* women are clearly in transition. Although individual women, especially pious homemakers, may be averse to separating their sense of self-identity from that of tradition, the image of ideal Korean womanhood is changing. It remains to be seen what kind of ideal type will emerge from the ambiguity and uncertainty of the present and how the women's relation to the immigrant church and to the greater American society fashions that new image.

As these women demonstrate, Christianity affects *ilse* women's daily lives significantly, though in complicated ways. The final chapter will disclose these women's struggle for a new life between the two gigantic religiosocial realities—the immigrant Korean Church and America.

CHAPTER 5

The Dynamics of *Ilse* Christian Women's Adaptation to Society

Survival primarily requires an individual's adjustment to his or her given social milieu. As mentioned in the previous chapters, educaton has significantly contributed to the social members's adaptation process. Education in the Korean language is *kyoyuk* (교육: 教育), which means "teaching" and "rearing." As the term *kyoyuk* indicates, education innovates a person's identity, that is, self, through teaching the social rules and norms, the collective consciousness, and by shaping a person in the social mold.

Korean *ilse* women now live in a new land, America. What is their major educational institution here in the United States? How does education affect these women's lives? Does the education of the immigrant women facilitate the fulfillment of their personhood in the new social situation?

Furthermore, immigration means work outside the home, a new experience to most of the *ilse* women. Again, from the Meadean point of view, this new social experience must trigger women's new self-image in America. But, what have their work experiences in the American society been like and how have they affected these women's self-development in the United States? In other words, how does the American society treat *ilse* women, members of a racial minority?

This final chapter will analyze women's social experiences in the United States as viewed from the perspective of educaton and work. Particular attention will be paid to the adaptation of these women to life in America within the dynamics of their two major social foci, particularly the workplace and school, that is, the church.

WOMEN AND EDUCATION

The Yi dynasty shaped women through education, both formal and informal, based on Confucian social and educational principles of hierarchical gender roles and status. However, postcolonial (1945 and after) governments in South Korea guaranteed the constitutional equality of men and women and thereby legally improved the status of women. Yet Korean society has continued to employ education, both implicitly and explicitly, as a means of maintaining the mold of Yi women. For modern women, education has continued to be a powerful instrument for developing and maintaining the self-image of modern Korean women.

The Christian impact on the education of modern Korean women in terms of shaping women's self-identity and self-development is substantial. Early Christianity, which arrived in Korea during the last decade of the Yi dynasty, brought about great improvements in the education of women and played an important role in opening up Korean society and culture to modern (i.e., western) influences, including the new religion itself.[1] But this was made possible largely by the early Christian church's accommodation to and legitimation of the Confucian role and status of women prevailing in the later Yi period. From this point of view, Christianity helped to perpetuate the traditional self-image of Korean women through its Christian doctrines. In other words, the Korean Christian churches have brought with them to America a blend of Confucian and Christian teachings on the place and role of women in home and society. The basic questions posed here in the discussion on religion in the lives of Korean women in America are: What is the educational situation of *ilse* Christian women in the United States? What are the main sources of learning for these women, and how do they affect the women's self-development? Focusing on these questions, the section of the *ilse* woman's contemporary education in the United States will report on the role of education in the adaptation of *ilse* Christian women to life in the United States.

Old Wisdom and New Knowledge

The Bible is the major textbook of Christian education. In recent years, feminists have been arguing about the significant impact of the Bible on women's self-development.[2] Feminists commonly argue that the Bible is a product of patriarchy and communicates a subordinate and devalued image of women. How do Korean immigrant Christian women, then, understand the Bible? What is its impact on them?

Among the women who were interviewed, the prevailing view is that the Bible is the Word of God, a book written by inspired men. Not one of the interviewees mentioned the Bible as a literary classic or a book of human wisdom. Seeing it as a holy book, they set the Bible apart from other books and submit to its authority. However, their interpretation of it and the implications they draw from it are diverse.

Most of the women, homemakers as well as working women, regardless of their religiosity, tend to believe in the literal truth of the Bible. Na In-Wha, the pious pastor's wife whose sole source of reading is the Bible,[3] said, "Jesus said that no human beings can either add or omit even one letter in or from the Bible" (Matt. 5:18). Like Na In-Wha, most women defend the infallibility of the Scripture by asserting their belief in God's infinity and human beings' finitude. Women worship the Bible as an absolute authority which requires their unconditional acceptance of and obedience to its commandments. Such an airtight belief system shuts off many women from experiencing confusion and contradiction between the written word and the reality of their situations. Consequently, these women do not see conflict between biblical and modern knowledge because they believe the Bible provides the rationale for their conduct. Even highly educated scientists, such as medical doctors, defend scriptural inerrancy and accept the notion of woman as the property of men.

Dr. Suh Jai-Mi explained that she very seldom reads the Bible because she has no time. Yet, she acknowledged the authority of the Bible and said:

> I believe the Bible as the Word of God; therefore, everything in the Bible is true. I even believe that God made women out of Adam's ribs [Gen. 2: 21–23]. It is very possible for Him, because for God, nothing is impossible. Human knowledge is so limited. We can never understand God's Wisdom. Practically speaking, I often experience God's miracles. For example, we doctors declare a death sentence to some patients because it is impossible to cure them. But in reality we often see those who had received a death sentence fully recover and live in an unbelievably healthy condition. It cannot be explained by modern medical knowledge.

Therefore, I do believe everything written in the Bible. There is no conflict between the Bible and modern science. The Bible is above modern science and God is omnipotent.[4]

In contrast, a number of the women expressed their uncertainty and skepticism regarding the factual validity of the Bible, though they believe it as the Word of God. Nonetheless, the women in this case blamed themselves for their shallow faith; they view their skepticism as an act of evil. For Kil Young-Sook, the wife of a physician and an elder of Fellowship Church, the Bible is also her major reading material:

> Frankly speaking, we [she and her husband] have lots of questions about the Bible. I mean, we can't believe lots of things in the Bible. Sometimes, my husband raises some questions; but, I tell him not to question. "Questioning the Bible is not virtuous" [성경을 의심하면 덕이못되요]. As far as the Bible is concerned, we have to read it without raising questions and accept everything unconditionally. If we cannot believe the Bible, I think, we are trapped by evil.[5]

As Mrs. Kil demonstrates, many women try to accept the Bible unconditionally and to repress their skepticism. Their unanimous answers to the question "Is there any conflict between the Bible and modern science?" are "I want to believe the Bible unconditionally," or "I want to accept the Bible as the Truth," or "I try not to question, because questioning the Bible is a sin." Many refused to give a direct answer to the question as to whether or not they see a conflict between Scripture and modern science. By speaking abstractly, these women tried to avoid potential conflict and self-confusion. Women's interpretations of and attitudes toward the Bible suggest some important issues: a literalist interpretation of Scripture inhibits human reasoning, that is to say, it shuts off the development of secular knowledge; second, it provides justification for women to hold on to old values and norms. Is its impact on women negative or positive?

These women admit that the biblical implications for women's roles and status are complex and have several possible interpretations. Some accept its teachings literally, while others question the applicability of some of the passages to their lives. Such passages include ones addressing women's submission to men based on the church's teachings (Eph. 5:22–24; 1 Cor. 14:34–35) of what is taught as Paul's writings. For example, Dr. Suh, who believes in the inerrancy of the Bible and the notion of women's biological inferiority to men, repudiates Paul's teachings as an archaic remnant of patriarchy. Like her, some women agree with the view that Paul's teachings were the product of his specific social context and cannot be applied uncritically to women today. The women holding this attitude are most likely to admit their relative flexibility in interpreting the Bible and affirm the change in women's roles and status in modern society.

It is not surprising, therefore, that many of these "biblically flexible" women expressed their support for the ordination of women. After preaching at Korean churches, I have often encountered young married women who lead their daughters by their hand to wherever I may be at the time and say to the young ones:

> See, Look at Kim *Moksa-nim.* Isn't she great? Study hard and grow up and become a minister like Kim *Moksa-nim.*[6]

It has been my experience that women of all ages, but older women in particular, become exhilarated and even declare gratitude to God for this expansion of women's roles and status within the United Methodist Church. Many times, after preaching or leading a worship service, I have been warmly and tightly embraced by older women who come forth from the pews with tears and exclamations of happiness at being with an ordained woman minister. The most moving and unforgetable incident, which overwhelmed me some years ago, vividly reflects some women's thrill at witnessing a change in women's public roles. An elderly woman came running up to me after a worship service and said while jumping up and down and hugging me:

> You are the first *yŏja Moksa-nim* (여자목사님: 女子牧師任: female pastor) I have ever seen in my life. You are great! You did what we have not been able to do. You fulfilled our *han!* Thanks to God who raised women out of a pit and now use them for His glory.[7]

Even though most Korean women in the United States think they accept the authority of the patriarchal biblical teachings, many are increasingly less likely to apply it to their lives without qualification. From my numerous encounters with Korean *ilse* women of all ages, a pattern seems to have emerged: young married women with young daughters and elderly women (who now are widowed and living with or apart from their children in the United States) support changes in the public roles of women that sometimes contradict or are not supported by a literal interpretation of the Bible. The young married women, those in their twenties and early thirties, are new to the role of wife and mother and are not yet entrenched in the duties of domestic life. Many of them also have had or continue to hold jobs outside the home. It is possible that these women are seeking role models, not only for their own young daughters but also for themselves, and for ways to live a Christian life without relying excessivly on Korean tradition. Also, the elderly have left behind their entrenchment in conventional living, since many are widows with middle-aged, independent children. For these women, life does not center around fulfilling wifely and motherly expectations; obedience to husbands and self-sacrifice to children are part of their past. It is time for them to enjoy the rewards of their past obedience and sacrifice, for an earthly compensation that has until now remained unfulfilled. More significantly, many of these elderly women have experienced and suspected the futility of their past role play. Therefore, for them, to see a female pastor is an occasion for vicarious self-affirmation and reward for their own sufferings.

In contrast to the young mothers and elderly widows, it is the established middle-aged women with extensive responsibilities to family and work who seem to accept literal interpretations of the Bible, particularly with regard to women's submission to men. Thus, they deny the legitimacy of changes in women's roles (within the church leadership) away from existing patriarchal ones. Kil Young-Sook, who insists on the unconditional acceptance of the Bible, strongly defended the maintenance of patriarchal system and said:

> I believe that Apostle Paul is right. Women should be silent, and men should be placed over women [in gender hierarchy]. Therefore, I do not believe in women's ordination and priesthood. Women should not be ministers. It is against the Scripture. Women should remain silent and serve the Church as *chŏndo puin*. They should help *namja Moksa-nim* (남자목사님: 男子牧師任: male pastor) and take care of the children's education in Sunday School.[8]

For such women, even ordination does not confer upon women the authority and right to serve the church in a ministerial capacity.

Although educational and professional training of female physicians and lawyers renders some women competent and legitimate in the eyes of these traditional women, female pastors, who also undergo extensive educational and professional training, are not bestowed with such credibility and legitimacy.

Kang Jin-Sook, whose major reading is the Bible, is a physician who strongly reacted against the idea of female ministers:

> Sister! I was actually so angry and even offended when a female minister was appointed to our church as an associate pastor in charge of the Youth Program. How dare a women be a minister? I don't trust women ministers. Above all, where in the Bible does it say that a woman can be a minister? The Apostle Paul said that women should remain silent in the church. The priesthood of women is against the Bible.[9]

Though she herself holds a leadership position in the health care profession, she defends patriarchal leadership within the Christian church. She sees no contradiction concerning women's roles, since the Bible supplies her with the rationales for dividing the world into two separate entities, the religious and the secular.

For such women, the Bible is used to preserve old norms and gender roles and to prevent the change in and promotion of contemporary women's roles and status. With respect to these women, some feminists' claims that the Bible has a negative impact on the self-image(s) of women is justified.

To summarize, this section presents the multiplicity and complexity of the biblical impact on the self-development of contemporary Korean immigrant ilse women in the United States. The more religious the women are, the more literal is their adoption of the Bible into their lives and the more they tend to preserve traditional images of women within the church. Hence, Scripture provides rationales for the "religious women" to accept and maintain traditional social conventions and so to perpetuate patriarchy within the church.

On the other hand, despite their traditional positions regarding women's roles in the church, the majority of the interviewed women demonstrated some tension between their interpretation of the Bible and their application of its teachings to daily life. Though they accept the Bible as the authority on Christian living, they apply it selectively and sometimes even in contradictory ways. The effect of the Bible, the ultimate progenitor of old religious norms, seems to cause confusion when women actually try to live according to those norms. In particular, professional women and less religious, American-educated women are likely to question the validity of following the "old wisdom," traditional biblical teachings, in contemporary American life.

Self-Sustainer

The Confucian society of the Yi dynasty mandated a monolithic social morality, *namjon yŏbi*, which precluded and excluded any other principles of male-female status and roles. Accordingly, women's selves were molded in the context of the patriarchal home and family largely through informal education. In this way, such education enabled their survival in that society. Christianity and the immigrant church in the United States, as the major social enclave of most contemporary Korean immigrant women, perform functions similar to that of *namjon yŏbi* (for Yi women) in shaping women's consciousness and behavior in America.

However, unlike the women in the Yi dynasty, most *ilse* women have received modern secular education, and a large percentage of them have earned bachelor's degrees.[10] But only a very small minority of women seek or participate in continuing formal education (i.e., beyond the undergraduate or vocational level) after immigration. For most of them, the only form of additional education they receive is Bible-centered.

Almost all the interviewees regularly attend a Bible class, offered by their respective churches at least once a week, in addition to Sunday worship and Wednesday evening service. The majority also attends a "Sunday Bible Study" before the main worship service. There are monthly women's prayer meetings and *sokhoe* (속회),[11] where the emphasis is on the study of the Bible. The church, as an institutionalized social agent, educates its women informally yet systematically, because women are the predominating participants. Through the study of Scripture, women learn and cultivate their intellectual ability, but only insofar as it is specifically geared to the Bible.

That Bible class teachers are mainly men, usually church elders or visiting pastors, clearly reflects the patriarchal tradition of the Korean church and culture in which women learn from men. Kim Ai-Kyung, the wife of a physician and an elder of Fellowship Church, describes the patriarchal traditions in her church education:

I was born in a devout Christian family, but my husband came from a Buddhist family. He has been going to the church for only ten years. Until recently, he didn't read the Bible. He was very skeptical about it. I used to tell him about the Bible and he listened. But now, our positions are reversed. I am a born-Christian and have read the Bible throughout my life. But he knows the Bible much more than I do and teaches me now. How did it happen? Well, our pastor asked him to teach the Adult Bible Class. Therefore, he studied. Since that time, he leads the class and teaches the Bible in our church.[12]

As she explains, teaching the Bible is still a man's job, and women's consciousness in the church is shaped by men's teachings, as the women of the Yi period had been taught and shaped by what men deemed to be correct behavior. Through male instructors, churches systematically educate Korean women in America in accordance with patriarchal Korean Christian tradition.

However, unlike the Yi dynasty, the church, as the major social authority, is not coercive in its religious education. Most women become their own teachers and cultivate themselves through their own daily readings of the Bible at home and in the workplace. Also, books related to the Bible and the Christian faith, such as *The Daily Bible Study* and testimonials, serve as complementary sources of women's self-education.

Given this trend, this important question arises: Why do these immigrant women read the Bible and the religious books so fervently? The answer emanating from these interviews is inseparable from the urgency of adjusting to life in the United States. In other words, learning the Bible is an existential matter, one which determines whether or not they survive in the new context. This is to say that *ilse* women, who for the most part live in a social context of conflicting social values and lifestyles, seem to struggle against the confusion, tensions, and sense of powerlessness that can arise in their immigrant life situation. Many women have no hope of ever gaining a command of English and learning about American values and ideas. They fear losing the ideas and values of their old country. Given this situation, in which they risk becoming ignorant of both the American and Korean worlds—and hence, anonymous and powerless—they cling to Christian education, focused on the Bible, to clarify any possible confusion and to prevent moral conflict and loss of identity in their immigrant lives. The following account describes this social function of the Bible among immigrant Korean women.

Min He-Yun came from a very prestigious family of the highest social class in post-1945 Korean society. She studied religion at a Methodist university in the United States and also holds a master's degree. In every aspect, she belonged and still belongs to the upper class in both American and Korean terms. She is highly intelligent and rational in her thinking. She used to work as a professional, but she became a homemaker by choice and, at the same time, a pious and fundamentalistic believer. The Bible supplies her with the knowledge to clarify all situations in her life:

> I live on the Bible. My days start and end with prayer and with reading the Bible. If I could do nothing but read the Bible all day long, I would be very happy. As you know, I studied religion in my undergraduate years. I read Tillich and Bultmann, and the books of many other theologians. I was quite influenced by them and became very liberal in thought. I used to criticize the Bible and the literal interpretations of it because they didn't make any sense at all, especially for us living in the era of highly developed modern technology of the twentieth century. But, I have realized that I was wrong. How? Well, it is a long story. Briefly speaking, after I joined Holiness Church, my religious views became entirely changed. Moreover, my personal experiences in my then job critically affected my religious views. I worked as the Director of the Dietary Department of [Mt. Sinai] Hospital in Boston for more than ten years. Oh, I enjoyed that job so much. My job was not limited to just programming and administrating. I used to teach and lead seminars. I went here and there and met lots of people. I especially loved to talk with elderly people in the nursing homes. And I enjoyed dealing with blue-collar workers. You know, they were so cute; they were simple and listened to me. I loved to work with them. Those people liked me and respected me. But after we moved to New Jersey when my husband was transferred (in his company), I took a job at [Littlebrook] Hospital for a while. Oh, I hated that job so much. You know, I was so disappointed by people and institutionalized American bureaucracy. What do I mean by that? Well, people had no dignity and decency. Employees, as well as patients and their families, abused social security benefits. Ooooo—they made me angry and upset. Above all, I didn't have freedom at all in the new job as I had had in the previous one. I had to pursue my work routinely like a machine. I couldn't teach people or lead seminars. Especially, I

couldn't influence the blue-collar workers by talking with them and teaching them. There was no love and respect. It was boring and terrible to work there; therefore, I resigned . . .

But the problem was after the resignation. How could I stay at home? What could I do all day long at home? As you know, I am very outgoing and energetic. Can you imagine me staying home doing nothing? I was very depressed for a while. My son and daughter were studying and active at school, and my husband was also busy with at the office. They all seemed to be progressing and developing, but I felt that only I in the family was regressing. Therefore, I thought very seriously about going back to school, I mean seminary, to study theology and to prepare my second career—but I hesitated. At that time, I had just joined Holiness Church and had begun to experience the authentic Christian faith. I was very much afraid that modern and liberal religious studies would tear my faith away. Tillich and Bultmann, or any other liberal theologians, actually make us confused and destroy the pure Christian faith. Therefore, I decided not to study at a seminary and began earnestly to read the Bible. I wanted to educate and improve my life, as my husband and two children were doing, through Bible study. Otherwise, I would go insane because of depression and the feeling that I'm regressing . . .

Oh, I was so right; I am so happy with my decision not to go to seminary. The Bible just comforted me. It also helped me think about myself and gave me strength and endurance to become a good Christian woman. It is too, too sweet to understand biblical wisdom. Now, I have a whole day to pray and read the Bible. All day, I pray for my husband and children. I am the most rich and progressive woman in my family because my family depends on my prayers and spiritual power. Without the Bible, I cannot accept and fulfill my life.[13]

As indicated by her story, Min He-Yun chose the Bible as the source of knowledge that would help her accept and justify her situation. In a sense, she is a self-supporter: she survives and flourishes in her specific situation. As a woman and an ethnic and racial minority person, she experienced the helplessness of trying to exercise professional power in the White American bureaucratic structure. Moreover, her class consciousness and high educational level caused her to struggle in a context of American egalitarianism. She wanted to teach and lead, but her ambition to become a somebody, a leader, was not realized. She feared losing her self-esteem and pride, in terms of social class, by working as an ordinary person.

Yet plain homemaking was not a viable alternative for her. As an energetic and ambitious woman, she needed to channel her energy elsewhere; she needed a public sphere of recognition and empowerment.

In this frustrating situation, Mrs. Min consciously rejected modern secular knowledge (reasoning) and pulled herself away from her personal reality as well as from her host (American) society. From an observer's point of view, she retreated into her own cave, the home and church, but from her point of view, she asserted herself in the religious world and at home. She relied on the Bible to justify and support her new situation. In her circumstance, the Bible, that is, Christian education, served as the means of legitimating her exit from the secular world of her profession, as well as from the greater American society, rather than challenging her to innovate her situation in that secular reality. While turning away from her unsatisfactory life situation, she at the same time adopted a way to accept it. For many *ilse* women, simultaneous escape from and acceptance of the given reality through Korean Christian education is a mode of adapting to life in America.

Peter Berger asserts that human beings, unlike animals, use legitimating structures in order to survive, either in the process of mechanical acceptance or reconstruction of the environment in a given situation.[14] Religion, particularly Christianity in the Western world, has served as a major legitimating structure. Many women, like Min He-Yun, use Christian education based on the Bible in order to legitimate their present situation, and act very much in accordance with Berger's theory.

However, for many immigrant women, like Min He-Yun, legitimation of a given situation means escape from reality, rather than innovation, and the escape is a means of acceptance of and adjustment to the given situation. Such women use their given social reality against which to define themselves, so that reality is essential for their "self against culture" personal stance. I call these Christian immigrant *ilse* women's mode of accepting and adjusting to reality through escape "elusive adaptation." Christian education justifies and sustains the "elusive adaptation" of these women to life in the United States.

The majority of the interviewees, particularly housewives and those who are religiously pious, intentionally try to block themselves from learning about and becoming involved in the host

American society. For such women, Christian educational materials, Korean fiction, Korean newspapers, and Korean television programs and videotapes serve as the secondary sources of their education. All educational materials are Korean-made, that is to say, they reflect Korean culture and values. By living almost exclusively in Korean enclaves, most immigrant women seem to isolate themselves from the surrounding host society.

Only a few women read English-language newspapers or magazines and watch American television programs. This can be understood in view of the problem that Korean women have with the English language, for the majority admitted their difficulty with the language and the consequent communication problems with their American-educated children. However, even the professional women who are American educated and work in the mainstream of American society and have fluent command of English show this tendency toward "elusive adaptation." They also tend to legitimate their life situations with the Bible. Grace Hurh, a pious Christian and one of the most Americanized Korean immigrants, reveals an elusive adaptation to life in America. She attained her bachelor's and master's degrees in the United States and has been in this country for more than forty years. Further, she has been working as a professional educator in American educational institutions throughout her life. She said in her interview:

I used to subscribe to *The New York Times, The Wall Street Journal*, and various American magazines. But, I discontinued all of them. I still read some written materials in English, but only in relation to my job. I also do not watch T.V. any more. Nothing interests me and helps me. But, reading the Bible is the best education and solace. It clarifies my vision. It is so good to read the Bible. It is also so comforting. I am fifty-nine years old. I may retire in a few years. How much more can I accomplish in my profession as an Asian woman? Can I become the president of this institution? Of course not. I came up to the top level as a Director of Education in this institution, even though I am well qualified to be the president. So, why do I need to bother to absorb more knowledge and information in order to promote myself? . . .

You know, I received my Master's Degree in the 1950s. At that time, there were very few Korean women who had advanced degrees, like a Ph.D. or master's, especially American degrees. If I had returned to Korea after my graduation, I might have been "somebody" now. I actually planned to go back, but my mother told me not to come back because I was in my late twenties and past the prime time of marriage and therefore would have a hard time finding a husband. Things may be different for women now, but at that time, who would have take an "Old Miss" with a degree from America? Anyway, until I retire, I'll just remain in this job . . .

As I get older, the Korean community is more meaningful to me. I work as a director of the church school in my church. They need me, and I enjoy working for them. Now, all I want is to rest in Heaven some day.[15]

Grace Hurh shares her depression and helplessness as a minority woman in the host society. It is obvious that she finds it difficult to assimilate with America on her terms; therefore, she has given up on "making it" in American life. In contrast, the Korean immigrant church provides her with meaning and recognition and so becomes an existential support in her life. It was apparent from her interview that through formal and informal self-education based on the Scripture, she has altered her consciousness and attitudes toward the church and thereby justifies her withdrawal from the host society. In this sense, the church provides her with an existential base. Grace Hurh's example indicates that elusive adaptation can be found even among American-educated professional women. She intentionally evades assimilation to American society and, at the same time, comes to terms with her social reality. In this process of self-sustainment, the Bible and the church are primary sources of adaptation to life in America as an immigrant woman.

Like Grace Hurh and Min He-Yun, many women—businesswomen and professionals as well as housewives—tend to justify their adhesive adjustment to the chuch and exibit elusive adaptation to American society, voluntarily alienating themselves from the host country. In other words, the more women are involved in learning the Bible, the more tightly they are attached to the church. The more women adhere to the church, the more they tend to escape from American society. From this point of view, Christian education indirectly encourages women to lead a sectarian lifestyle, being away from the major world and living in a state of "mini-Korea" in the United States. Although it sustains the lives of immigrant women, the immigrant church hinders their inculturation into American society. Consequently, Korean traditions and culture dominate such women's lives, and the women maintain traditional roles and status and preserve their traditional self-image.

However, Christian education does not have much effect on some women, especially working women. Oh Young-Ran, a single, successful business woman, said regarding her relationship to Christian education:

> Except Sunday and Wednesday services and the Sunday Bible Class, I hardly read the Bible. I try to believe the Bible, but it does not convince me. I prefer to read the Talmud. It is much more pertinent to my life and is very helpful for understanding problems in life and solving my own. But, when I am in "real" trouble, I try to read the Bible.[16]

For Ms. Oh, the Bible is more like a "magic book" or a "good luck charm" than an actual guide to living. Christian education does not seem to provide her with the necessary rationales for her particular lifestyle.

Like Oh Young-Ran, Helen Choi, a professional educator, also rarely reads the Bible. Her reading materials, most of which are in English, are mainly related to her job. Lee Bong-Hee, another professional, though she insistently emphasizes that she is a born-again Christian, rarely reads the Bible. She explains that her reading materials cover a broad spectrum, encompassing professional literature as well as readings on social justice, anthropology, psychology (such as the works of Eric Fromm), and religion. These three women also reveal a keen interest in current news affairs. They say that they try not to miss listening to the news.

One very interesting finding is that the women who read secular books tend to be working women. They are all Christians, but the Bible is not the focus of their education. Their educational materials are directly related to their jobs or to secular life in general, and they are sensitive to the world outside the Korean immigrant church. Two women out of the three are also single and economically self-supporting. This fact may be a self-explanatory phenomenon, in that working women, particularly self-supporters, are more sensitive to and have a favorable attitude toward the host society because their subsistence, that is, existence, directly relies on it. For these women, Christian education is both essential to their existence and also confusing. They do not find a proper place for the Bible in their lives. Christian education, therefore, provides them with neither a traditional self image nor a newly integrated Korean-American one. Attaining secular knowledge, they become their own teachers and self-sustainers in America.

Appendix Self

Except for two college drop-outs, all the interviewees completed undergraduate studies, and some went further to receive master's degrees. However, for most of the women, any type of formal/institutional education ceased after marriage. In the immigrant Korean church environment, women's aspiration for higher education seems to be discouraged and such schooling very difficult to achieve. This is in stark contrast to the period of early Christianity in Korea during the late nineteenth century, when women's educational institutions were established and the development of women's intellectual capacity encouraged and improved.

Yoon He-Rim who acquired a Master of Divinity degree and pursued studies in a doctoral program at Drew Graduate School (while I was writing my doctoral dissertation) might be viewed as a model of an *ilse* woman struggling to develop her academic potential and improve her self-image as a Christian woman. Her story conveys the difficulty of doing both. Mrs. Yoon married a medical doctor who came from a devout Christian family. Her father-in-law had studied medicine in the United States and had spent most of his time in Korea as a medical missionary. Therefore, her husband was born in Korea, and his mind-set was formed by Korean Christian values and culture. She was an outgoing mother of three grown-up children and was financially well off. She was relatively free from undertaking household chores and child rearing. From a distance, she appeared to have no hindrance to pursuing her studies. However, she explained her difficulties in studying as a Christian woman:

> I really don't have much time to study. It is awfully hard and frustrating to attend class without completing reading assignments. If you don't read, you can't participate in the seminar, and actually, you don't know what's going on. Why don't I have time to study since I don't work and also have a housemaid to take care of my housework? Many people do not understand my problem. You know, my husband doesn't like my studying. Like most Korean men, especially Christian men, he is a man of patriarchy. He believes that women should stay home and take care

of housekeeping. But, I am not a domestic person. My interests are not only in housework. When I was in college, I was very active in women's Christian organizations and was the president of such organizations. I am also still active in these groups and lead a statewide organization. I should have been born a man because my nature is very masculine. I cannot stay home and just do homemaking. Anyway, it took twenty years to persuade my husband and to get his permission to study. Therefore, I cannot neglect my duties as a good Christian woman and housewife . . .

Every morning, I get up early to prepare my husband's breakfast and help him dress. When he is around, I never open my books. None of my family members ever sees me studying. When no one is at home, it is my time to study. But, most of the time, I have some errands to do. I have to take my parents or parents-in-law shopping or to the doctor's office. I have to go to organizational meetings. I also accompany my husband to most of his conferences or social meetings. Furthermore, I have to entertain many guests and attend social gatherings for my husband's social and professional life. I also entertain my colleagues in the different civic and Christian organizations I'm involved in. I try to be a perfect Christian housewife. Therefore, sometimes I don't sleep because I have to read and write papers at night while every one else sleeps. Everybody thinks that I have a luxurious life. In some ways, yes. But, it is too tough to be a student and a good housewife. If I neglect my wifely and motherly duties, my husband won't let me study. Also, it would give a bad image of a Christian woman. Doing all these things—I often wish I were a superwoman. And also, I always feel guilty at home and at the church because I study . . .

Then, why do I study? I came from a conservative Presbyterian tradition. The development of women's leadership was not only discouraged but also ignored. As you know, women's position in the church is terrible. We are "nobodies." Therefore, I wanted to study as much as male ministers and prepare myself as a church leader so that I may help improve women's status, so that men cannot ignore my leadership. You know, people in the church, especially men and women in our generation, don't like ambitious women who cultivate their potentials. I mean, they really reject those women who pursue higher academic degrees. Therefore, when I go to the church, I never stand or walk straight. Constantly, I bend my back forward and bow to every one, so that I may not offend or threaten the people. Gee, it is hard. When I come home from church on Sunday, I feel exhausted, and my whole body aches because I was forced to bend my back all day long and because my nervous system is too sensitive to my behavior and to the attitude of others toward me. You know, by the time my body is recovered from that ache, it is already Sunday again. Then, I force to squeeze myself again. Oh, I always suffer this body pain. [17]

Interestingly, I never saw her squeezing herself and bending down on the campus. There she was straight and assertive. What Yoon He-Rim emphasizes is the difficulty of maintaining her "double-self." She seems to be caught between the church, which represents Korean culture and her "social self," and her desire to develop her "subjective self" through knowledge and innovation of her role and status. Mrs. Yoon poignantly demonstrates the predicament of *ilse* women trying to survive in the Korean church while developing a self apart from the church.

Korean Christianity, then, is detrimental to those women who want to develop their own potential as persons and to improve their roles and status through formal education. Consequently, those women who view themselves as "good Christians" must develop double selves in order to fit into two social environments, the church and the world outside the church.

The discouraging of female education by immigrant Korean Christianity not only limits *ilse* women but seems to extend its force to the next generation as well. Sin Mal-Hee was an *iljŏm ose* woman in her early thirties and a wife of a young *ilse* pastor. She completed her high school and college education in the United States and worked as a licensed medical technologist in New York City hospitals until she married. She was very assertive, energetic, and outgoing. She was also a progressive thinker. Though she was a licensed medical technologist, she never used her professional skills after marriage. Therefore, she began to take night courses in nursing at a local college to prepare for a new career. However, her determination to cultivate her potential and to pursue a career other than that of traditional homemaking triggered a family crisis: her devout Christian pastor-husband has adamantly opposed her attempt at changing her role as a Korean woman through education. After many days and nights of bitter argument with her husband, she became outraged and cried:

I'd rather die than live like this. Two months ago, I had my fifth baby in my six year marriage. I am exhausted staying home with

these five small children and my mother-in-law. Taking care of
the children and my mother-in-law suffocates me. I want fresh
air for myself. All day long I just wrestle with them. I want to get
out of the house. Why do I have to have all these hardships by
myself? He wanted children, especially sons, and turned me into
a birth-giving machine, but he does not even change the diapers.
I am still too young and energetic to stay at home and consume
all my time and energy only on housekeeping . . .

If anything happens to my husband, I alone have to raise all
these children. I need a career in order to educate and support
them. I have not used the knowledge and skill of medical technology since my marriage, so I forgot everything. I also don't like
that job. I am interested in nursing. Therefore, I enrolled in a
nursing course last semester. You know my father—he's always
financially and morally supportive of his children. He encourages me to study. He said that in order to be a good pastor's wife,
I have to be better than my husband. If I want, he said, he will
financially support me even to do a Ph.D. . . .

Anyway, I was so happy to take two night courses for nursing last semester while my stomach was like a mountain because
I was pregnant with my fifth baby. Two nights a week, I went to
school. Phew—I felt like I was breathing and living in fresh air.
Just getting out of the house made me feel so vital. I studied so
hard. Sometimes I stayed late in the lab and did my experiments.
Oh, I enjoyed it so much . . .

But, I never neglected my duties at home as a wife, mother,
daughter-in-law, and pastor's wife. I have never opened my books
in front of my family, especially, my husband. After I bathed the
children and put them to bed, I studied twice a week for about
two hours only and slept only a few hours. I was so tired, but I
was so happy to go back to school and to learn. After I had my
fifth baby two months ago, I again enrolled in one course and
was looking forward to going back to school. But, yesterday, my
husband commanded me to cancel the enrollment today. He told
me that it is so selfish of me to study. Am I selfish? No, I am not.
I want to get my life back. I want to study and make my life
progressive. Above all, even just for a moment, I want to get out
of this house and to be free from all these burdens. I want to
have my own time even for a short time and develop myself.
What should I do now? Should I stop going to school? I feel like
I am going to be crazy. Why did my husband want me to stop
studying? . . .

He said I would be a bad example for the other women in
the church. A pastor's wife should be a role model, staying home

and helping her husband and rearing the children and just taking care of housework. He said that my studying is an act of evil and ruins his church and other women. Am I trapped by evil? Am I ruining his church? I am very concerned about his ministry and our church. I do everything as a pastor's wife for our church. I provide food for the congregation every Sunday. I follow him to *sokhoe,* Bible Study classes, prayer meetings, and visitations. I have put forth all my effort to help him and our church. Why can't I have just one night for my studies? Once he had approved of my studying, but now, he's canceled it. What's going on? My husband said, "If you really want to study, learn how to use a computer so that you can work for the church as an unpaid secretary." But, I have no interest in secretarial work. I am no good in that kind of thing. I want to be a nurse and help people who are ill. Once, he granted me permission to study and now forces me to stop. Again, he permits me to study the computer in order to make me his secretary. What is he doing? I am totally confused and angry. I feel like I'm going to be insane.[18]

Sin Mal-Hee has been wrestling with her problems and crying out in order to survive in two unavoidable settings, the Korean church, which represses women's self-cultivation through other than traditional means, and the secular world of American education, which encourages women's professional and personal development. As her anguished voice conveys, Korean Christian culture in America seems to perpetuate the image of woman as an appendix to men.[19] Even younger Korean women, who have grown up in the United States, struggle between self-cultivation and survival in their immigrant Christian context. Unlike the women discussed above, those for whom patriarchal Christianity has functioned to suppress their desire for self-cultivation through higher education, for a few, Christianity has worked as a catalyst, motivating and igniting their educational aspirations and fostering a new self-image. Nevertheless, these women are entrapped in the contradiction between the Gospel message and their social reality. Lee Bong-Hee, a born-again Christian and professional woman in the educational field, reflected upon her entrapment and said:

I really wanted to see you before this interview to discuss my problem. I have seriously thought about preparing for a new career as a minister. As you know, there is nothing to hinder my studies. My two daughters are in graduate school, and I have no husband to take care of. I studied religion at [M] Graduate School, but I never completed the program; so I always wanted to study theology again. I also heard that seminaries provide some scholarships for students, especially women. I really want to go to seminary and prepare for my old age in ministry. I have been in the present profession for more than twenty years. I am assistant director of my department. I don't think the institution will appoint me as director. I will most likely remain a permanent assistant in this White American institution. I have been there too long and I don't want to end my life as an assistant. I want to become a minister and serve the Korean church and our people. That is my only hope, but I hesitate to apply to seminary now . . .

Originally, I came from a very conservative Christian tradition. I have been taught that women should not be at the altar. I am still skeptical about the ordination of women. Rationally, I didn't believe that teaching, but my faith says that I should accept the teaching. I am very confused now. Above all, I believe that the Gospel message is "liberation." Jesus' teaching is actually one of "liberating" women from old oppressive traditions. However, the Gospel message and the situation of the present church are too contradictory, and I've heard that the United Methodist Church produces a considerable number of Korean clergywomen. Of course, you are one of them. But, where are they? What are they doing? I don't see any of them serving Korean churches. Can I serve the church after studying? Above all, what do you think about the ordination of women? I am fifty-four years old now. If I cannot serve the church as a minister, why should I spend my money and time for nothing? I don't want to waste money, time, and energy for an uncertain future at this age. I also heard that it is very tough even for male ministers to get churches. How, then, can I as a woman compete with them? I am really troubled in making a decision to study and change my career. I want to hear your testimony.[20]

Lee Bong-Hee seems to be caught between what she believes to be the Gospel's message of liberation and the oppressive social situation of the church. Further, as an Asian woman, she faces racism in the White American society, represented by her workplace, which in principle supports and encourages equal rights of women, including education, while preventing upward mobility for racial minorities. As Mead asserts, an individual, as a social member, cannot transcend his or her social context, so these women, particularly career-minded women, struggle between two social forces— the Korean immigrant church and the host American society. In principle, Christianity encourages women's education and the development of a new self, while the reality of the church hinders it. At the same time, Korean women, as minorities, do not have much hope of attaining their potential in White American society. Consequently, women living within these social conflicts seem to be frustrated, confused, and regressive, rather than progressive and in pursuit of new "self formation."

Helen Choi, a professional educator, explained her rather helpless and regressive situation:

> Throughout my life, I have worked in American educational institutions. I have worked as an education program coordinator at this college [where she currently is employed] for about ten years. I once had hope of pursuing a doctoral degree and advancing myself as a career person. So, I began my doctoral studies at Seton Hall College. I received a full scholarship because the program was sponsored by the U.S. government in support of bilingual programs. I completed all the course work and the comprehensive exams, but I gave up pursuing the degree. I am an ABD [all but dissertation]. You know, there is not much chance for us minority women. Of course, our language, appearance, and culture are the obstacles. But, the major problem is still White racism. Can I become a president of this college? My ceiling is too low, no matter what degree I attain. What do I do with the doctoral degree? Maybe I am justifying my laziness. But, as a minority Asian woman, I don't see much hope in this society. I rather want to work for the Korean community when the time comes. Korean immigrants have so many serious problems. With my experience, I want to help them. Especially, I want to work to improve Korean immigrants' consciousness about current problems, like generation and communication gap, as well as cultural differences. We may not have equal rights and privileges as Whites do, but our children have to live as equals of White Americans and together build a better American society. With that hope, I want to work for our community. Then, I don't need a Ph.D.[21]

As Helen Choi describes her professional limits and renouncement of career ambitions, it is apparent to her that the host American society, while nurturing the hopes and ambitions of higher education among Korean women (and women in general), in fact denies them the rewards of achievement: minority women are not promoted to positions of policy making and administration. The absence of desired reward for advanced studies has an inhibiting effect on some women's motivation to pursue higher education. Therefore, *ilse* women are doubly bound—by Korean patriarchy, sexism in general, and White racism.

In short, Korean immigrant *ilse* women's educational prospects appear gloomy at present. The Korean church, the major social and religious institution, seems to hinder women's education (outside the church). However, one interviewee, Lee Bong-Hee, interprets the Gospel message as a liberating force. The rest of women interviewed receive dual messages from the larger American society, the host social authority. In principle, American academia attracts and encourages minority women's self-cultivation and improvement of self through education, but the reality of racism discourages those same women. Consequently, the women seem to retreat from the hope and prospect of continuing their education.

In Mead's terms, what kind of self-image do Korean immigrant women develop in the United States? It is very difficult to draw a clear picture of *ilse* women's self-image. They struggle in order to adjust to and survive in their complicated social situations. However, it seems quite clear that women are no longer merely receptive to their social situations, that is, they are not mere mechanical "social selves." Although few in number and varied in approach, *ilse* women are questioning and challenging their religious and cultural traditions and White American racism. They are starting to resist the necessity of becoming "appendix selves" to patriarchy and to White racism. Furthermore, they are preparing themselves to move toward integration into American society. They are becoming "subjective human beings," improving their lot in their own way. These women are in the midst of creating a new self-image, even though their social conditions may not provide the most promising educational context.

WOMEN AND WORK

Second-Class Persons

All of the businesswomen interviewed for this research are self-employed: they are either shop owners or independent saleswomen working on commission. Professionals and semiprofessionals are predominantly engaged in medical and educational work, as physicians, nurses, and academic administrators, in American institutions. Relatively speaking, these women are in a socially privileged class, and their social status is seemingly quite high. The nature of their jobs and their status, as owners and professionals, requires a considerable degree of autonomy if they are to perform their work effectively. According to Epstein's theory,[22] the workplace produces an individual's specific and unique self, based on his or her role and status on the job. Have the gender roles and social status of Korean working women actually been elevated by their participation in work outside the home? Pursuing this question, I will explore the social status of *ilse* women with respect to financial management as a means of implementing woman's autonomy. This will then be evaluated in relation to the degree of religiosity of the women and to the particular situation of each woman in the American work environment.

As has been true in traditional Korean society, *ilse* women in the United States, in general, also serve as financial managers in their households. Most housewives manage entirely those finances related to housekeeping, and they call their financial responsibilities "small management," referring to relatively small amounts of money spent on such items as groceries, clothes, and daily expenses for children and the family. But such major items as the mortgage or car payments, which involve relatively large amounts of money, are considered the husband's prerogative, and women name the husband's domestic financial management responsibilities "big management." The division of financial management into big and small and women's involvement in "small matters" are reflections of gender hierarchy.

People of lower social status, in general, have little or no power to engage in decision or policy making. The Civil Rights struggle in America[23] and the feminist movement vividly demonstrate efforts by the powerless to establish their own power and autonomy. From this point of view, Korean immigrant women, who possess a low status in the gender hierarchy, may have little or no power in matters of financial decision making. Moreover, past research suggests that women's financial contribution is directly related to decision making and to status,[24] that is, the more women contribute financially, the stronger are their voices in decision making and the higher their status.

However, this study shows that Western understandings of economically determined power and powerlessness are not necessarily applicable to Korean immigrant women. *Ilse* housewives who do not financially contribute to the family income and are involved in "small management" demonstrate enormous power in decision making. Moreover, women's status in the home does not necessarily correlate with their income-earning capacity. Min He-Yun, an American-educated *ilse* woman and zealous Christian housewife, is an example:

I take care of everything belonging to the house, grocery bills, shopping for clothes, house repairs, and even renovation of the house. A few months ago, our kitchen was totally expanded and upgraded. You would be shocked to know how much money and work were involved. I oversaw all of it myself—from the selection of the construction company to the closing of the contract, determining the budget, and the finishing details. I do all the small details, but my husband does only the big things: mortgage, insurance, and investments, along with his business transactions. I also don't have my own savings account. Our house is in both names, my husband's and mine, but our major financial investment is my husband's share in his business. I do not know anything about his business, but he told me that whatever he owns is mine, and it is very big. I don't care about money. Even though I have no money of my own, I can do anything, if I need to do it. My husband listens to me . . .

As you know, our church grew so fast, and the old American church which we rented for our [Korean church] services was too small. Therefore, our church had a special fund-raising project in order to buy a big church. At that time, I expanded my house and spent a lot of money and felt so guilty. I justified the renovation of my house by referring to King Solomon in the Bible. You know, Solomon built a luxurious palace before he erected God's temple, and God still blessed him. However, later, Solomon built a Great Temple for God, and he was more blessed. So, I thought that my house remodelling could be justified. But, it always bothered me that I lived in a big house and God lived in such a small church. I really wanted to contribute a great amount of money for either buying or building a big church, as Solomon did, so I persuaded my husband that we should donate a bulk of our money to our church building fund. I told him that we have been so blessed and that I was afraid of God's punishment if we didn't pay Him back. Therefore, he pledged a large sum of money—enough for buying a big luxurious house in a New Jersey suburb [I later found out that Mrs. Min had sold one of her homes in order to contribute to the fund.] . . .

My husband was appointed chairman of the building project, and the fund-raising went very well. Especially, our church women's financial and moral contribution was unbelievably great. I know that many women persuaded their husbands to donate large amounts of money. You know, men listen to their women. Men seem to work hard, but behind them, there are always women who actually do the work. Without women, I think, men cannot do anything, and also, the church would be in great trouble. Anyhow, our church recently bought this beautiful church building for $2.5 million, and we are very thankful to God.[25]

As if to disapprove western views that powerlessness in decision making stems from economic powerlessness, Min He-Yun, as a housewife who makes no financial contribution to her household at all, demonstrates her implicit yet significant power in decision making. Like her, *ilse* housewives play an enormous role in the decision making that applies directly to the family and the church. As women in the Yi dynasty put forth their men as symbolic facades and exercised power behind them, so immigrant women also accept and adjust to the gender hierarchy of their families and churches. That is, they accept their second-class status, yet they exercise great power in the sphere assigned to them.

This study finds that religious women, housewives as well as professionals, demonstrate a tendency toward "dual adjustment." That is, they demonstrate competence and relative independence in some matters (usually outside the church) but accept and maintain their second-class status within the church. In this way, they maintain patriarchy. Dual adjustment is more vivid in the lives of working women, whose sense of self and expertise in the workplace do not accord with those at home and in the church. In fact, women intentionally retain their lower status by reducing their incomes or by transferring their financial power to their husbands.

Sa Mi-Ja was a registered nurse but left that profession two years ago in order to start her own business, a dry cleaning shop in a small town in western New Jersey. Her purpose for starting the business was financial. The income of her husband, who holds a Ph.D. and works as an engineer in an American institution, does not suffice to meet the educational costs of their two daughters (one is already in college, and the other is in high school). During her interview, she spoke about her business and matters of financial management:

> Business is very good. I learned a lot about business through this shop. I think I have a pretty good sense of business. But, my husband actually runs this store behind me. I supply only the physical labor and presence because he cannot work here during the day because of his job. Every day he stops at the shop on the way home from his work and takes the cash box. If he cannot come, I take the cash box to him. I don't even open it. I don't know how much we make through this business. He takes care of everything and I am here only for physical labor.[26]

Though Sa Mi-Ja runs the store, she does not express a sense of independence or autonomy. She still remains an appendix self to her husband. Again, western theories which set forth a correlation between women's financial contribution and their status is not applicable to Mrs. Sa's case. Like Sa Mi-Ja, Dr. Whang (Ha Yul-Nyu) subordinates her financial power to that of her husband. Dr. Whang is a pediatrician and runs her clinic in the basement of her house, while her husband runs a farm in rural New Jersey. Still, her husband takes care of her business and household financial matters, except for matters of small management. She said:

> My medical vocation is my calling. Through this job, I serve God. I do not know anything about the financial situation of my clinic and the house. My husband takes care of all big things like our income, and I do only small things. I don't even know how much money I make.[27]

Justifying her vocation and renunciation of her power in economic management with her religious faith, Dr. Whang seemed in the interview to be trying to claim a lower status for herself and to elevate her husband's. Moreover, Chang Ok-Hee, who believes in real female superiority based on her religious faith and practical experience, while at the same time justifying male social supremacy through the Bible, spoke of her struggle to reduce her income as a nurse in order to boost and elevate her husband's male ego and social image and status.

> To tell you the truth, I make much more money than this man [pointing to her husband, who was sitting next to her during the

interview—she had told him to come along]; therefore, I try hard to avoid any overtime in order to reduce my income. Sometimes, I am very sorry to my colleagues because I always avoid overtime work. You know, hospital work needs nurses all the time. There are lots of overtime opportunities. Often, overtime is mandatory because we are short-handed. My basic salary exceeds his. If I do overtime, my income will be too much—compared to his—and so, when overtime work falls on me, I just try so hard to find other nurses to cover my overtime assignments. You know, it is awfully hard to avoid the needs of the hospital, but by reducing my income, I think, my husband can keep his ego and male superiority. Gee, it is hard to make myself lower than my husband all the time. But, I still believe that women are much superior.[28]

Like Chang Ok-Hee, *ilse* Christian working women seem to expend much thought and energy on maintaining their traditional lower status and raising that of their husbands. Self-subordination, in this sense, is rational and calculated.

Unlike these women, whose work can be done by men and women alike, businesswomen whose job is to sell "women's things" (and mainly cater to other women), such as boutique or jewelry shop owners, absolutely separate their work from their husband's status. They express their full competence and power in handling their business, including financial matters, and insist that their husbands do not get involved in "women's [trivial] business." Many such women say, "Oh, my husband does not know anything about my business. I do very well in my business." The women are quick to add, "Oh, but my husband makes much more money than I do." During the interviews, such women make concerted efforts to convince me that their husbands' earning power is superior to their own and that they, as wives, are merely supplementing their husbands' incomes. In this way, these businesswomen protect their husbands's egos and preserve the patriarchal notion (and practice) that women should earn less than men.

The tendency toward and degree of these women's protection and elevation of male status, while at the same time accepting and maintaining their lower status as females is clearly an expression of their religiosity. The more religious the woman, the more she tends to uphold her second-class status.

According to Mead, an individual's personal experience is also social and is therefore a reflection of the social group to which the individual belongs. From this point of view, observations from the interviews point to the Korean immigrant church, the religious and social institution, as being detrimental to the elevation of women's status in the United States. But what impact does the American workplace have on women's status?

As indicated above, several women hold prestigious jobs and relatively high-status positions in American institutions. Such women seem to have developed a substantial degree of autonomy and decision-making power in professional matters. Nonetheless, these women express a decisive ambivalence toward the role of the American workplace in aiding self-development. For example, Paik Eun-Jin was a medical student in Korea. Her father was also a medical doctor, and she came from an upper-class family. As a daughter of a privileged family, she came to America to study in the 1960s but changed her major to medical technology because she found medical school too difficult. She lowered her aspirations and became a licensed medical technologist after completing her education in the United States. She has worked in the laboratory of [Randolph] Hospital in New Jersey for more than sixteen years. As her brief history will indicate, immigration to the United States for many Korean women implies descending the ladder of social class from their original position. Moreover, the social degradation of men's status in America, as I have briefly mentioned earlier, is much more conspicuous in Korean community. Consequently, self-development which improves a woman's status is not usually a prospect. Paik Eun-Jin also shared her experiences with racism and classism in an American institution and its negative impact on her self-development:

> I am one of few employees, including two Filipino women, who have worked in the chemistry department for more than sixteen years. The present supervisor, a White woman, who came after us, was selected and promoted to become a department supervisor. Well, I didn't expect at all that I would be a supervisor no matter how long I work here. Anyway, she is O.K. But, I often get upset working with these White women colleagues. You know, these White women do not work hard, and they have an imperialistic attitude to us, Asians and other racial minority people. They often leave all the difficult and dirty work to us, me and Don, a Chinese man, and the Filipino women. In front of the supervisor, they act like they work hard, but if she is not around, they gather together

and gossip a lot. Why do we have to work hard while they play around? I complained about them several times to the supervisor, but she doesn't do anything . . .

Furthermore, when she assigns me to set up the SMAC machine[29] in the morning, she always appoints only one helper for me. Of course, I am the most experienced person, but it is not fair—she always assigns two helpers when White women set up the same machine. And on holidays, like last George Washington's Birthday, the supervisor assigned only the hard-working people, like me, Don, and Sue [a Filipina] to cover the entire department. But usually, with White technologists, she assigns four to share the workload. But we do not complain because we are afraid that she'll put us on evening shift, which we don't want to work. You know, these white women try to treat us [indicating her Asian colleagues, four women and one man] as their subordinates, even though we have become longtime colleagues. Often, they try to exploit us. Anyway, all of us racial minorities work hard. Therefore, they always expect hard work from us. Well, I used to like my job, but no more. I have no ambition. All I think about now is going home and lying down on the floor and watching Korean video movies. But, I will work until I retire because I have worked here a long time, and the hospital has very good retirement benefits.[30]

Mrs. Paik's experiences in the workplace have denigrated her social status and consequently her self-image in two ways. First, she has stumbled down from her original position of high status in the Korean class structure by working in a position with people who would not be considered her social equals in Korea. Second, within the structure of status and power in her workplace, she has been thrown to the bottom rungs because of White racism against Asian minorities. Therefore, in absolute terms, she has been denigrated and, in relative terms, although she may earn more than her White colleagues, has been demeaned. Racism (also classism) at work has made her feel defeated and powerless. And this racism-based hierarchy in the workplace implicitly enforces the subordinate status of racial minorities and discourages the development of Korean immigrant women's new subjective self.

As in the case of Paik Eun-Jin, the social class of many Korean immigrants, males as well as females, became lower after immigration. Mainly owing to language barriers and lack of American diplomas, most men and women have not been able to obtain white-collar jobs and thereby maintain the class status they had held in Korea. Consequently, their aspirations shrink and their status and self-esteem decline.[31] The denigration of male social status has a direct critical effect upon women since, as described above, Korean tradition requires the status of the latter to be lower than that of the former. In other words, the status of women directly depends on that of men. Consequently, *ilse* women experience double oppression and discrimination, since they are simultaneously subject to subordination by their husbands at home and by racist White Americans at work. For *ilse* Korean women, developing a new subjective self in America would require their liberation from this double social bondage.

However, not all Korean women quietly complain and reduce their self-expectations. Though rare, there are women who, unlike Paik Eun-Jin, articulate their anger and frustration toward institutionalized White American classism, so closely aligned with racism and sexism. Fifty-eight-year-old Joan Smith is a woman who came to the United States in the 1950s from one of the highest Korean social classes, in terms of name and power, in order to study. She earned bachelor's and master's degrees in philosophy and married a Caucasian-American who was a high-ranking official in the U. S. government. She is highly intelligent, energetic, and outgoing. However, until her husband's death in May 1990, she had never worked outside the home. But with the loss of her husband, she was forced to find work. While searching for a job, she bitterly experienced American racism, classism, and ageism. She said:

> I really regret not going to work before while my husband was still alive. All these years, I was kept in a terrarium. I didn't know anything about the world that was going on around me. I was absolutely confined at home. I did not know about my husband's pension or insurance policies, the house mortgage, etc. Do you think I am rich with my husband's pension and insurance money? Hah! Actually, my husband left me with all these debts. I am wrapped up with all these debts. I put this house on the market, but as you know, real estate business is way down now. Also, my second son is in law school, and I have to pay his educational expenses. Above all, psychologically, I am too depressed. I have to get out of this house and meet people. Therefore, I tried so hard to get a full-time job. But, I never realized how difficult it is to get a job. I went to lots of employment agencies. They all asked for typing and computer skills. I am very good in typing;

therefore, I went to school for computer training. Now, I am very good with the computer too. But, there is no full-time job. Since my husband's death, I have worked as a temporary all over the place. Gee, lately, I am always financially and psychologically unstable. This temporary work drives me crazy. I desperately need a steady income and psychological tranquility . . .

I am a fast learner and a hard worker. Above all, I have a master's degree in philosophy. Most of the work I have done requires only a high school education. Anyway, I had excellent references from all the places I had worked. About a few weeks ago, I finally got a full-time job. Oh, I was so happy. But, once I began to work, I had problems. American women don't work hard. They also didn't teach me my work, yet they still expected me to do all the work for them. I learned by myself and worked hard. But, these women constantly told me to do this and that. I got so angry, but I didn't say anything and did whatever they asked. In the middle of the second week, the White woman manager called me at home around eight o'clock in the evening and said I was fired as of that day. She then told me to continue to work for the rest of that week until a woman who was on vacation comes back the following week. I was so shocked and felt humiliated. How dare she call me at home? Why couldn't she tell me that day before I left? I was so angry and asked her why I was fired. She said that I didn't understand English and that I do not learn fast enough. What nonsense! I am educated more than anyone else in that company. I have a master's degree. I have also lived with an American man in America for forty years. I may still have an accent, but I have no problem with English at all. Also, I am a very effective and fast worker and have excellent work records—so, I went to the company to meet the president next day. I wanted to know what the real situation was. Useless— these White people. Anyway, I found that the White woman manager had used me as a temporary. A woman who had resigned wanted to come back; therefore, the manager fired me and rehired the previous employee, who is also another White woman. You know, these White people just used me on a temporary basis, and they would not give me the same rights and benefits that they have. They treated me as a "spare tire" because I am an old Asian woman. When they needed help, they temporarily used me, and then they threw me away when they no longer needed me. What the White people are doing is against the anti-discrimination laws. It is racial and age discrimination. I have grounds for a lawsuit. If my husband were still alive, I would surely sue them. But, now,

I don't have the money, time, and energy to do that. I just need a solid job.[32]

Joan Smith raises profound issues of ageism, racism, and classism, which most minority people still experience in White American society. Paula Giddings argues that African-Americans, especially women, were used as "spare tires" to fill the needs of the U.S. labor force during World War II.[33] She states that African-American women were in demand to work as nurses and skilled or semiskilled workers, even in fields where Whites had prevailed, in order to fill the jobs that were left open by American men's entry into military service. However, after the war, when the men returned home, Black women faced severe competition with Whites, men and women, and Black women were forced to go back to the home, as the returning soldiers were given priority over all women in obtaining employment.

Korean *ilse* women seem to face similar problems. They are confronted with racism and classism, in addition to sexism, which Black women have been experiencing for generations. Korean women also acutely suffer age discrimination. In the Korean culture, aging has traditionally been viewed as a natural phenomenon, and women, particularly in their old age, were secured by, and received respect from, their offspring and community. However, in American society, where individualism and pragmatism prevail, human value tends to be measured only by one's economic contributions. Consequently, aging is viewed only as "consumption," and its value is denigrated. In brief, the American workplace, as a host social context, places definite limits on the development of Korean immigrant women, as it does upon women in general and upon all racial minorities, even though some of these women are engaged in high-status professions. Therefore, American society itself does not seem to offer promising grounds for the self-development of Korean women.

Nevertheless, some Korean immigrant women show positive attitudes toward work. Sa Mi-Ja, an owner of a dry cleaning shop, offered her view of work in terms of its self-transformative effects, when compared to the depressive and unproductive lifestyle of homemakers:

I think it is good to work. I see lots of women who are very bright and talented who just stay home and bury their gifts. They seem to be very depressed and don't have any freedom. I have a few monthly *kye* (계) meetings.[34] Most of the housewives in the groups hurry home about the time when their children or husbands come home, but we working women stay and continue to enjoy our meeting. The working women I know seem to have much freedom and confidence. Also, those women who do not work spend lots of time and energy on church work. Serving the church and God is good, but I think, if they use their talents to improve their lives, that is also good. I want to work as long as my body allows.[35]

Although she had relinquished her business autonomy by transferring all financial responsibilities to her husband, in principle, Sa Mi-Ja advocates women's working outside the home and conveys a somewhat progressive attitude. Such a positive and self-affirming outlook on work is a significant indication of change in *ilse* women's lives. Even Kil Young-Sook, a strong advocate and representative of Korean culture and church tradition, suggests a similar change of lifestyle as a Korean woman:

I have never worked in my life, but I am thinking about opening a business. Next year, my youngest daughter will go to college. Then, what am I going to do at home? I have to do something. I am really thinking hard about what I want to do at this time.[36]

Despite the ambivalent situation created by the tension between the Korean and American social conditions, Korean immigrant women's consciousness and attitudes toward work are in flux. They are beginning to think about the focus of their lives. *Ilse* women are not mere "social animals," simply accepting their socially, culturally, and religiously prescribed lot, but have begun, in their own ways, to evaluate their social experiences and to challenge their Korean tradition and White American norms. They have embarked on the path to change.

Career Development

Commencing work outside the home represents the most conspicuous change that has taken place in *ilse* women's lives since their immigration to the United States. Among twenty-two interviewees, including four pretests, all of the women, except one permanent housewife (Kil Young-Sook), have worked or are currently working outside the home for pay in the United States. Eleven women out of twenty-two had worked in Korea before immigrating. However, the majority of those women were engaged in the medical field as nurses or doctors. A few women worked for a short time while they were single in order to fill the transitional gap until marriage, and two women worked as secondary earners in order to supplement the family income. Therefore, except for the medical professionals, most *ilse* women found work to be a new experience and, through that work, encountered a new social reality they must accept in their immigrant lives in the United States. As a consequence, the concept of a woman's career other than homemaking is still unfamiliar to most women, though the majority show a relatively positive attitude toward women's work outside the home.

Among the interviewees, the main motivation for women's work is to contribute financially to their families, rather than to develop careers. Kim Ai-Kyung, who has been running a boutique in northern New Jersey for thirteen years said:

> I have already been here in this spot for thirteen years. When I first began this store, I didn't know anything about this business, but now I have become an expert. I have established a good number of steady customers and the business is good. When I started this business, my husband did his residency training at the hospital and made very little money. I had to help him financially. I still need to work because my first son is in medical school. The second son, who is working now, is also thinking about going to graduate school next year. Therefore, I plan to work several more years until they complete their advanced studies. But, my financial contribution is not as critical as before. I have sometimes thought about selling this store and staying home. But then I ask myself, If I do not work, what will I do? I cannot just stay home. Therefore, I continue to run this shop—but I have never thought of this job as my career. Maybe, in a few years, I will quit. Then, I will fully devote myself to serving God for the rest of my life. That is my wish.[37]

Many women, like Kim Ai-Kyung, work for financial reasons as well as to fill up their time and so regard their work as a temporary measure that will end when they can serve God. In the interviews, none of them clarified what they meant by serving God; however, they implicitly expressed their view that to serve God involved returning to the traditional homemaker role and becoming more involved in their spiritual development and church activities.

My general impression of these women is one of discontent and unfulfillment. They have spent enormous amounts of time and energy on rearing children and housekeeping. They are accustomed to serving and developing others. Most women have not developed any hobbies or talents other than those involving traditional duties. After the children grow up and leave the home, their accustomed roles become less significant, and these women feel a certain emptiness. They seem to seek a channel through which their power and energy can be consumed. God is the ultimate object of their service because the church is their primary existential context. Therefore, to most women, career development offers little appeal. Kim Ai-Kyung spoke of the following in her interview:

> If my future daughter-in-law wants to work and develop her career, it is fine with me as long as my son approves of her working. But, if she has a child, she has to stay home and raise her children. Child rearing is a woman's primary job. I will not take care of her children. I will serve God. I respect Mrs. Thatcher and other professional women, but I have no desire to become a professional woman.[38]

Most women like Kim Ai-Kyung still view homemaking, especially child rearing, as the primary and permanent career of women and work outside the home as temporary. Above all, serving God and the church is the highest calling of a woman after she fulfills her primary duties as wife and mother. However, for most women, serving God implies their physical and spiritual devotion to being men's assistants. Grace Hurh, a devout Christian and a lifelong professional, even rebuked a woman's career development as an egocentric act and emphasized women's vicarious service for others:

> Women's career orientation is evil because it begins from egoism and self-centeredness. Childbearing and rearing should be the highest priority of a woman. Once married, the family and home should be the center of women's lives. Everything that women do should be a service to the family, others, and the church, so that through those services, God should be glorified.[39]

Several women share Grace Hurh's view, holding the view that developing a woman's career outside the home is a selfish endeavor. Therefore, service for the family, the church, and ultimately God is considered women's "privileged" career.

The focus of *ilse* women's lives in the United States is still upon others, as determined by their social conventions. Also, the tendency toward vicarious living conspicuously increases with their religiosity, that is to say, the more religious the women are, the more they live for and through others instead of living their own lives. From this point of view, the Korean immigrant church hinders *ilse* women's career development, which can potentially be a source of personal enrichment and fulfillment in family and public life.

What, then, is the situation of the host society outside the Korean church in relation to the career development of *ilse* women? Is it encouraging a new self-development through career development, or is it problematic? Dr. Suh, an anesthesiologist, explored her struggle for survival in her professional world:

I used to work very hard. When I came to America, I was insecure about my profession. Everything was new, and I had a language problem. So, if any doctors asked me to cover their work, I used to do it. And especially after my divorce, my financial situation was terribly bad. I had to pay the mortgage, other bills, and also raise my son. Therefore, I always did overtime work. I took every opportunity which my colleagues offered me to work in their place— Saturdays and Sundays, holidays, morning or night duties. I didn't care; as long as there was work, I grabbed it. If anyone wanted to get rid of on-call or weekend/holiday duties, they came to me first and asked me to work for them. Like a dog, I picked up every crumb [of overtime] that was dropped, especially by the White male doctors. You know, they loved me. They always said that I was so nice and kind. But now, I no longer pick up the crumbs. Unless it is my duty, I do not take overtime work. My son is at Harvard, and I am O.K. financially. Also, I have enough experience, and I am very good in anesthesiology. In terms of technique, I am far superior to them, especially those young doctors. Do you know how those doctors, especially the White males, treat me? Since the day I started claiming my equal rights, oh, they don't like me. They still expect me to pick up their garbage and unwanted crumbs like a dog. Now, they see me as a threat and a competitor. Behind my back, they talk about me a lot. They try to find mistakes in my work in order to harm me. They want to get rid of me. If they cannot find any fault with my work, they make an issue about my accent. Now, I am more tired than before because my nerves are on edge—I am hyper alert to their potential criticisms.[40]

As Dr. Suh reveals in her statement, Korean immigrant *ilse* women, as a minority group in America, struggle to survive in the midst of White American imperialism manifested in racism, classism, ageism, and sexism. It is very common to encounter White male notions that Asian women are passive and docile. These stereotypes often translate themselves into racist and sexist behavior in the workplace. From this point of view, the host American society is also an inhospitable social environment in which the process of *ilse* women's self-creation through career development is to take place.

Encountering the multiple barriers to career development—and hence, self-development—immigrant Korean women are highly conscious of their state of victimization and powerlessness as women and as minorities. Many are beginning to rationalize their social experiences and assert their rights, albeit still subtly, as equals to White Americans and to men in general. Though they may not yet have a fully articulated image of self, they appear to be searching for new identities as minority Asian, and in particular Korean, women in the United States.

CHAPTER 6

Conclusion

I have often heard that Korean women are domestic, obedient, and submissive. Even some highly educated and intelligent men of other ethnicities joke that they want to marry Korean women because they obey men and treat men like kings. In outward manner and appearance, Korean women may be submissive, yet obviously this "submissiveness" is a product of Korean society and culture. Under the pervasive influences of the five-hundred-year Confucian Yi society, the monolithic social and ethical rule of *namjon yŏbi* and *hyŏnmo yangch'ŏ* produced obedient yet self-sacrificial women. In other words, to survive in that society women had no other choice than adjusting to the culture. As George H. Mead affirms, an individual's adaptation to one's social circumstance is what is most essential for survival; and the individual's primary/social self emerges from the act of adapting.

Korean immigrant *ilse* women in the United States must struggle for survival amid a quite different social milieu. First, women themselves have been changed by education. Second, the home is no longer a sanctuary for many such women. Either by volition or by inescapable circumstances, the majority of women are pushed into workforce, into the society outside the home which was once the province of men only. Now some of these women work with men and often compete with them.

Third, their social context is pluralistic in terms of values, lifestyles, and cultural forces. They live mainly in two indispensable social realities: the Korean immigrant church and the host American society. Therefore, in order to survive in America, *ilse* women have no other choice than to adjust to both of these social contexts. How do they adjust? From the research, I postulate three distinctive modes of adaptation. In other words, *ilse* women may develop their selves in three unique ways.

181

1. *Elusive Mode*. Homemakers whose major social context is the Korean church tend to escape from the confrontation or conflict between themselves and the church. In other words, they try not to see themselves and not to confront their situations. Blocking themselves from the social force or phenomena outside the church, and escaping from the major American society, they adhere to the church. They erect religious walls around themselves based on the church's patriarchal teachings combined with the Confucian cultural traditions in order to justify their perspectives and to protect themselves. In so doing, many deceive themselves and do not fully develop their potential in areas other than in homemaking. Consequently, they perpetuate the Korean women's traditional image of obedient homemaker. For them, the church functions as the "Christian Yi dynasty." Supplying the legitimating principles, the church seems to perpetuate patriarchy as women's bulwark.

2. *Dualistic/Schizophrenic Mode*. On the other hand, many women, mainly professionals and entrepreneurs, who face the challenge or confrontation in the adjustment to the two different social contexts, the church and workplace, also develop distinctive adaptation modes. These are women who experience themselves as "nobodies" in the church but as "somebodies" outside the church. They tend to show unique modes of adaptation and develop two personas/masks. In the church, they act as traditional and obedient women. But outside the church, they act as independent individuals. Like some "elusive" women, they are also apparently deceptive. Psychologically speaking, the women of this group are often similar to the schizophrenics.

3. *Ambiguous/Confused Mode*. Most women in this mode seem to be confused. They are very ambiguous about the process of adjusting to their immigrant situation. They are not sure who they are or what they have to do. They experience the incompatability or disparity between their beliefs and the social realities. They are often angry, confused, frustrated, and even depressed. Interestingly, the Korean immigrant church does not have any words or provide any support to the women in the last two categories. The church is silent or ignorant about them.

Min He-Yun, a pious and intellectual Christian housewife, articulated the church's attitude to those women who struggle to survive in the new social environment in America. She asked about the purpose of my research after her interview. When she heard that the aim of this study is to determine the extent of the church's helpfulness to Korean immigrant women as they adjust to life in America, she commented quite spontaneously: "*No, the church is not helpful at all.*"

My research shows that none of these women seem to be wholistic persons, that is, healthy social beings. Radically speaking, most of them seem to be pathological, not inately, but sociologically. From my feminist theological point of view (I am an United Methodist ordained minister), men and women should equally reveal the healthy and wholistic image of God because they were created in the likeness of God who is understood perfection. However, in belittling themselves and developing only one skill, homemaking, women may not fully cultivate their potential. Thus, the self is deformed.

From the sociological and ethical point of view, men and women should interact with dignity and integrity. They have to live in mutual love and repectful relationship; then, as companions, they may cooperate to establish a just society where human equality and value are esteemed. The present noncultivation of women's potential, the rich human resources of half of the human beings, is not only a waste of women's energy and power but also that of the church and society. Moreover, by disempowering women, men become overempowered. Clearly, social and ethical injustice results.

Moreover, women's pathological symptoms, that is, their social malfunction and maladjustment, may cause significant social problems. As mentioned before, women, particularly religious housewives, tend to escape from the major society and to adhere to their ethnic culture and traditions by hiding themselves inside the church. This "elusive/adhesive adapatation" may exacerbate social division and disintegration rather than unity. Also, working women's social experiences such as ageism, classism, racism, and sexism within society seem to discourage their social adjustment to the American context. All these social and ethical factors contribute to breeding women's distorted selves, creating partial and unhealthy human beings.

Therefore, these women urgently need treatment. How can these women be treated to become healthy and wholistic persons? In other words, how can these women perfect their selves and become healthy social members of the United States? Here, as the initial step, I suggest the transformation of the Korean immigrant church because the church is the primary social context where women should adjust and their consequential selves emerge as a result of adaptation.

Accordingly, my research points out the significance of the Korean church's prophetic role. Max Weber describes two kinds of church leadership: prophetic and priestly.[1] The prophetic role is visionary. A prophet transforms a religious group or a society with his or her vision. But the role of priests is to maintain the prophetic tradition.

From the Weberian view, the Korean immigrant church faithfully plays the priestly role by preserving and perpetuating Christianized-Confucian gender hierarchy and patriarchal tradition. However, the Korean church powerfully demonstrated its prophetic role during the Korean independece movement. Today, the situation of the Korean immigrant *ilse* women asks for the church's same prophetic vigor and vision.

Furthermore, the transformation of the Korean immigrant church is not sufficient in itself. The whole society, the host American society, should be transformed. As my research has disclosed, the *ilse* women's victimization by White American values and standards such as ageism, classism, sexism, and racism point to the fact that the society as a whole has to be redeemed from the age-old White prejudice and bigotry. For the social transformation, I as a person holding a religious vocaton also suggest the cooperation and reformation of the greater church in America.

The power of the Christian church in the United States is apparently sizeable: 86.5 percent of Americans are Christians.[2] Though this figure includes occasional as well as regular church goers, the impact of the church in the United States cannot be ignored. In today's pluralistic American society, the church is definitely not the only infrastructure providing legitimating principles for social reality; yet, without a doubt, the ideas and practices of the church affect social processes, and people look to the church to guide and translate these processes. The 1992 American presidential election process succinctly demonstrated the church's impact upon the American public mores.

For this reason, I recommend that the church, Korean and American, as one of the major social contexts should mobilize its prophetic power to raise public consciousness and transform its system and structure to the point at which the fulfillment of human equality and dignity are upheld. When we truly establish a just society where all people, black and white, yellow and red, men and women, old and young, rich and poor, gays/lesbians and straights, physically abled and disabled, christians and non-christians, respect one another and live in cooperation and sharing, the wholistic self may emerge. Human fulfillment may be attained.

APPENDIX 1: QUESTIONNAIRE

Demographic Information

1. Name
2. Age
3. Education: final degree; name of school; location
4. Marital status
5. Immigration time and motif
6. Occupation

Church Questions

1. How long have you been a Christian?
2. What made you a Christian?
3. What church do you attend now?
4. Why do you go to that particular church?
5. How often do you attend the church (including Sunday worship, other activities, meetings, and Bible classes)?
6. What do you like the most/least among the church activities (programs), including worship?
7. Are you active in the church? How? What programs/or activities are you interested/involved in?
8. Are you happy in your church?
9. Do you feel any contradictions between the church's teachings and practice in life situation?
10. Is the church important to your life in America? Does your church make your life happier? If so, how?
11. Do you have any suggestions for the church to help improve women's life?

Faith Questions

1. How do you think about God?
2. How do you think of Jesus?

3. What do you think about the Bible? Is it the actual word of God? Do you believe that everything written in it is true?

4. How do you think about the Bible in relation to science?

5. Do you believe that the first woman was made out of the first man's rib? Do you agree with Paul's view that man is the head of woman?

6. Among the women in the Bible, who comes closest to your image of an ideal woman? Which woman interests you most? Why? Would you explain your ideal type of woman?

7. How often do you read the Bible? How important is the Bible to you?

8. Besides the Bible, what books or magazines do you read?

9. How often do you pray? Do you believe in the power of prayer? For whom and what do you mostly pray? Do you pray for your self? If so, what is the content of your prayer?

10. Do you believe life continues after death? How does this belief affect your present life?

Biographical Questions

1. Would you share your personal history? From childhood to now (briefly).

2. How did you marry? Did you choose your husband? If not, did someone arrange it?

3. What do you think about divorce/remarriage?

4. When you have decisions to make, such as which school to choose for your children, whether to purchase property, or which options related to your work outside the home to select, with whom do you discuss the quandary? Whose opinion influences you most?

5. Who most affects your choice of dress or hairstyle? Do you dress differently when you go to church (as compared to other places)? If so, would you explain how and why? Whose opinion affects you most?

6. What are your special gifts and talents? How do you develop them?

7. What makes your life important? What makes you feel most alive?
8. Are you happy with your own self?
9. If you were to die now, what message(s) would you leave to your daughter(s)? What would you want to do most?

Economic Questions

1. Did you work outside your home before you came to America?
2. Do you do paid work now? Would you tell me why you work?
3. Are you happy to work? Does your present work lead to the career you want?
4. If you are not a job holder, would you tell me why? Is it your decision to be a housewife? How do you spend most of your time? What is your greatest pleasure?
5. Are you financially independent? Do you have your own savings account, investments, or property?
6. (To working women only:) Do you sense any conflict between your work and your church life? Does your church help you become independent?

Sociopolitical Questions (Optional)

1. Do you have close friends? Church friends? Koreans only? Any Caucasians or others?
2. How often do you meet and spend time with three of your closest friends?
3. What do you do for relaxation?
4. What is your opinion on abortion? How do you think about euthanasia?
5. What do you think of feminism?
6. Racial conflict is a dominant factor in American life now. Korean grocers have experienced conflicts with Blacks in Brooklyn and Harlem. What do you think Christians should do about these kinds of social problems?

7. Do you vote or have you ever voted? Who or what most influences your voting?

8. How do you think about Christians' concerns and participation in politics?

9. Would you tell me anything else about the church and women in general? For example, clergywoman, woman lawyer, homosexuality, interracial marriage, etc.

APPENDIX 2:
PRIMARY SOURCES:
INTERVIEW MATERIALS

HOUSEWIVES

Tape 1.   Name: Kil Young-Sook
          Date: September 12, 1990.
          Time: 2 Hours
          Place: Oakland, N.J.
          Membership: Fellowship Church; former UMW president
          Demographics: 53 years old; mother of three daughters;
          wife of a medical doctor and church elder; B.A. in
          Korea; immigrated in 1967.

Tape 2.   Name: Min He-Yun
          Date: September 6, 1990.
          Time: 2 hours
          Place: Short Hills, N.J.
          Membership: Holiness Church; UMW president
          Demographics: 48 years old; mother of two children;
          wife of a businessman (Ph.D. and church elder);
          former dietician; B.A. and M.A. in the U.S.; came for
          studies in 1961.

Tape 3   Name: Na In-Wha
          Date: September 9, 1990.
          Time: 1.5 hours
          Place: Pastor's Office in Holiness Church, N.J.
          Membership: Holiness Church
          Demographics: 41 years old; mother of two children;
          pastor's wife and previously a R.N.; B.S. in Korea;
          immigrated in 1973.

Tape 4   Name: Pai Il-Mi
          Date: August 31, 1990.
          Time: 1.5 hours
          Place: Madison, N.J.

Membership: [Y] Church
Demographics: 46 years old; mother of two children;
pastor's wife; B.A. in Korea; came for husband's
studies in 1978.

Tape 5   Name: Park Jung-Ja
Date: September 22, 1990.
Time: 2.5 hours
Place: Scarsdale, N.Y.
Membership: Word Church; former Sunday School
principal.
Demographics: 56 years old; mother of two children;
wife of a businessman and church elder; associate
degree in education in Korea; immigrated in 1968.

Tape 6   Name: Ye Soon-Jong
Date: August 17, 1990.
Time: 2.5 hours
Place: Short Hills, N.J.
Membership: Holiness Church
Demographics: 43 years old; mother of three children;
wife of a medical doctor and elder of the church;
B.A. in Korea; immigrated in 1970.

WOMEN IN BUSINESS

Tape 7   Name: Ahn Sung-Sim
Date: August 30, 1990.
Time: 1.5 hours
Place: Fort Lee, N.J.
Membership: Fellowship Church
Demographics: 59 years old; widow; mother of one
daughter; real estate broker; B.A. in Korea and
graduate school drop-out in the U.S.; came for
studies in 1960.

Tape 8   Name: Chung Myung-Soon
Date: September 8, 1990.
Time: 2 hours
Place: Korean restaurant, New York City.

Membership: Word Church
Demographics: 56 years old; mother of two children; owner of a restaurant (with assistance of husband); college drop-out in Korea; immigrated in 1973.

Tape 9   Name: Kim Ai-Kyung
Date: July 31, 1990.
Time: 1.5 hours
Place: Leonia, N.J.
Membership: Fellowship Church; former UMW president.
Demographics: 51 years old; mother of two sons; wife of a medical doctor and church elder; boutique owner; B.A. in Korea; immigrated in 1970.

Tape 10   Name: Sarah Lim
Date: August 27, 1990.
Time: 1.5 hours
Place: Fort Lee, N.J.
Membership: Fellowship Church
Demographics: 52 years old; mother of two sons; wife of a UMC minister; real estate broker; B.A. in Korea; came for husband's studies in 1962.

Tape 11   Name: Sa Mi-Ja
Date: August 29, 1990.
Time: 1.5 hours
Place: Irvington, N.J.
Membership: Fellowship Church
Demographics: 45 years old; mother of two daughters; wife of an engineer (Ph.D) and church elder; former R.N.; owner of dry cleaning shop; B.S. in Korea; immigrated in 1970.

Tape 12   Name: Yang Byung-In
Date: August 26, 1990.
Time: 2 hours
Place: Franklin Lakes, N.J.
Membership: Fellowship Church; former UMW president.
Demographics: 51 years old; mother of two children;

wife of a businessman and church exhorter; jewelry shop owner; B.A. in Korea; came for husband's studies in 1966.

PROFESSIONALS AND SEMIPROFESSIONALS

Tape 13   Name: Chang Ok-Hee
Date: August 30, 1990.
Time: 2 hours
Place: Fort Lee, N.J.
Membership: Word Church; former UMW president.
Demographics: 49 years old; wife of a computer programmer and church deacon; R.N.; B.A. in Korea; immigrated in 1970.

Tape 14 Name: Helen Choi
Date: August 19, 1990.
Time: 1.5 hours
Place: Paramus, N.J.
Membership: Word Church
Demographics: 55 years old; mother of two sons; wife of a chemist; Educational Coordinator at [M] College; B.A., M.A. & ABD in the U.S.; came for studies in 1956.

Tape 15   Name: Ha Yul-Nyu
Date: September 21, 1990.
Time: 1.5 hours
Place: Fort Lee, N.J.
Membership: Fellowship Church
Demographics: 54 years old; mother of two sons; wife of a farm owner and church elder; medical doctor; B.S. in Korea; accompanied husband to job transfer in 1971.

Tape 16   Name: Grace Hurh
Date: September 18, 1990.
Time: 3 hours
Place: Madison, N.J.
Membership: Holiness Church; Sunday School Director
Demographics: 59 years old; mother of three children;

wife of an engineer (Ph.D.) and church elder; Education Director at state-run pre-school institution; B.A. M.A. in the U.S.; came for studies in 1951.

Tape 17 Name: Suh Jai-Mi
Date: August 17, 1990.
Time: 1.5 hours
Place: Fort Lee, N.J.
Membership: Holiness Church
Demographics: 46 years old; divorcee; mother of one son; medical doctor; B.S. in Korea; immigrated in 1970.

Tape 18 Name: Lee Bong-Hee
Date: September 16, 1990.
Time: 1.5 hours
Place: Leonia, N.J.
Membership: Fellowship Church
Demographics: 54 years old; widow; mother of two daughters; assistant editorial director at [W] university; B.A. in Korea and M.A. in the U.S.; came for studies in 1958.

PRETESTS

Tape 19 Name: Oh Young-Ran
Date: July 22, 1990.
Time: 1.5 hours
Place: Word Church.
Membership: Word Church.
Demographics: 48 years old; single; owner of a travel agency in New York; college drop-out in Korea; came for studies in 1974.

Tape 20 Name: Kang Jin-Sook
Date: August 25, 1990.
Time: 2 hours
Place: Rifton, N.Y.
Membership: [L] Church in upstate, N.Y.
Demographics: 51 years old; mother of two sons; wife

of a medical doctor; medical doctor; B.S. in Korea; immigrated in 1971.

Tape 21   Name: Paik Eun-Jin
Date: April 19, 1990.
Tome: 1.25 hours
Place: Morristown, N.J.
Membership: [C] Church in Morristown, NJ
Demographics: 51 years old; mother of three children; wife of an engineer (Ph.D.); medical technologist; B.S. in the U.S.; came for studies in 1961.

Tape 22   Name: Yoon He-Rim
Date: summer, 1990.
Time: 1.25 hour
Place: Madison, N.J.
Membership: [A] Church in N.Y.
Demographics: 44 years old; mother of three children; wife of a medical doctor and church elder; B.A. in Korea and M.Div. in the U.S.; a graduate student (in Ph.D. program); immigrated in 1970.

Notes

PREFACE

1. See Anne Wilson Schaef, *Women's Reality* (Minneapolis: Winston Press, 1985).
2. Won Moo Hurh and Kwang Chung Kim, "Religious Participation: Ethnic Roles of the Korean Church," *Journal of the Scientific Study of Religion*, 20 (3/1990). About 70 percent of Koreans in the United States are affiliated with their ethnic churches, and women make up about two-thirds of the church membership. Also refer to Pyong Gap Min, "The Structure and Social Functions of Korean Immigrant Churches in the United States" (the revision and expansion of the paper presented at the Annual Meeting of the Association for Asian Studies, Washington, DC; March 18, 1990). The authors argue that the major social function of the Korean churches in America is to serve as community centers; therefore, even non-Christians join Korean ethnic churches after immigration.

1. INTRODUCTION

1. G. H. Mead, *On Social Psychology*, ed. Anselm Strauss (Chicago, University of Chicago Press, 1964), 199.
2. Ibid., 200–46.
3. Ibid., 250–92. The term *society*, defined by Mead, is not a material entity; society is a set of common beliefs and attitudes, which the members share and which shape individuals' consciousness and lifestyles. Therefore, society is constituted by social agents or institutions, such as family, churches, schools, and organizations, which actualize the social mores.
4. *Ilse* means "first generation," and commonly refers to those who immigrated to the United States after their personalities (beliefs and lifestyles) had been shaped in the traditional Korean culture. *Iljŏm ose* (일점오세 : 一點五世) refers to members of the "trans-generation," those who came to America in their teens. Their personalities have been molded in two cultures, Korean and American; they are the

"hybrid" Koreans. *Ise* (이세 : 二世) refers to "second generation" individuals who were born in America and whose identities are more likely identified with Americans than with Koreans.

2. WOMEN OF YESTERDAY: WOMEN OF THE YI DYNASTY

1. Out of respect for Korean culture, Korean names in this book are written according to the Korean traditional order: the family name comes first, and the given name follows. When a first name comprises two "words" (which would be two *letters* in Korean), it is hyphenated for clarity. Bibliographical citations give all names—English and Korean—in standard American order.

2. See Max Weber, *The Protestant Ethic and the Spirit of Capitalism* (New York: Charles Scribner and Sons, 1958). Weber illustrates how the Protestant ethic, based on Calvin's doctrine of predestination, affected people's rationalization of their lifestyles in modern capitalist society. Weber asserts that religion powerfully functions to mold human mind and behavior.

3. Yung-Chung Kim, *Women of Korea* (Seoul: Ewha Womans University Press, 1976), 83.

4. Ibid., 92. According to traditional Korean calculation, at the moment of birth, a child is considered to be one year old; therefore, the American equivalent of marriageable age would be thirteen or fourteen for boys and twelve or thirteen for girls.

5. Tales from Korean folklore often describe the self-sacrifice of women as devotion to their family. *Sim Ch'ŏng Jŏn* is one of the most popular. According to the story, Sim Ch'ŏng, a kind and gentle girl who was deeply devoted to her blind father, threw herself into the ocean as a sacrificial offering to appease the Ocean Spirit; in return, her father gained sight. This story is one of the many conveyed to generations of Korean women in order to inspire women's self-sacrifice for men and the family.

6. See Jean Baker Miller, *Toward a New Psychology of Women* (Boston: Beacon Press, 1986). Miller argues that by expending their time and energy on the development of others, especially that of men and their achievements, women engage in a process of self-negation and self-devaluation.

7. Most of the primary sources about women's lives in the Yi period are part of Korean culture's oral tradition. The famous story of Han Sŏk-Bong poignantly describes how women in the Yi dynasty fulfilled their lives through self-sacrifice. According to this true story, Sŏk-Bong's mother had endured severe ordeals in order to educate her

son. Because of her sacrificial devotion, Sŏk-Bong became the most renowned Chinese calligrapher in the Yi dynasty. Through her son's success and fame, she gained social recognition, elevated status, respect, and the admiration of others. She was forever known as "the mother of Han Sŏk-Bong."

8. Kim, *Women of Korea*, 85. It is also interesting to note that typically, only "abnormal" and "illegal" people, such as burglars, wife-stealers (men who were too poor to obtain wives would steal sleeping women, married or unmarried), prostitutes, and other socially marginalized women, roamed about at night in traditional times. "Normal" women would go outside only on business, for example, to visit an ill member of the natal family.

9. *Chang-ot* is a large drape-like shawl that was used for covering a woman's face and body when she ventured outside her home. The material used for *chang-ot* distinguished a woman's social status. Women in the *yangban* class (intellectual and military ruling class) used silk, and lower-class women used cotton.

10. The Yi dynasty had strict, hierarchical socioeconomic-political class distinctions. In general, three distinctive classes, besides that of the royal family, existed: *yangban* (양반: 良班); *sangmin* (상민: 常民); and *ch'ŏnmin* (천민: 賤民). The *yangban* class was the intellectual and military ruling class. The *sangmin* could be regarded roughly as members of the "middle-class," people who were mainly engaged in small trade. (It is misleading to think that a middle class as exists in western societies existed in Yi Korea. In general, those of the *yangban* were in the upper class, and all others were in the lower classes. The *sangmin*, however, were free and independent, that is, they were not servants or slaves and possessed commercial skills with which to earn a living.) The *ch'ŏnmin* were the people of the lowest class, those who were engaged in service-oriented occupations and considered as slaves and servants. The opportunity for upward mobility was almost nonexistent in that society.

11. Kim, *Women of Korea*, 85.

12. Hesung Chun Koh, "Women's Roles and Achievements in the Yi Dynasty," in *Korean Women in Transition*, ed. Eui-Young Yu and Earl H. Phillips (Los Angeles, CA: California State University, 1987), 30.

13. Ibid., 38–42; also, Yung-Chung Kim, in *Women of Korea*, 129–38.

14. See Weber, *Prostestant Ethic*; also, see Peter Berger, *The Sacred Canopy* (Garden City, NY: Doubleday, 1969), particularly the sections on religion and world-construction (3–28), and world-maintenance (29–51) and the problem of theodicy (52–80).

15. Kim, *Women of Korea*, 154. Kim here refers to Yi Ik, *Songho Saesol* (Collected Essays of Songho), vol. 3, no. 1.

16. *Ŏnmun* refers to the Korean character system (the vernacular) which was created for the use of women and lower-class men at the initiation of Se-jong the Great, the fourth king of the Yi dynasty.

17. Koh, "Women's Roles and Achievements in the Yi Dynasty," 41.

18. Kim, *Women of Korea*, 155.

19. Dong-won Lee, "The Changes of Korean Family and Women," in *Challenges for Women: Womens Studies in Korea*, ed. Sei-wha Chung, trans. Chang-hyun Shin et. al. (Seoul: Ewha Womans University Press, 1986), 233.

20. Kim, *Women of Korea*, 84.

21. There are numerous stories and books about women's sacrifice and martyrdom for men and families. As mentioned previously, *Sim Ch'ŏng Jŏn* and the story of Han Sŏk-Bong's mother represent those women who fulfilled their duties sanctioned by the society. *Ch'un Hyang Jŏn* is another popular story which elevates women's loyalty to men. Ch'un-Hyang endured severe ordeals and overcame sexual harassment in order to keep her chastity and loyalty to her prospective husband. Finally, she married her prospective husband, who became a local magistrate. Her suffering and ordeals were rewarded through her husband's success.

22. Kim, *Women of Korea*, 218. The name, given by the last Queen Min, means "the learning hall of pear blossom." The emblem of the royal household was the pear blossom.

23. Ibid., 220. The author refers to writings by D. L. Gilford "Education of the Capital of Korea," *The Korean Repository* (August 1886), 409–10 and *The Gospel in All Lands* [1888], 373 which express the Mary Scranton's views on education of Korean women.

24. See Colleen McDannell, *The Christian Home in Victorian America*, 1840–1900 (Bloomington: Indiana University Press, 1986).

25. Kim, *Women of Korea*, 216. The author cites an excerpt from the article in *Tongnip Sinmun*, May 12, 1896.

26. Eui-Young Yu, "Women in Transitional and Modern Korea," in Yu and Phillips, " *Korean Women in Transition*, 21.

27. Sin Sa Im Dang who lived during the Yi period, was a well-known poet, artist, and calligrapher, as well as a wise mother who raised her son, Lee Yul-Kok, as a great scholar of Taoism. Hwang Jin-Yi was also a great poet and a strong-willed woman, who was a famous *kisaeng*.

28. Koh, "Women's Roles and Achievements in the Yi Dynasty," 34–42.

29. On festivals such as New Year's Day, children kow-towed to their parents, both mother and father, and showed their gratitude and respect. On the wedding day, the new bride and groom ceremoniously

kow-towed to the parents and parents-in-law and expressed their obedience and veneration. Children, especially son(s), took care of their parents in their old age. Parents lived in the home of their son(s) and with the families of son(s). Above all, women became ancestors after they died and received equal veneration with men through ancestor worship. In such ways, women's role performance in marriage was rewarded.

30. Karl Marx, "Contribution to the Critique of Hegel's Philosophy of Right," in Karl Marx and Friedrich Engels, *On Religion* (Chico, CA: Scholars Press, 1964), 42.

31. I, myself, have experienced exclusion from the religious ceremony. My parents had five children—four girls and one son, the last child. Though I was the eldest daughter, my father the "liberal" would preside over the ancestor worship service with his small baby son. The rest of the family were excluded.

32. I had frequent contacts with the student as a counselor and an alumna. Having completed her doctorate, she teaches at E University in Seoul Korea. The citation is a paraphrase of her comments made during a casual conversation in January 1991.

33. Kim, *Women of Korea*, 133. Also see Dong-sik Yu, *Hankuk Mukyo ŭi Yŏksa wa Kujo* (Seoul: Yonsei University Press, 1975), 282. In a 1932 survey, 68 percent of the registered shamans were women. Further, Alan Carter Covell suggests that more than 95 percent of the registered shamans were women in the 1970s. See Alan Carter Covell, *Ecstacy: Shamanism in Korea* (Elizabeth NJ: Hollym International, l983), 19.

34. For further information, see Dong-sik Yu, *Hankuk Mukuo ŭi Yŏksa wa Kujo*.

35. See Youngsook Kim Harvey, *Six Korean Women* (St. Paul: West Publishing Co., 1979). The author thoroughly describes the symptoms, suffering, and ineffective medical treatments related to *sinpyŏng*.

36. See Covell, *Ecstasy*. The author interprets *naerim kut* as a conjugal event of the spirit and the afflicted.

37. Harvey, *Six Korean Women*, 129–69, for the cases of *Namsan-Mansin* and *Ttonggol-Mansin*. In *Namsan-Mansin*'s case, the shaman mother was the major economic provider for the family, and her son functioned as her manager. In the latter case, *Ttonggol-Mansin* became the major financial provider, and her husband became dependent.

38. Ibid., 133. Governor-General of Chosen, "Chosen no mugeki" (Korean Shamanism), *Chyosa siryo*, 36 (1932), 10–12.

39. In *Six Korean Women*, Youngsook Kim Harvey vividly describes the ordeals which shamans and their families endure in Korean society today. The social discrimination was much more painful and difficult

to endure in the hierarchical Yi society. Since being a shaman is one of the most socially disgraceful vocations a Korean can undertake, the spirit-possessed person and her or his family attempt to avoid that fate by all means possible to them. Yet the only solution is acceptance.

40. See Dong-sik Yu, *Hankuk Mukyo ŭi Yŏksa wa Kujo*, particularly "Shaman's Function," 203–12.

41. *Kut* is the major ritual of Shamanism. It consists of music, dancing, food, and people. The purpose is to secure well-being of the living and the dead and reconciliation between the spirits and the living.

42. Kim, *Women of Korea*, 131. Citing the *Yijo Sillok* (The Annals of the Yi Dynasty), the author describes the Shamanistic practices observed by the Confucian kings during times of national crisis.

43. Ibid., 130. Yŏnsan-kun's *ilgi*, vol. 49, May, 9th year of Yŏnsan-kun, Pyongin-jo.

44. Ibid., 130–32. The story of *Chillyŏn-kun* vivifies *kuksa*'s influence on the royal family. Queen Min, the mother of the last Yi king, Sun-jong, hired as her advisor the shaman-woman who foretold the date of Queen Min's return to the palace from her exile in *Kanghwa-do* (a region north of Seoul). Luckily, her augury came true. As a reward, Queen Min bestowed upon her a special title, *Chillyŏn-kun*, and appointed her as the religious priest of the royal court. Queen Min received advice from *Chillyŏn-kun* in her decision making and erected a Shamanistic temple in her court. There, she offered daily prayers to the spirits and observed Shamanistic rituals for the health and security of her son, King Sun-jong. The queen also employed *Chillyŏn-kun*'s son in a high government post.

45. Yu, *Hankuk Mukyo ŭi Yŏksa wa Kujo*, 207–13.

46. Refer to Jung Young Lee, *Korean Shamanistic Rituals* (New York: Mouton Publishers, 1981); In-hoe Kim, *Hankuk Musok ŭi Chonghap chŏk Koch'al* (Seoul: Koryo University Press, 1981); Laurel Kendall, *Shamans, Housewives, and Other Restless Spirits* (Honolulu: University of Hawaii, 1986). These references are helpful for understanding the nature and variety of *kut* in Korean Shamanism.

47. Kendall, *Shamans, Housewives, and Other Restless Spirits*, especially Kendall's discussion of *Mugam*, 10–12. *Mugam* is dancing performed by the spectators dressed in the shaman's clothes.

48. I can vividly remember my mother supplying the family with good luck charms and amulets prescribed by shamans. She placed them in my book bags and under my pillows so that evil spirits could not attack me.

49. When I was a child, I often accompanied my mother to obtain advice from shamans in order to increase good luck for her husband and children, especially her only son. If there was a problem in the

family, even my father, who was a physician and life-time devotee of modern science, would implicitly encourage my mother to contact shamans for their advice. It is commonly acknowledged that even Christian women visit shamans and consult with them on their family problems and use the amulets and provisions prescribed by shamans. For example, whenever my sisters—Christians—living in the United States, visit Korea, they always consult with shamans. If necessary, they spend an enormous amount of money for *kut*. They often bring the good luck charms and amulets to their home in Los Angeles.

50. Lee, *Korean Shamanistic Rituals*, 153–66. Also, see Kendall, *Shamans, Housewives, and Other Restless Spirits* on the role of Korean women as household priestesses.

51. *Kosa,* a ritual that takes place in the home, is initiated and directed by women, usually the grandmother or mother. It is a ceremony that reaffirms the amicable relationship between spirits and the family and reassures the former of the latter's loyalty in return for safe and prosperous guardianship of the household. *Ttŏk* (rice-cake) is the main food offered with water to the spirits. *Kosa* is held regularly (monthly and seasonally) to ensure the spirits' blessings upon and protection of the family.

52. My mother used to conduct *kosa* on the first day of each month. She cooked an enormous potful of *siru ttŏk* (시루떡 : steamed rice-cake) and offered a big piece of that cake and water to spirits in every single room of the house, outside the house gates, and in the front and rear gardens. Then she went into every room and prayed for her husband and for each one of her children, especially for her only son. At the end of the ceremony, she would go out to the garden and call the various spirits of the "outside world" and offer them *ttŏk* and water, asking them all to protect her household. Then, she distributed the *ttŏk* to the entire neighborhood.

53. See Maxine Hong Kingston, *The Woman Warrior* (New York: Vintage Books, 1977). "Warrior woman" is an epithetical term. Warrior woman is the one who acts as a courageous warrior to guard and protect her husband and children. Nothing stops her from doing things, even unrealistically superhuman ones, for her family's welfare. She often becomes a martyr for her family (particularly for husband and children).

54. See Emile Durkheim, *The Elementary Forms of the Religious Life* (New York: Free Press, 1965).

55. Max Weber, *The Sociology of Religion*, trans. Ephraim Fischoff (Boston: Beacon Press, 1963), 80–137. A specific social context produces its representative individual as well as her or his religious beliefs, lifestyles, and socioeconomic-political values. Those who best survive

and flourish are called an "ideal type." For example, in Confucian society, a man who embodies the Confucian beliefs and lifestyles is an ideal man. In a capitalistic society, an ascetic, hard-working individual is an ideal type.

56. Kim, *Women of Korea*, 85–86.

57. This custom continued to be popular in modern Korea, (although its frequency and form has slightly changed), as I am able to relate from my personal experience. Instead of calling me by my proper name, Ai Ra, my maternal grandmother and aunts, who were born and raised in the Yi dynasty and so were shaped by its social values, used to call me *munyŏli* (문열이: gate opener), since as the first child born by my mother, I had opened the latter's womb.

58. The mother of Han Sŏk-Bong is a celebrated example of an ideal nameless woman. Being poor, she worked day and night at her home as a dressmaker for members of the upper class. With the money she earned, she educated her son. He grew up to become the most famous calligrapher of Chinese letters in Yi Korea. With the fame of her son, she gained immortality in Korean history as "the mother of Han Sŏk-Bong." No one to this day knows what her own given name was. This demonstrates the importance of male-oriented self-sacrifice and its attendant reward (immortality, albeit a nameless one) in traditional Korean society.

59. Lee, *Korean Shamanistic Rituals*, 167–70.

60. See Harvey, *Six Korean Women*. Harvey explores the contrast between a shaman's life of sacrifice in her personal life and her life of public service of healing. Shamans and their families endure unbearable social stigma and unjust treatment by others. Yet shamans practice their vocation of healing as work that is mandated by the spirits.

61. In order to restore Korean sovereignty and independence from ten years of Japanese colonial rule, thousands of Koreans marched in protest on March 1, 1919, and proclaimed to their national independence. Many people were arrested and killed by the Japanese police, and their families were subjected to severe torture. It was a historic moment in Korea's ever-recurring struggle for national liberation from foreign powers. The story of Yu Kwan-Soon has been transmitted from generation to generation through education in schools and at home.

62. Berger, *Sacred Canopy*, 4–51. Berger argues that human beings not only accept and adapt to the given social situation but also reconstruct the social system or structure in order to legitimate their existence. Religion in the Western world has served as a principle of self-justification. For example, the doctrine of theodicy was used to justify and maintain American slavery; at the same time, the same doctrine was used to support the abolition of slavery and social reform.

Berger's point is that religion supplies the basic principle of world construction.

63. Hakwon Sunwoo and Sonia (Shinn) Sunwoo, "The Heritage of the First Korean Women Immigrants in the United Sates," in *Koreans in America*, ed. Byung-Suh Kim, et al. (Fayette, MO: Association of the Korean Christian Scholars in North America, 1977), 142–69; Eun Sik Yang, "Korean Women of America," *Korean Women in Transition*, 168–81.

64. Eun Sik Yang, "Korean Women of America," *Amerasia*, 11 (February 1984), 3. The article gives a precise account of the history of early Korean immigrant women in Hawaii. This same article also is in *Korean Women in Transition*, 168–81.

65. Sunwoo and Sunwoo, 145, "Heritage of Korean Woman Immigrants," 145. The authors cite as their source Lee Houchins and Chang-su Houchins, "The Korean Experience in America, 1903–1924," *Pacific Historical Review*, (November 1974), 550.

66. Yang, "Korean Women of America," 10. More than 40 percent of the immigrants were Christians before coming to Hawaii. The author suggests that the percentage among women could have been much higher than the above figure indicates.

67. For further information, see Alice Yun Chai, "Women's History in Public: 'Picture Brides' of Hawaii," *Women's Studies Quarterly*, 1–2 (Spring/Summer 1988), 51–62.

68. Yang, *"Korean Women of America"*, 7.

69. Sunwoo and Sunwoo, *"Heritage of Korean Women Immigrants,"* 149. The interviews vividly disclose the first immigrant women's yearning to seek personal freedom and liberation from oppression in the Yi dynasty.

70. Ibid.

71. Ibid.

72. Yang, *"Korean Women of America,"* 7–10.

73. Yu, "Women in Transitional and Modern Korea," 21. The data were previously cited in the section on education in the Yi dynasty.

74. I met several "picture brides" in San Francisco in the 1960s through my ex-husband's two aunts, both of whom had been "picture brides." Most of these women had not received much education before coming to America, but regardless, they all displayed strength of character and an independent cast of mind.

75. Yu, "Women in Transitional and Modern Korea," 22–25.

76. Ibid., 23.

77. Ibid., 23.

78. Ibid., 17.

79. Ibid., 20.

80. Ibid., 18.
81. *Shinhan Minbo*, May 26, 1927 (cited in Eun Sik Yang, "Korean Women of America," 20).
82. I have written the name Maria Hwang in western manner: The first name is followed by the family name. In this way, I signify the Americanization of the early immigrant women.
83. Yang, "Korean Women of America," 5.
84. This acquaintance died about ten years ago. The quotation is a paraphrase of her words based on my recollection.
85. Sunwoo and Sunwoo, "Heritage of Korean Women Immigrants," 150.
86. Yang, "Korean Women of America," 7.
87. Ibid., 25.
88. Janet E. Giele, "Gender and Sex Roles," in *The Handbook of Sociology*, ed. Neil J. Smelser (Newbury Park, CA: Sage Publications, 1988), 306.
89. Yang, "Korean Women of America," 14.
90. Sunwoo and Sunwoo, "Heritage of Korean Women Immigrants," 154–55.

3. WOMEN OF TODAY (1954–PRESENT): IMMIGRANT *ILSE* WOMEN IN THE UNITED STATES

1. Eui-Young Yu, "Women in Traditional and Modern Korea," *Korean Women in Transition*, ed. Eui-Young Yu and Earl H. Phillips (Los Angeles: California State University, 1987), 22.
2. Hyung Cho, "The Position of Women in the Korean Work Force," in *Korean Women in Transition*, ed. Eui-Young Yu and Earl H. Phillips (Los Angeles: California State University, 1987), 100.
3. Tape 18. (See Appendix 2: Primary Sources). The specific tape number identifies with a respective interviewee and provides her biographical information.
4. In the 1950s and 1960s, most drug stores were operated out of homes. Women were able to serve as pharmacist and shopkeeper while watching their children and taking care of domestic chores. This was considered one of the least disruptive ways for women to assist their family economically, and in general, pharmacy work was considered quasi-domestic work, not a career.
5. Tape 9.
6. Hesung Chun Koh, "Women's Roles and Achievements in the Yi Dynasty," in *Korean Women in Transition*, ed Eui-Young Yu and Earl H. Phillips (Los Angeles: Calfifornia State University, 1987), 32.
7. *Han* is a uniquely Korean expression describing the psychological

state of a person's "unfulfilled wish/desire." *Han* has been believed to cause psychosomatic illnesses and psychological disorders. The soul of a person who died with *han* was believed to become a *mangnyŏng* (망령: "restless spirit") and roam around the living world instead of resting in the other world. A *mangnyŏng* would cause all kinds of evil and hurt the living until his or her *han* is fulfilled. For a more detailed explanation of *mangnyŏng* in relation to *han*, see Laurel Kendall, *Shamans, Housewives, and Other Restless Spirits* (Honolulu: University of Hawaii, 1986), 89–112.

8. Karl Marx's "Capital, Book 1," in Karl Marx and Friedrich Engels, *On Religion*, (Chico, CA: Scholars Press, 1964), 135.

9. Tape 12.

10. In Korean custom, after marriage, Mrs. (*yŏsa*: 여사: 女史: or *puin*: 부인: 婦人) is suffixed to her maiden name. For example, Chung *yŏsa* (*puin*) identifies Mrs. Chung.

11. Tape 8.

12. In order to distinguish those women who (try to) remain in Korean tradition from the others (still a minority) who have adopted western names or married non-Koreans, I use the western style of naming— given name first and family name last (e.g., Sarah Lim)—for the more Americanized women.

13. Tape 10.

14. Tape 1.

15. Tape 5.

16. See Max Weber, *The Protestant Ethic and the Spirit of Capitalism* (New York: Charles Scribner and Sons, 1958). Weber argues that the characteristic lifestyle of the Protestant is rationalistic asceticism, which means that Protestants, in general, become rational ascetics.

17. Yung-Chung Kim, *Women of Korea: A History from Ancient Times to 1945*, (Seoul: Ehwa Womans University Press, l976), 228–31.

18. *Moksa* means "minister." *Nim*, a suffix attached to a person's position or title, expresses respect and honor. It is akin to the English "Sir," "Honorable," or "Lord."

19. This citation is paraphrased from a statement made by a woman during "Women and Self-Awareness Section," a session of the Korean-American United Methodist Clergywomen's Conference held in Los Angeles on August 12, 1990.

20. "Alumna-sister" refers to a woman who had graduated earlier than the speaker from the same school or university. It is a typical Korean idiomatic expression, referring to one who is older than one-self as well as an alumna. Influenced by Confucian principles of hierarchy, instead of calling a person by her or his name, it is common to refer to people as sister, brother, aunt, uncle, mother, father, etc., and

to address older people as grandmother, and grandfather, even if they are not blood relatives.

21. Tape 3.

22. *Sorok-do* is the name of an isolated island located in the southern part of Korea. It was well known as a convalescent center for leprosy victims and their families. The life there was one of absolute isolation from the rest of the world. The Korean government shipped the invalids and their families there. Therefore, *Sorok-do* implies "doom" or a "death sentence."

23. Tape 7.

24. Won Moo Hurh and Kwang Chung Kim, *Korean Immigrants in America* (Cranbury, NJ: Associated University Presses, 1984), 41–42. The authors state that in 1905, John G. Meyers, a British merchant of the Continental Settlement Company, illegally recruited 1031 Koreans (802 men, 207 women, and 22 children) and sent them to Merida, Yucatan, promising them that immigration to Mexico would bring them large fortunes. However, those immigrants were sold in Mexican slave markets and were severely exploited. After the discovery of this incident, the Korean government banned immigration. Moreover, the Japanese colonial government (1910–45), which governed Korea after its annexation by Japan, legally prohibited Korean immigration. The Japanese relied on the Korean labor force to work on farms and in factories in their attempt to propel Japan onto the global arena as a modern world power. The Japanese also counted on Koreans to serve in the Japanese Imperial Army during the Second World War, men as mercenary soldiers and women as prostitutes so-called *chŏngsindae* (정신대: comfort women) to Japanese soldiers. Third, the U.S. "Oriental Exclusion Act" of 1924, which granted a quota of 100 immigrants per year, prohibited Koreans from entering the United States until the end of the World War II.

25. For further information, see Bok-Lim Kim et al., *Women in Shadow* (La Jolla, CA: National Committee Comcerned with Asian Wives of U.S. Servicemen, 1981). Also Kim's article, "Case Work with Japanese and Korean Wives of Americans," *Social Casework*, 53 (1972), 273–79.

26. Hurh and Kim, *Korean Immigrants in America*, 50–51.

27. Ibid., 49–52.

28. Ibid., 51.

29. Tape 2.

30. Tape 14.

31. Tape 16.

32. Hurh and Kim, "Religious Participation of Korean Immigrants in the United States," *Journal of the Scientific Study of Religion*, 20 (March 20, 1990), 1.

33. Edna Bonacich, Mokkerrom Hossain, and Jae-hong Park, "Korean Immigrant Working Women in the Early 1980s," in *Korean Women in Transition*, ed. Eui-Young Yu and Earl H. Phillips (Los Angeles: California State University, 1989), 222.

34. Tape 13.

35. Tape 20.

36. Tape 5.

37. Tape 5.

38. Tape 19.

39. See Cynthia Fuchs Epstein, *Women in Law* (Garden City, NY: Doubleday, Anchor Press, 1983). Epstein explains that work structures women's personalities, behavior, and self-image. She documents the self-image of women developed through work from her interviews with young women lawyers. When she interviewed women lawyers who had recently entered the profession, most of them did not show much confidence in their jobs. They also did not dress formally. Several years later, when she met them again, all of them showed firm confidence. They also displayed, to some degree, consensus in their dress and manners. According to her theory, work shapes one's personality and self-identity.

40. *Sinparam nanda* is a typical Korean Shamanistic expression which means that the spirit(s) is driving a shaman into ecstasy. It is a very common Korean idiom used to describe extraordinary excitement, enthusiasm or exhilaration. *Kitpal nallynda* (to wave a flag) is a unique Korean idiom expressing self-congratulatory action for extraordinary achievement or victory. For the celebration or commemoration of victorious acts, Koreans used to wave flags. When a woman says, "I am waving my flag," she is expressing pride at herself and sense of achievement and contentment with herself. It is an indirect expression of self-advancement and self-praise.

41. Tape 19.

42. Hurh and Kim, *Korean Immigrants in America*, particularly 73–100.

43. Pyong Gap Min, "The Structure and Social Functions of Korean Immigrant Churches in the United States" (revision and expansion of a paper presented at the Annual Meeting of the Association for Asian Studies, Washington, DC, March 18, 1990), 7.

44. Ibid., 4. Also, see Hurh and Kim, "Religious Participation of Korean Immigrants," and Illsoo Kim, *New Urban Immigrants: The Korean Community in New York* (Princeton: Princeton University Press, 1981).

45. Hurh and Kim, "Religious Participation of Korean Immigrants," 13.

46. Tape 2.

47. While at the Korean Clergywomen's Conference in Los Angeles in August, 1990, this clergywoman, spoke of her frustration and reluctance in giving up her own ministry and following her husband.

48. Tape 19.

49. Tape 17.

50. Tape 10.

51. Emile Durkheim, *The Elementary Forms of the Religious Life* (New York: Free Press, 1965), 13–33.

52. In theory, the church is considered the house of God, embracing all people regardless of sex, age, race, etc. Paul Rutledge, in his work *The Role of Religion in Ethnic Self-Identity* (Lantham, MD: University Press of America, 1985), describes the inclusive nature of the Vietnamese churches in the United States. In fact, prior to immigration, the majority of the Vietnamese immigrants had been Buddhist. Since immigrating, most of them have practiced Christianity, in a mixed form with Buddhism, as their major religion. Churches have embraced Buddhists and other Christian groups, such as Catholics, because these churches function as community centers. Won Moo Hurh and Kwang Chung Kim also point to the Korean immigrant church's inclusive nature as a community center in the Korean immigrants' unique adjustment process, "adhesive adaptation and ethnic confinement." See their "Religious Participation," 129–37.

53. Tape 19.

54. See Heisik Oh, "Marriage Enrichment in the Korean Immigrant Church" (D. Min. diss., School of Theology at Claremont, 1987).

55. Tape 17.

56. Tape 2.

57. Min, "Structure and Social Functions of Korean Immigrant Churches," 11–12. In this paper, Min, a male sociologist, observes that the Korean churches in the United States and Korea are more sexist than any other social institutions in terms of their organizational structure.

4. THE RELIGIOUS FACTOR IN THE LIVES OF KOREAN *ILSE* INMMGRANT WOMEN IN AMERICA

1. Peter Berger, *The Sacred Canopy* (New York: Doubleday, 1969), 105–77.

2. Barbara Hargrove, *The Sociology of Religion* (Arlington Heights, IL: AHM Publishing Corp., 1966), 65–134.

3. Robert N. Bellah, *Beyond Belief* (Berkeley and Los Angeles: University of California Press, 1970), 20–50.

4. Rosemary Ruether, *Sexism and God-Talk: Toward a Feminist Theology* (Boston: Beacon Press, 1983); Elizabeth Schüssler Fiorenza, *In Memory of Her: A Feminist Reconstruction of Christian Origins* (New York: Crossroad, 1983). Ruether argues the church's structural perpetuation of sexism, and Fiorenza emphasizes the need for new hermeneutics in order to correct sexist interpretation of the religious ideas influencing women's selfhood.

5. I Corinthians, chapter 13, emphasizes love as the center of Christian life. Most homes are decorated with some variation of verse 13 of chapter 13: "Meanwhile these three remain: faith, hope, and love; and the greatest of these is love."

6. Tape 5.

7. Tape 3.

8. Tape 2.

9. Tape 6.

10. Tape 20.

11. Tape 16.

12. Ernst Troeltsch, *The Social Teaching of the Christian Churches* (Chicago: University of Chicago Press, 1981), 1:331–43.

13. Tape 9.

14. Tape 14.

15. Emile Durkheim, *The Elementary Forms of the Religious Life* (New York: Free Press, 1965), 62.

16. For general scholarly information on Buddhism and Shamanism, see Dong-sik Yu, *Hankuk Musok ŭi Yŏksa wa Kujo* (Seoul: Yonsei University Press, 1975); also, Naomichi Takasaki, *The Entrance to Buddhism*, trans. Sa Sung Hong (Seoul: Woo Ri Publisher, 1988).

17. Tape 1.

18. See Donald Light Jr. and Suzanne Keller, *Sociology* (New York: Alfred A. Knopf, 1985), 104, on the theory of Charles Horton Cooley's self-development. According to Cooley, self is developed through the reflection of others. In this sense, others act like mirrors.

19. Nelle Morton, in *The Journey is Home* (Boston: Beacon Press, 1985), 74–77, identifies Christian patriarchy as "the perpetuator of female oppression."

20. Tape 5.

21. Tape 18.

22. Tape 13.

23. See Ana-Maria Rizzuto, *The Birth of the Living God: A Psychoanalytic Study* (Chicago: University of Chicago Press, 1979).

24. Tape 16.

25. Tape 15.

26. The interviewee is a friend of one of my younger sisters. It is a

Korean custom to address persons who are not members of one's family in terms of family relation as an indication of respect; so one uses such terms as *sister, aunt, brother, uncle*, etc., instead of using first names. This practice is a reflection of Korean culture—which respects and treasures human relationships—by strengthening collective identity, and maintaining a social order.

27. Tape 20.

28. Tape 2.

29. I understand Jesus as a transformer and revolutionary in view of such acts as the cleansing of the temple (Mark 11:15–16). The whole thrust of Jesus' ministry, such as the miraculous acts of healing the sick and restoring the disabled (blind, mute, deaf), can be understood as acts of re-creation and innovation, rather than as acceptance of the chaotic and unjust present. See also, H. Richard Niebuhr, *Christ and Culture* (New York: Harper & Row, 1951), particularly the section on Jesus as a "Transformer of Culture," 190–229.

30. Tape 19.

31. Tape 14.

32. Max Weber, *The Protestant Ethic and the Spirit of Capitalism* (New York: Charles Scribner and Sons, 1958), 181.

33. Tape 13.

34. Tape 12.

35. Tape 5.

36. Tape 8.

37. Tape 19.

38. Eui-Young Yu, "Women in Traditional and Modern Korea," *Korean Women in Transition*, ed. Eui-Young Yu and Earl H. Phillips (Los Angeles: California State University, 1987), 24.

39. During the 1980s, he was pursuring his doctoral work at Drew Graduate School, where I was doing my graduate studies. The citation is paraphrased from my memory of frequent conversations with this pastor.

40. The woman referred to here is a familiar acquaintance of mine and receives counselling from me. After her move away from New Jersey, most of the counselling has been done over the telephone. The citation was paraphrased from a telephone counselling session held on February 5, 1991.

41. Durkheim, *Elementary Forms of Religious Life*, 121–49. Durkheim explains that the Australian totemic religion, as the original indigenous form of religion (though challenged and suspected by sociologists), is nothing but a symbolic representation of the collective consciousness of the Australian aborigines. Clan members define certain animals or plants as totemic entities and set them aside and worship them as sacred. Through rituals, the symbolic acts, the members share the

same beliefs and lifestyles and strengthen their collective identity.

42. As mentioned earlier, in Korean custom, a woman keeps her natal name throughout her whole life, even after marriage.

43. Many of these women defend hierarchical family order through the story of creation in Genesis, chapters 1 and 2, and Ephesians 5:22–24.

44. Tape 3.

45. Niebuhr, *Christ and Culture*. See in particular the section on Christ of Culture, 83–115.

46. Tape 17.

47. Tape 1.

48. Tape 3.

49. Tape 5.

50. Pyong Gap Min, "Immigrant Entrepreneurship and Wife's Overwork" (a paper presented at the Annual Meeting of the American Sociological Association, Washington DC, August 13, 1990), 10.

51. Tape 16.

52. Tape 8.

53. Tape 2.

54. Tape 19.

55. Tape 6.

56. Tape 2.

57. Tape 17.

58. *Kimch'i* can be considered the representative of Korean food and culture. It is the very basic vegetable dish. The salted *paech'u* (so-called Chinese cabbage) or fresh turnip is fermented with garlic, ginger, scallions, pickled or fresh fish, and hot red pepper. It is very spicy and hot, which may symbolize the Korean temperament, passion, and intimacy in human relationships.

59. Tape 12.

60. Tape 9.

61. Tape 1.

62. The solitary living of the elderly, especially women, is a serious issue in the Korean community and a unique one among ethnic groups in the United States today. It is very common for older Korean women (even in their sixties and seventies) to work as housemaids for Korean families. Moreover, many elderly people live in their own apartments instead of depending on their children. For example, when my aunt, Kim Mi-He, was in her late seventies, she lived alone in a government-subsidized apartment for senior citizens on the West Coast. She was a typical traditional woman who had devoted her whole life to the well-being of her husband and five children. However, in her old age, she became self-supporting and lived a very lonely life. In her building, which comprised fifty apartments, elderly Koreans occupied sixteen

214   NOTES

units, thus accounting for almost one-third of the residents. She died in 1992.

63. A woman used to be buried in her husband's tomb if her husband died before her. This is called *"hapjang"* (합장: 合葬: togetherness-burial). This custom reflects the social status of a woman as a property of her husband.

64. In Korea, originating from the Confucian Yi dynasty, a married woman is not allowed to return to her natal home, on any occasions. Marriage, for a woman, was used lead lead her to a total uprooting and disconnection from her natal family. Though the degree of separation may be different, this custom is, in general, still viable today. The custom indicates the shift of a woman's loyalty and obligation from her natal home to husband's.

65. The citation is a part of Aunt Kim Mi-He's will and testament spoken to me on January 15, 1991, while on her deathbed. She died on April 13, 1992. I truly pray for her to rest in heaven. May eternal peace be with her.

66. Unmarried and childless people are still considered "imperfect beings" in Korean society. Therefore, only childless and poor elderly people who have no families to depend on go to nursing homes. Koreans consider living in a nursing home to be the most miserable fate because it is regarded as a consequence of one's unactualized and unfulfilled moral duties, i.e., raising a family.

67. Tape 5.
68. Tape 6.
69. Hargrove, *Sociology of Religion*, 289–307 (particularly 297). She illustrates the characteristics of sects, including avoidance of or escape from "this world."
70. Tape 14.
71. Tape 17.
72. Weber, *Sociology of Religion*, 138–150.
73. Tape 3.

5. THE DYNAMICS OF *ILSE* CHRISTIAN WOMEN'S ADAPTATION TO SOCIETY

1. See the discussion of education in chapter 2.
2. See Mary Daly, *Beyond God the Father: Toward a Philosophy of Women's Liberation* (Boston: Beacon Press, 1973). Also see Hyun Kyung Chung, *Struggle to be the Sun Again* (Maryknoll, NY: Orbis Books, 1990). Both authors illustrate the negative impact of the Bible on women's self-image.
3. For this interviewee, the Bible is the sole source of education

and information. She does not read newspapers, not even Korean newspapers, nor does she listen to news on the radio or TV. She proudly confesses that she does not know anything outside her church.

4. Tape 17.

5. Tape 1.

6. During my doctoral studies at Drew University Graduate School, I served Word Church as a Christian Education Director for Sunday School for about a year. I regularly preached to the children and received positive responses to changes in women's roles from the children and their parents, especially the mothers.

7. The citation is paraphrased from my recollection of the past encounter. This memorable occasion took place one Sunday in November 1988, when I visited one of the United Methodist churches in Washington, DC. For most of the women in the congregation, it was their first opportunity to meet a clergywoman. After my benediction, women surrounded me and showed their surprise and excitement to see a Korean clergywoman for the first time in their lives. In particular, one elderly woman, who was in her eighties and wore the Korean traditional dress and *jjok* (쪽: an old-fashioned woman's hair-style of braids fastened into a bun at the nape of the neck) could not hide her excitement and thankfulness to God. She danced around the fellowship hall and embraced me and cried tears of happiness and relief. Repeatedly, she shouted, "Hallelujah! Hallelujah! Amen, Amen!"

8. Tape 1.

9. Tape 20.

10. Pyong Gap Min, "Immigrant Entrepreneurship and Wife's Overwork" (paper presented at the Annual Meeting of the American Sociological Association, Washington, DC, August 18, 1990), 16. According to Min's research, 48 percent of married Korean immigrant working women in New York City completed at least four years of college.

11. *Sokhoe* literally means "regional meeting" or "section meeting." Korean churches divide the congregation into regions, appoint a leader for each region, and hold regular prayer and Bible study meetings for members of each group. It is a Korean version of Wesleyan class meeting in the Methodist tradition.

12. Tape 9.

13. Tape 2.

14. Peter L. Berger, *The Sacred Canopy*, (New York, Doubleday, 1969), 3.

15. Tape 16.

16. Tape 19.

17. Tape 22. This citation is mostly paraphrased based on my notes

and memories collected from the conversation during lunch meeting with her at a Chinese restaurant in Madison, New Jersey in summer, 1990.

18. As my counselee, Sin Mal-Hee used to visit me in order to explore her frustration, anger, and confusion in her marriage life. After she moved out to southern New Jersey, her counselling continued by phone. The citation is a paraphrase of comments made during a telephone counselling session on February 5, 1991.

19. Rosabeth Moss Kanter, *Men and Women of the Corporation* (New York: Basic Books, 1977), 69–103. Kanter argues that the self-image of a (female) secretary is identified with (her) boss and that (her) identity is developed as the boss's appendix.

20. Tape 18.

21. Tape 14.

22. See Cynthia Fuchs Epstein, *Women in Law* (New York: Doubleday, Anchor Press, 1983); Also see Rosabeth Moss Kanter, *Men and Women of the Corporation.*

23. See Paula Giddings, *When and Where I Enter: The Impact of Black Women on Race and Sex in America* (New York: Bantam Books, 1984). Giddings succinctly yet profoundly illustrates the history of the Black struggle for autonomy and power.

24. Janet Giele, "Gender and Sex Roles," *The Handbook of Sociology*, ed. Neil J. Smelser (Newbury Park, CA: Sage Publications, 1988), 296.

25. Tape 2.

26. Tape 11.

27. Tape 15.

28. Tape 13.

29. SMAC stands for Sequential Multiple Analyzer with Computer. This machine analyzes twenty-four body chemicals, such as glucose and cholesterol. It is a highly sophisticated and complex machine and requires expertise to operate it.

30. Tape 21.

31. See Won Moo Hurh and Kwang Chung Kim, *Korean Immigrants in America* (Cranbury, NJ: Associated University Press, 1984), 38–55. These authors portray general and detailed aspects of Korean immigrants' lives in the U.S. and argue that the life satisfaction and aspiration of the immigrants generally shrank after immigration.

32. Joan Smith is a longtime acquaintance and counsellee of mine. The citation is carefully paraphrased based on a telephone counselling session of February 11, 1991.

33. Giddings, *Where and When I Enter*, 232–58.

34. *Kye* is an informal, private financial club system through which

Koreans traditionally have saved and invested money. After modernization of the banking system, it became the major financial source for women and was socially justified as a means of social gathering for women. Commonly, members meet once a month and pay their dues. Each month, in rotation, one woman collects all the dues as hers to keep. The woman who receives the entire sum of money from the members usually treats all the members to food, and so all the women have a social time, sharing gossip and information. After the meeting, they may go to a movie or shop, or visit friends together. The *kye* can be considered an informal means of liberating homemakers from traditional housekeeping and socially sanctioning their participation in the outside world in a limited fashion. The *kye* is still popular among many *ilse* women (also men in business) in the United States.
35. Tape 11.
36. Tape 1.
37. Tape 9.
38. Tape 9.
39. Tape 16.
40. Tape 17.

6. CONCLUSION

1. Max Weber, *The Sociology of Religion*, trans. Ephraim Fischoff (Boston: Beacon Press, 1963). See especially the sections entitled "The Prophet" and "The Religious Congregation, Preaching, and Pastoral Care," 46–59, 60–79.

2. See "Portrait of Religion in U.S. Holds Dozens of Surprises," *New York Times*, April 10, 1991, sec. 1, pp. 1, 18. The article signifies that Christianity is still a dominant religion in America.

BIBLIOGRAPHY

Babbie, Earl. *The Practice of Social Research.* Belmont, CA: Wadsworth Publishing Co., 1986.

Basow, Susan A. *Gender Stereotypes: Traditions and Alternatives.* Monterey, CA: Brooks/Cole Publishing Company, 1986.

Bellah, Robert N. "American Civil Religion in the 1970's." *American Theological Review,* sup. ser. 1 (July 1973), 8–20.

———. "Civil Religion in America." In *Religion in America,* ed. William G. McLaughlin and Robert N. Bellah, 3–23. Boston: Houghton Mifflin Co., 1968.

———. *Beyond Belief.* Berkeley and Los Angeles: University of California Press, 1970.

Berg, David N. and Kenwyn K. Smith, eds. *The Self in Social Inquiry: Researching Methods.* Newbury Park, CA: Sage Publications, 1985.

Berger, Peter L. *The Sacred Canopy.* New York: Doubleday, 1969.

Bonacich, Edna, Mokkerron Hossain, and Jee-hung Park. "Korean Immigrant Working women in the Early 1980's." In *Korean Woman in Transition: At Home and Abroad,* ed. Eui-Young Yu and Earl H. Philips. Los Angeles: Center for Korean-American and Korean Studies, California State University, 1987.

Boo, Minza Kim. "The Social Reality of the Korean American Women: Toward Crashing with the Confucian Ideology." In *Korean American Women,* ed. Inn Sook Lee, 65–93. Fayette, MO: Association of Korean Christian Scholars in North America, 1985.

Browning, Don S. *Religious Thoughts and the Modern Psychologies: A Critical Conversation in the Theology of Culture.* Philadelphia: Fortress Press, 1987.

Chai, Alice Yun. "Korean Women in Hawaii, 1903–1945: The Role of Methodism in their Liberation and in their Participation in the Korean Independence Movement." In *Women in New Worlds,* ed. H. F. Thomas and Rosemary Skinner Keller, 328–44. Nashville: Abingdon, 1981.

———. "Freed from the Elders but Locked into Labor: Korean Immigrant Women in Hawaii." *Women's Studies: An Interdisciplinary Journal,* special issue, *As the World Turns: Women, Work, and International Migration,* ed. Karen Brodkin Sacks and Nancy Scheper-Hughs, 13 (March 1987), 223–24.

———. "Women's History in Public: 'Picture Brides' of Hawaii." *Women's Studies Quarterly,* 1–2 (Spring/Summer 1988), 51–62.

Chai, Ch'u. *The Sacred Books of Confucius and Other Confucian Classics.*

Ed. and trans. Ch'u Chai and Winberg Chai. New Hyde Park, NY:
University Books, 1965.

Chan, R. T. *A Source Book and Chinese Philosophy.* Princeton:
Princeton University Press, 1969.

Chang, Kee Keun, ed. and trans. *Non-ŏ* (논어: 論語). Seoul: Myung
Moon Dang, 1988.

Cho, Hyung. "The Position of Women in the Korean Work Force." In
Korean Women in Transition: At Home and Abroad, ed. Eui-Young
Yu and Earl H. Philips. Los Angeles: Center for Korean-American
and Korean Studies, California State University, 1987.

Cho, Wha Soon. *Let the Weak Be Strong: A Woman's Struggle for
Justice.* Bloomington: Meyer-Stone Books, 1988.

Ch'oe, Kil-Sung. "Male and Female in Korean Folk Belief." *Asian
Folklore Studies,* 43 (February 1984), 227–33.

Christ, Carol P. and Judith Plaskow, eds. *Womanspirit Rising: A Feminist Reader in Religion.* San Francisco: Harper & Row, 1979.

Chung, Sei-wha, ed. *Challenges for Women: Women's Studies in Korea,*
trans. Chang-hyun Shinn et al. Seoul: Ewha Womans University Press,
1986.

Chung, Hyun Kyung. *Struggle to be the Sun Again: Introducing Asian
Women's Theology.* Maryknoll, NY: Orbis Books, 1990.

Cordasco, Francesco. *The Immigrant Woman in North America: An
Annotated Bibliography of Selected References.* Metuchen, NJ:
Scarecrow, 1985.

Covell, Alan Carter. *Ecstasy: Shamanism in Korea.* Elizabeth, NJ:
Hollym International, 1983.

Daly, Mary. *Beyond God the Father: Toward a Philosophy of Women's
Liberation.* Boston: Beacon Press, 1973.

———. *The Church and the Second Sex.* New York: Harper & Row,
1985.

Dawson, Milels Mender. *The Basic Thoughts of Confucius: The Conduct
of Life.* New York: Garden City Publishing Co., 1939.

Durkheim, Emile. *The Elementary Forms of the Religious Life.* New
York: Free Press, 1965.

Eliade, Mircea. *Shamanism: Archaic Techniques of Ecstasy.* Princeton:
Princeton University Press, 1974.

Epstein, Cynthia Fuchs. *Women in Law.* Garden City, NY: Doubleday,
Anchor Press, 1983.

Estrada, Alvaro. *Maria Sabina: Her Life and Chants.* Ed. Jerome
Rothenberg. Trans. and commentaries by Henry Munn with a retro-
spective essay by R. Gordon Wasson. Santa Barbara: Ross-Erickson,
1981.

Falk, Nancy Auer and Rita N. Gross, eds. *Unspoken Worlds: Women's*

Religious Lives in Non-Western Cultures. New York: Harper & Row, 1980.

Filstead, William J., ed. *Qualitative Methodology: Firsthand Involvement with the Social World.* Chicago: Rand McNally College Publishing Co., 1970.

Fiorenza, Elizabeth Schüssler. *In Memory of Her: A Feminist Theological Reconstruction of Christian Origins.* New York: Crossroad, 1983.

Fiorenza, Elizabeth Schüssler and Ann Carr. *Women, Work, and Poverty.* Edinburgh: T. & T. Clark, 1987.

Foubert, Charles H. "Being Black, Woman and Christian." *IDOC Bulletin: International Documentation Service,* 8 (August 1984), 3–25.

Fowler, James W. *Stages of Faith: The Psychology of Human Development and the Quest of Meaning.* San Francisco: Harper & Row, 1976.

Frazier, E. F. *The Negro Church in America.* New York: Shocken, 1964.

Freud, Sigmund. *Totem and Taboo.* New York: W. W. Norton and Co., 1950.

———. *The Future of an Illusion.* New York: W. W. Norton & Co., 1961.

Friedman, Barbara, et al. *Women's Work and Women's Studies 1973–74: A Bibliography.* New York: Barnard College Women's Center, 1975.

Gerth, H. H. and C. Wright Mills. *From Max Weber: Essays in Sociology.* New York: Oxford University Press, 1946.

Giddings, Paula. *When and Where I Enter: The Impact of Black Women on Race and Sex in America.* New York: Bantam Books, 1984.

Giele, Janet E. "Gender and Sex Roles." In *The Handbook of Sociology,* ed. Niel J. Smelser. Newbury Park, CA: Sage Publications, 1988.

Gilligan, Carol. *In A Different Voice: Psychological Theory and Women's Development.* Cambridge: Harvard University Press, 1982.

Goffman, Erving. *The Presentation of Self in Everyday Life.* New York: Doubleday, 1959.

Hargrove, Barbara. *The Sociology of Religion.* Arlington Heights, IL: AHM Publishing Corp., 1966.

Harvey, Youngsook Kim. *The Korean Mudang as a Household Therapist.* Honolulu: University of Hawaii Press, 1976.

———. *Six Korean Women: The Socialization of Shamans.* St. Paul: West Publishing Co., 1979.

Hegel, Georg Wilhelm Friedrich. *Hegel: Texts and Commentary.* Ed. and trans. Walter Kaufmann. Notre Dame: University of Notre Dame Press, 1977.

Hochschild, Arlie and Anne Machung. *The Second Shift: Working Parents and the Revolution at Home.* New York: Viking Press, 1989.

Hooks, Bell. *Feminist Theory: From Margin to Center.* Boston: South End Press, 1984.

Hsu, Francis. *Culture and Self: Asian and Western Perspectives.* New York: Tavistock Publications, 1985.

Hurh, Won Moo and Kwang Chung Kim. "Adhesive Sociocultural Adaptation of Korean Immigrants." *International Migration Review* 18 (1984), 188–217.

———. *Korean Immigrants in America: A Structural Analysis of Ethnic Confinement and Adhesive Adaptation.* Cranbury, NJ: Associated University Presses, 1984.

———. "Immigration and Religious Participation" (in Korean). *Korean Christian Review* (June/July 1985), 36–37.

———. "Religious Participation: Ethnic Roles of the Korean Church." *Korean Immigrants in America,* Cranbury, NJ: Associated University Press, 129–37.

Joas, Hans. *G. H. Mead: A Contemporary Re-examination of His Thoughts.* Trans. Raymond Meyer. Cambridge, MA: MIT Press, 1985.

Jung, Carl Gustav. *Psychology and Religion.* New Haven: Yale University Press, 1966.

Kanter, Rosabeth Moss. *Men and Women of the Corporation.* New York: Basic Books, 1977.

Kendall, Laurel. "Korean Shamanism: Women's Rites and an Chinese Comparison." In *Religion and the Family in East Asia,* eds. G. De Voo and T. Sofuo. Berkeley and Los Angeles: University of California Press, 1986.

———. *Shamans, Housewives, and Other Restless Spirits: Women in Korean Ritual Life.* Honolulu: University of Hawaii Press, 1986.

Kendall, Laurel and Mark Peterson, eds. *Korean Women: View from the Inner Room.* New Haven: East Rock Press, 1983.

Kim, Bok-Lim. "Casework with Japanese and Korean Wives of Americans." *Social Casework,* 5 (1972), 273–79.

Kim, Bok-Lim, Amy Izuno Okamura, Naomi Ozawa, and Virginia Forrest. Ed. Michael Sawdey. *Women in Shadow: A Handbook for Service Providers Working with Asian Wives of U.S. Military Personnel.* La Jolla, CA: National Committee Concerned with Asian Wives of U.S. Servicemen, 1981.

Kim, Byung-Suh, Won Moo Hurh, Young Pai, Seok Choong Song, and Hakwon and Sonia Shinn Sunwoo, eds. *Koreans in America.* Fayette, MO: Association of Korean Christian Scholars in North America (Special Spring Issue), 1977.

Kim, Hyung Chan. *The Korean Diaspora: Historical and Sociological Studies of Korean Immigration and Assimilation in North America.* Santa Rosa: Clio Publications, 1977.

Kim, Illsoo. *New Urban Immigrants: The Korean Community in New York.* Princeton: Princeton University Press, 1981.

————. "Organizational Patterns of Korean American Methodist Churches: Denominationalism and Personal Community." In *Rethinking Methodist History,* ed. Russell E. Richey and Kenneth E. Rowe, 228–38. Nashville: Kingswood Books, 1985.

Kim, In-hoe. *Hankuk Musok ŭi Chonghap chŏk Koch'al (General Study of Korean Shamanism).* Seoul: Koryo University Press, 1981.

Kim, Sil Dong. "International Married Korean Women Immigrants: A Study in Marginality." Ph.D. diss., University of Washington, 1979.

Kim, Yung-Chung. *Women of Korea: A History from Ancient Times to 1945.* Seoul: Ewha Womans University Press, 1976.

Kingston, Maxine Hong. *The Woman Warrior.* New York: Vintage Books, 1977.

Koh, Hesung Chun. "Yi Dynasty Korean Women in the Public Domain: A New Perspective on Social Stratification." *Social Science Journal,* 3 (1975), 7–19.

————. "Religion and Socialization of Women in Korea." In *Religion and Family in East Asia,* ed. George Devos and Takao Sofue, 237–57, Osaka, 1984.

————. "Women's Roles and Achievements in the Yi Dynasty." In *Korean Women in Transition: At Home and Abroad,* ed. Eui-Young Yu and Earl H. Phillips. Los Angeles: California State University, 1987.

Korean Gospel Weekly (Arlington, VA)., October 28, 1990.

Korea Times (Seoul), June 19, 1990.

Lee, Dong-won. "The Changes of Korean Family and Women." In *Challenges for Women: Women's Studies in Korea,* ed. Sei-wha Chung, trans. Chang-hyun Shin, et al. Seoul: Ehwa Womans University Press, 1986.

Lee, Jung Young. *Korean Shamanistic Rituals.* New York: Mouton Publishers, 1981.

Lee, Hyo-jae. "Han of Korean Women." In *The Story of Han,* ed. Kwang Sun Suh, 235–44. Seoul: Borhee Press, 1988.

————. *Kajok kwa Sahoe (Family and Society).* Seoul: Kyung Moon Sa, 1990.

Lee, Pu Duk. "The Contribution and the Hardship of the Women in Interracial Marriage" (in Korean), 1992. Typescript.

Lenski, Gerhard. *The Religious Factor.* Westport, CT: Greenwood Press, 1961.

Lerner, Gerda. *The Creation of Patriarchy.* New York: Oxford University Press, 1986.

Light, Donald, Jr., and Suzanne Keller. *Sociology.* New York: Alfred A. Knopf, 1985.

Light, Ivan and Edna Bonacich. *Immigrant Entrepreneurs: Koreans in Los Angeles, 1965-1982.* Berkeley and Los Angeles: University of California Press, 1988.

Lin, Yutang. *The Wisdom of Confucius.* New York: Modern Library, 1938.

Marshall, C. "Organizational Policy and Women's Socialization in Administration," *Urban Education,* 16 (February 1981), 205-31.

———. "The Stigmatized Woman: The Professional Woman in a Male Sex-typed Career." *Journal of Educational Administration,* 23 (February 1985), 131-52.

Marshall, Catherine and Gretchen B. Rossman. *Desigining Qualitative Research.* Newbury Park, CA: Sage Publications, 1989.

Marx, Karl and Friedrich Engels. *On Religion.* Chico, CA: Scholars Press, 1964.

McDannell, Colleen. *The Christian Home in Victorian America, 1840-1900.* Bloomington: Indiana University Press, 1986.

McDargh, John. *Psychoanalytic Object Relations Theory and the Study of Religion: On Faith and the Imaging of God.* Lanham: University Press of America, 1983.

Mead, George Herbert. *On Social Psychology.* Selected Papers edited and with an introduction by Anselm Strauss. Chicago: University of Chicago Press, 1964.

Miller, David L. *George Herbert Mead: Self, Language, and the World.* Austin: University of Texas Press, 1973.

Miller, Jean Baker. *Toward a New Psychology of Women.* Boston: Beacon Press, 1986.

Min, Pyong Gap. "The Structure and Social Functions of Korean Immigrant Churches in the United States." This is a revised and expanded paper which was presented at its Annual Meeting, Association for Asian Studies, Washington, D. C., March 18, 1989.

———. "Immigrant Entrepreneurship and Wife's Over-work: Koreans in New York City." Paper presented at the Annual Meeting of the American Sociological Association, Washington, D. C., August 13, 1990.

Morton, Nelle. *The Journey is Home.* Boston: Beacon Press, 1985.

Natanson, Maurice: *The Social Dynamics of George H. Mead.* Washington, DC: Public Affairs Press, 1956.

Niebuhr, H. Richard. *Christ and Culture.* New York: Harper & Row, 1951.

Nietzsche, Friedrich Wilhelm. *The Portable Nietzsche.* Ed. and trans. Walter Kaufmann. New York: Viking Press, 1982.

Oh, Heisik. "Marriage Enrichment in the Korean Immigrant Church." D. Min. diss., School of Theology at Claremont, 1987.

Park, Soon Kyung. *Minjok T'ongil kwa Kidoggyo (The Unification of the Korean People and Christianity).* Seoul: Hangilsa Publishers, 1986.

Park, Young-hai, ed. *Women of the Yi Dynasty.* Seoul: Research Center for Asian Women, Sookmyung Women's University, 1986.

Pleck, E. "Two Worlds in One: Work and Family." *Journal of Social History,* 70 (February 1976), 178–95.

Pope, Linston. *Millhands and Preachers.* New Haven: Yale University Press, 1942.

Rich, Adrienne. *Of Women Born: Motherhood as Experience and Institution.* New York: W. W. Norton and Co., 1986.

Rizzuto, Ana-Maria. *The Birth of the Living God: A Psychoanalytic Study.* Chicago: University of Chicago Press, 1979.

Robertson, Ian. *Sociology.* New York: Worth Publishers, 1987.

Robinson, John P. and Phillip R. Shaver. *Measures of Social Psychological Attitudes.* Ann Arbor: Institution for Social Research, The University of Michigan, 1973.

Ruether, Rosemary Radford, ed. *Religion and Sexism: Images of Women in the Jewish and Christian Traditions.* New York: Simon and Schuster, 1974.

———. *Sexism and God-Talk: Toward a Feminist Theology.* Boston: Beacon Press, 1983.

Russell, Letty M., Katie Cannon, Pui-lan Kwak and Ada Maria-Diaz, eds. *Inheriting Our Mother's Garden: Feminist Theology in Third World Perspective.* Philadelphia: Westminster Press, 1988.

Rutledge, Paul. *The Role of Religion in Ethnic Self-Identity: A Vietnamese Community.* Lanham, MD: University Press of America, 1985.

Schaef, Anne Wilson. *Women's Reality: An Emerging Female System in a White Male Society.* Minneapolis: Winston Press, 1985.

Shinhan Minbo (신한민보). Seoul, May 26, 1921.

Smelser, Neil J. *Handbook of Sociology.* Newbury Park, CA: Sage Publications, 1988.

Smelser, Neil J. and William T. Smelser. *Personality and Social System.* New York: John Wiley and Sons, 1970.

Sommer, Robert and Barbara B. Sommer. *A Practical Guide to Behavioral Research: Tools and Techniques.* New York: Oxford University Press, 1986.

Sunwoo, Hakwon and Sonia (Shinn) Sunwoo. "The Heritage of the

First Korean Women Immigrants in the United States." *Koreans in America*, ed. Byung-Suh Kim, et. al. Fayette, MO: Association of the Korean Christian Scholars in North America, 1977.

Takasaki, Naomichi. *Pulkyo Ibmun (The Entranc to Buddhism)*. Trans. Sa Sung Hong. Seoul: Woo Ri Publisher, 1988.

Troeltsch, Ernst. *The Social Teaching of Christian Churches*. Vols. 1–2. Introduction by H. Richard Niebuhr. Trans. Olive Wyon. Chicago: University of Chicago Press, 1981.

Turner, Jonathan H. *The Structure of Sociological Theory*. Chicago: Dorsey Press, 1986.

Weber, Max. *The Protestant Ethic and the Spirit of Capitalism*. New York: Charles Scribner and Sons, 1958.

———. *The Sociology of Religion*. Trans. Ephraim Fischoff. Boston: Beacon Press, 1963.

Yang, Eun Sik. "Korean Women of America: From Subordination to Partnership, 1903–1930." *Amerasia*, 11 (February 1984), 1–28. The same article is also in *Korean Women in Transition*, 168–81.

Yi, Hwang. *T'oegye Sŏnjip* (퇴계선집). Trans. Hyun-ho Yoon. Seoul: Hyun Am Sa, 1985.

Yi, Ping Hŏ Kag (빙허각이씨). *Kyuhap Ch'ongsŏ* (규합총서: 閨閣叢書). Trans. Ryang Wan Chung. Seoul: Bo Jin Je, 1975.

Yin, R. T. *Case Study Research: Design and Methods*. Beverly Hills: Sage, 1984.

Young, John D. *Confucianism and Christianity: The First Encounter*. Hong Kong: Hong Kong University Press, 1983.

Yu, Dong-sik. *Hankuk Mukyo ŭi Yŏksa wa Kujo (The History and Structure of Korean Shamanism)*. Seoul: Yonsei University Press, 1975.

Yu, Eui-Young. "Women in Traditional and Modern Korea." In *Korean Women in Transition*, ed. Eui-Young Yu and Earl H. Philips. Los Angeles: Centger for Korean-American and Korean Studies, California State University, 1987.

Yu, Eui-Young and Earl H. Phillips, eds. *Korean Women in Transition: At Home and Abroad*. Los Angeles: Center for Korean-American and Korean Studies, California State University, 1987.

INDEX

Alphabetization of names follows American order used in the Bibliography